LAST SONS OF AMERICA ™

PHILLIP KENNEDY **JOHNSON**
MATTHEW DOW **SMITH**
DOUG **GARBARK**

BOOM! ™
STUDIOS

LAST SONS OF AMERICA, January 2017.
Published by BOOM! Studios, a division of Boom
Entertainment, Inc. Last Sons of America is ™
& © 2017 Phillip Kennedy Johnson. Originally
published in single magazine form as LAST
SONS OF AMERICA No. 1-4. ™ & © 2015, 2016
Phillip Kennedy Johnson. All Rights Reserved.
BOOM! Studios™ and the BOOM! Studios logo
are trademarks of Boom Entertainment, Inc.,
registered in various countries and categories.
All characters, events, and institutions depicted
herein are fictional. Any similarity between any
of the names, characters, persons, events, and/
or institutions in this publication to actual names,
characters, and persons, whether living or dead,
events, and/or institutions is unintended and
purely coincidental. BOOM! Studios does not
read or accept unsolicited submissions of ideas,
stories, or artwork.

A catalog record of this book is available from
OCLC and from the BOOM! Studios website,
www.boom-studios.com, on the Librarians Page.

BOOM! Studios, 5670 Wilshire Boulevard, Suite
450, Los Angeles, CA 90036-5679. Printed in
China. First Printing.

ISBN: 978-1-60886-923-7
eISBN: 978-1-61398-594-6

WRITTEN BY
PHILLIP KENNEDY **JOHNSON**

ILLUSTRATED BY
MATTHEW DOW **SMITH**

COLORED BY
DOUG **GARBARK**

LETTERED BY
JIM **CAMPBELL**

COVER BY
TONCI **ZONJIC**

DESIGNER
MICHELLE **ANKLEY**

ASSOCIATE EDITOR
CAMERON **CHITTOCK**

EDITOR
ERIC **HARBURN**

SPECIAL THANKS
IAN BRILL AND MATTHEW LEVINE

FOREWORD

It's easy for an editor to decide whether an artist is ready to make the leap to pro work. Look through the portfolio, and within a minute or two, the editor knows if the artist is worth hiring. The proof is on the page.

For writers, there's no two-minute test. That's why breaking into comics as a writer is one of the steepest mountains to climb. Nobody wants to read your script. Truth be told, nobody really wants to read your pitch. But maybe, just maybe, someone will read your finished comic. And if it's good... and I mean the whole package, the story, the art, the color, even the lettering... there's a chance you'll get a chance.

Writers have to put in more time, more effort, and more expense to get themselves seen. No, that's not fair. But that's just the way it is. Phillip Kennedy Johnson put in

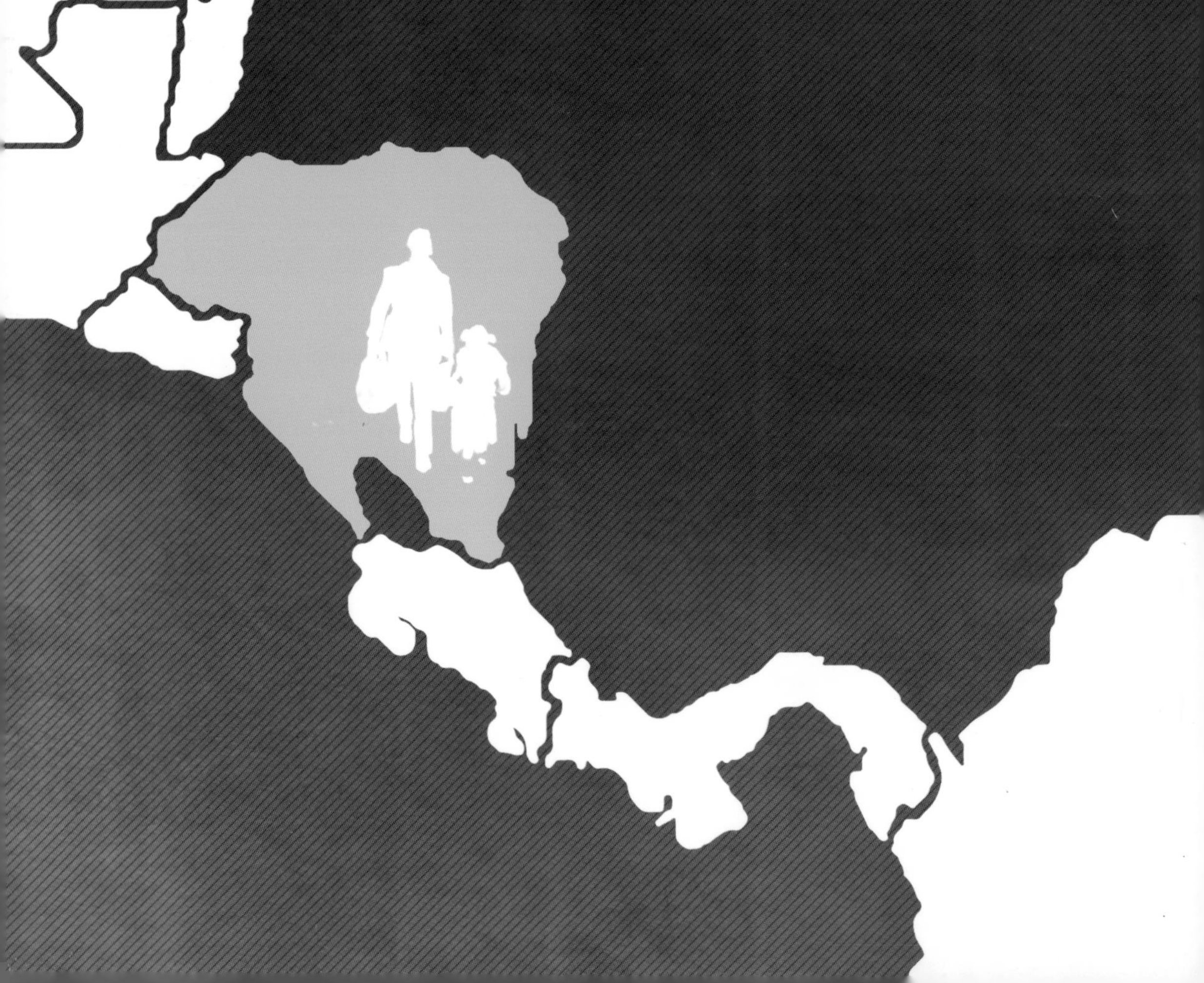

the work, and the result is this volume, the first of what I'm certain will be many.

I first met Phillip when he reached out to me via email with an essay he had written comparing two of the most American of art forms: comics and jazz. It was thoughtful, and it was well-written enough that I put in a good word to help him get the piece published at a comics website. When I later met Phillip in person, he showed me the comic he was working on, *The Lazarus Slaves, or The Damnation of George Washington Barlow*.

Note that I say "comic" rather than "script," because it consisted of finished pages by artist Scott Hampton, fully colored and lettered. Phillip had invested in his career by investing in actually making a comic. It was a great calling card, much more so than handing an overwhelmed editor a script or a pitch that's likely to go unread. If you want to make comics... you have to make comics. *The Lazarus Slaves* was impressive, a good concept well-executed, and showed a commitment to not only doing the work, but finishing the work.

The following year, I was having a drink with Phillip at a hotel bar during San Diego's annual pop-culture mecca. My friend Filip Sablik of BOOM! (the best man-hugger in comics) was at a nearby table and I made an introduction: "Phil, meet Fil." Phillip had finished pages from a number of different projects on his Kindle and showed them off. One of them was *Last Sons of America*, which you now hold in your hands.

I don't need to tell you much about this story; you're going to experience it yourself, and you should go into it unspoiled. But I will tell you that it has three things that every comic needs: characters you care about, a compelling concept, and terrific artwork. The art is by Matthew Dow Smith, who's been a friend for the better part of two decades, and his work here with colorist Doug Garbark perfectly matches the dystopian tale being told.

I'm proud of having played even a small part in helping *Last Sons of America* come into the world. Phillip's next BOOM! project, *Warlords of Appalachia*, has already been announced, and there's more on the way. This is what building a career looks like. I think you'll be glad you got in on the ground floor.

RON MARZ
Upstate New York
August 2016

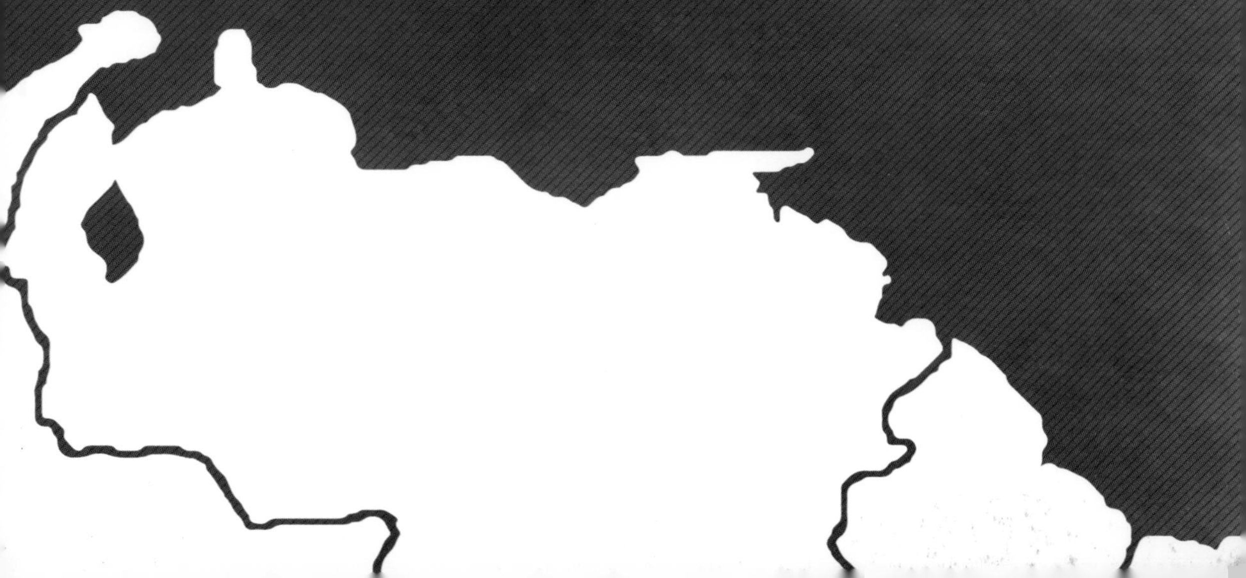

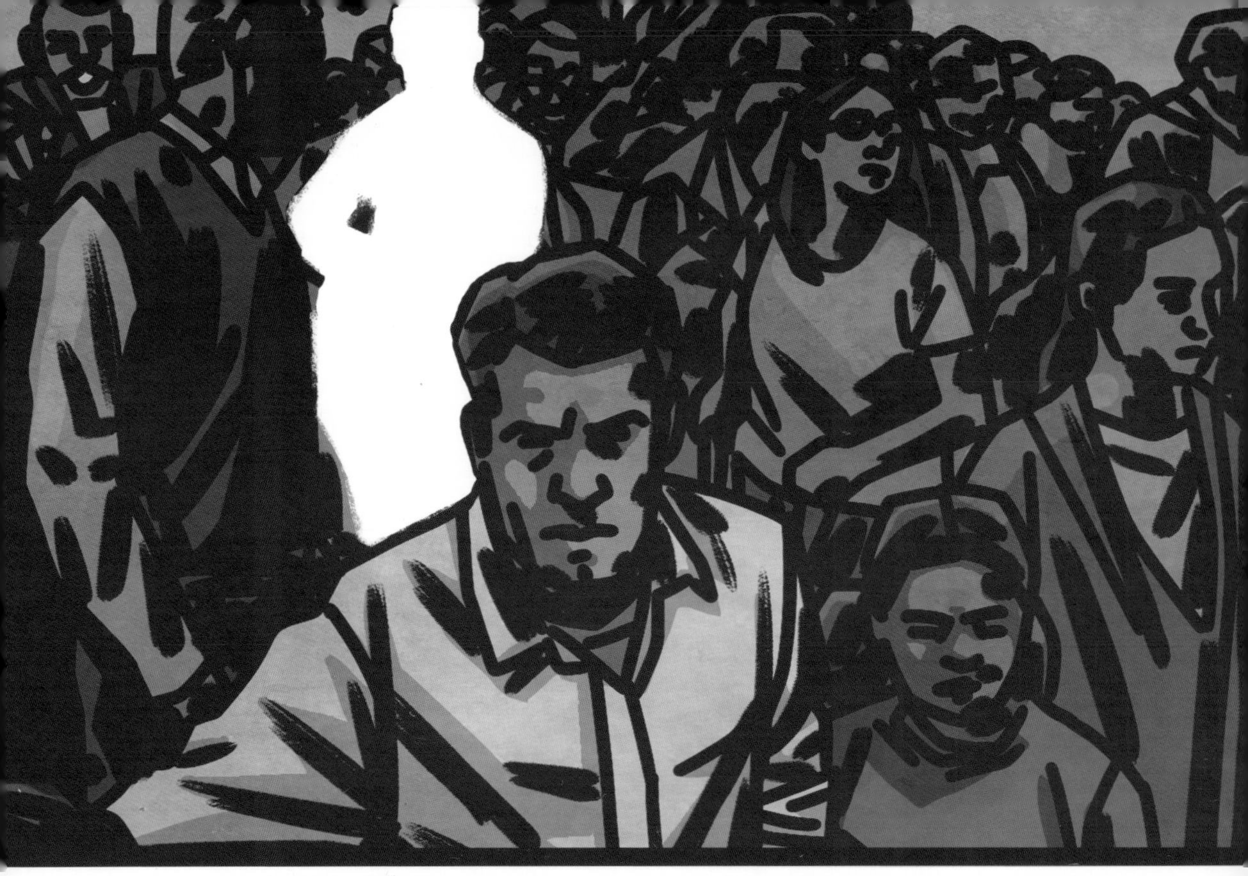

ONE

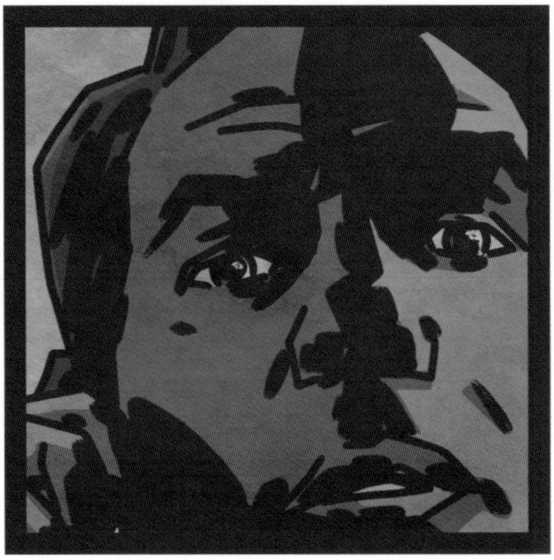

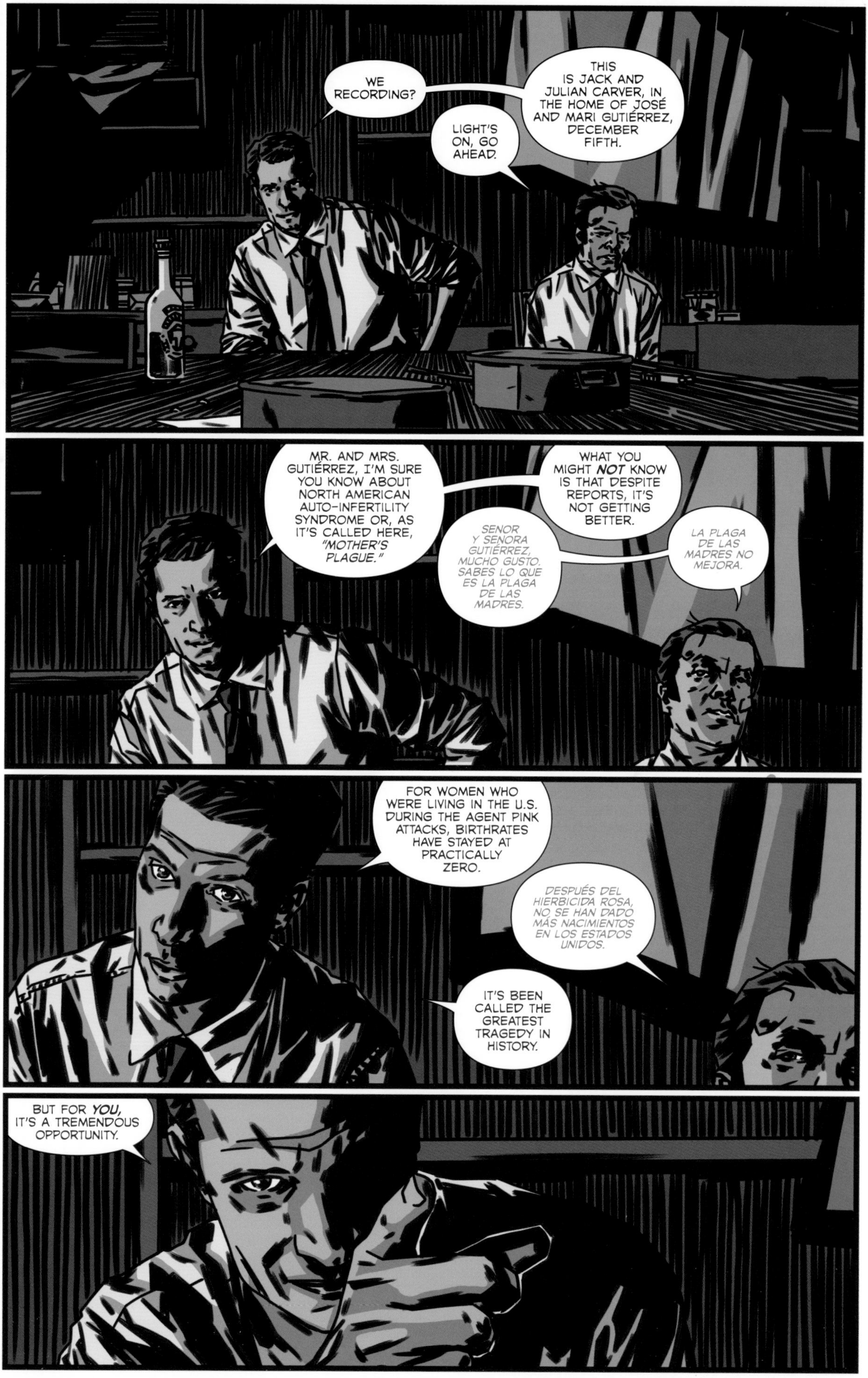
WE RECORDING?
THIS IS JACK AND JULIAN CARVER, IN THE HOME OF JOSÉ AND MARI GUTIÉRREZ, DECEMBER FIFTH.
LIGHT'S ON, GO AHEAD.
MR. AND MRS. GUTIÉRREZ, I'M SURE YOU KNOW ABOUT NORTH AMERICAN AUTO-INFERTILITY SYNDROME OR, AS IT'S CALLED HERE, "MOTHER'S PLAGUE."
WHAT YOU MIGHT NOT KNOW IS THAT DESPITE REPORTS, IT'S NOT GETTING BETTER.
SENOR Y SENORA GUTIÉRREZ, MUCHO GUSTO. SABES LO QUE ES LA PLAGA DE LAS MADRES.
LA PLAGA DE LAS MADRES NO MEJORA.
FOR WOMEN WHO WERE LIVING IN THE U.S. DURING THE AGENT PINK ATTACKS, BIRTHRATES HAVE STAYED AT PRACTICALLY ZERO.
DESPUÉS DEL HIERBICIDA ROSA, NO SE HAN DADO MÁS NACIMIENTOS EN LOS ESTADOS UNIDOS.
IT'S BEEN CALLED THE GREATEST TRAGEDY IN HISTORY.
BUT FOR YOU, IT'S A TREMENDOUS OPPORTUNITY.

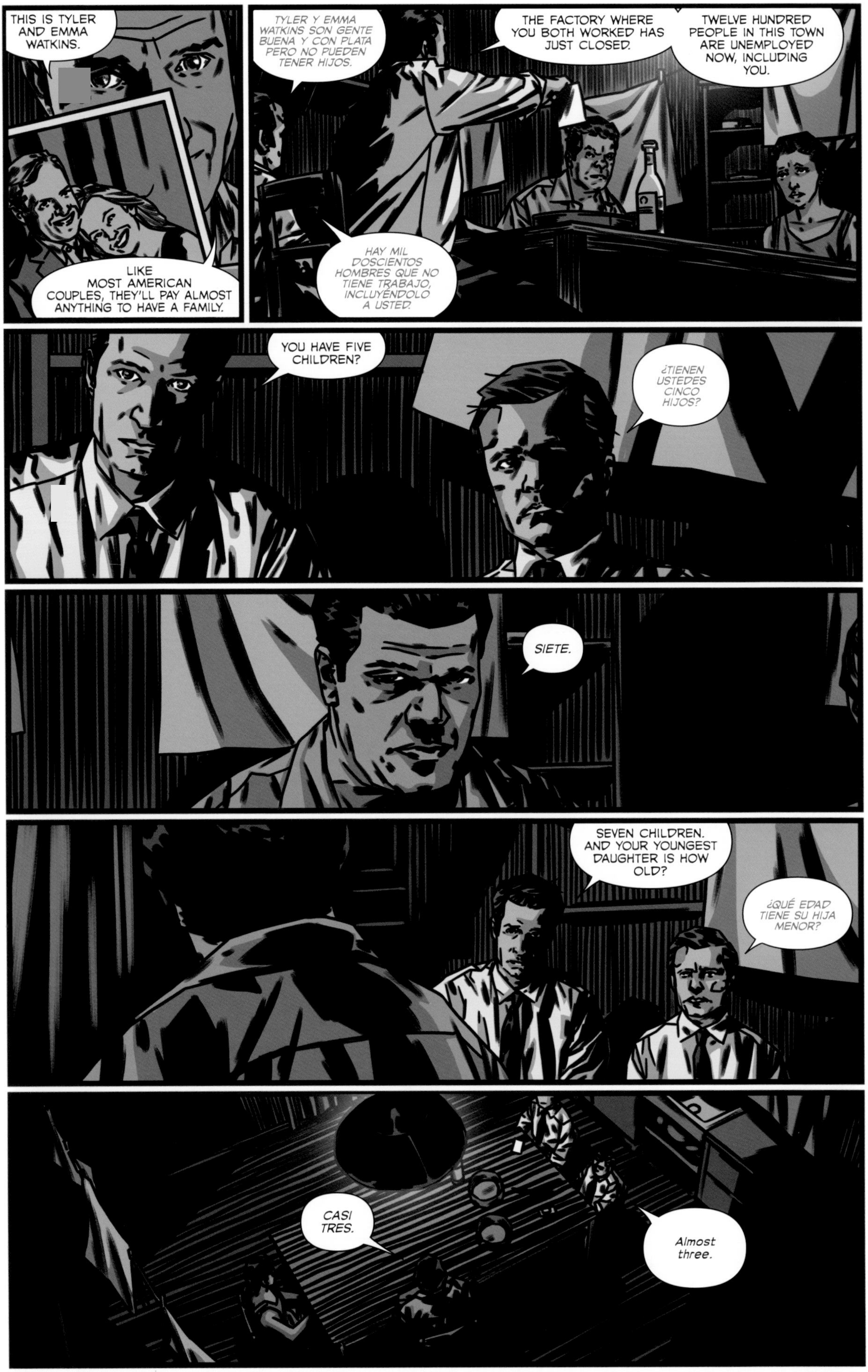

THIS IS TYLER AND EMMA WATKINS.
LIKE MOST AMERICAN COUPLES, THEY'LL PAY ALMOST ANYTHING TO HAVE A FAMILY.
TYLER Y EMMA WATKINS SON GENTE BUENA Y CON PLATA PERO NO PUEDEN TENER HIJOS.
THE FACTORY WHERE YOU BOTH WORKED HAS JUST CLOSED.
TWELVE HUNDRED PEOPLE IN THIS TOWN ARE UNEMPLOYED NOW, INCLUDING YOU.
HAY MIL DOSCIENTOS HOMBRES QUE NO TIENE TRABAJO, INCLUYÉNDOLO A USTED.
YOU HAVE FIVE CHILDREN?
¿TIENEN USTEDES CINCO HIJOS?
SIETE.
SEVEN CHILDREN. AND YOUR YOUNGEST DAUGHTER IS HOW OLD?
¿QUÉ EDAD TIENE SU HIJA MENOR?
CASI TRES.
Almost three.

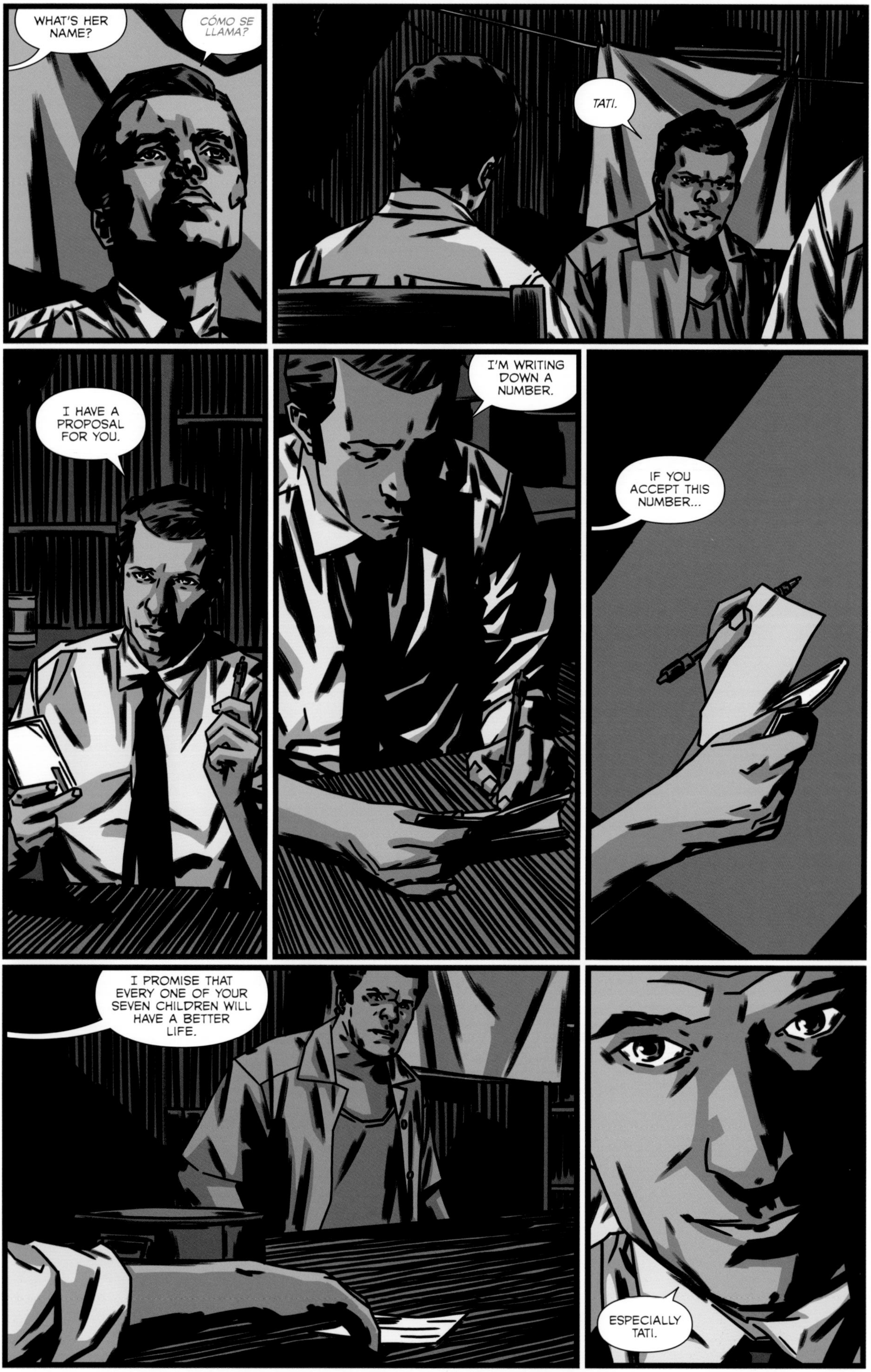
WHAT'S HER NAME?
CÓMO SE LLAMA?
TATI.
I HAVE A PROPOSAL FOR YOU.
I'M WRITING DOWN A NUMBER.
IF YOU ACCEPT THIS NUMBER...
I PROMISE THAT EVERY ONE OF YOUR SEVEN CHILDREN WILL HAVE A BETTER LIFE.
ESPECIALLY TATI.

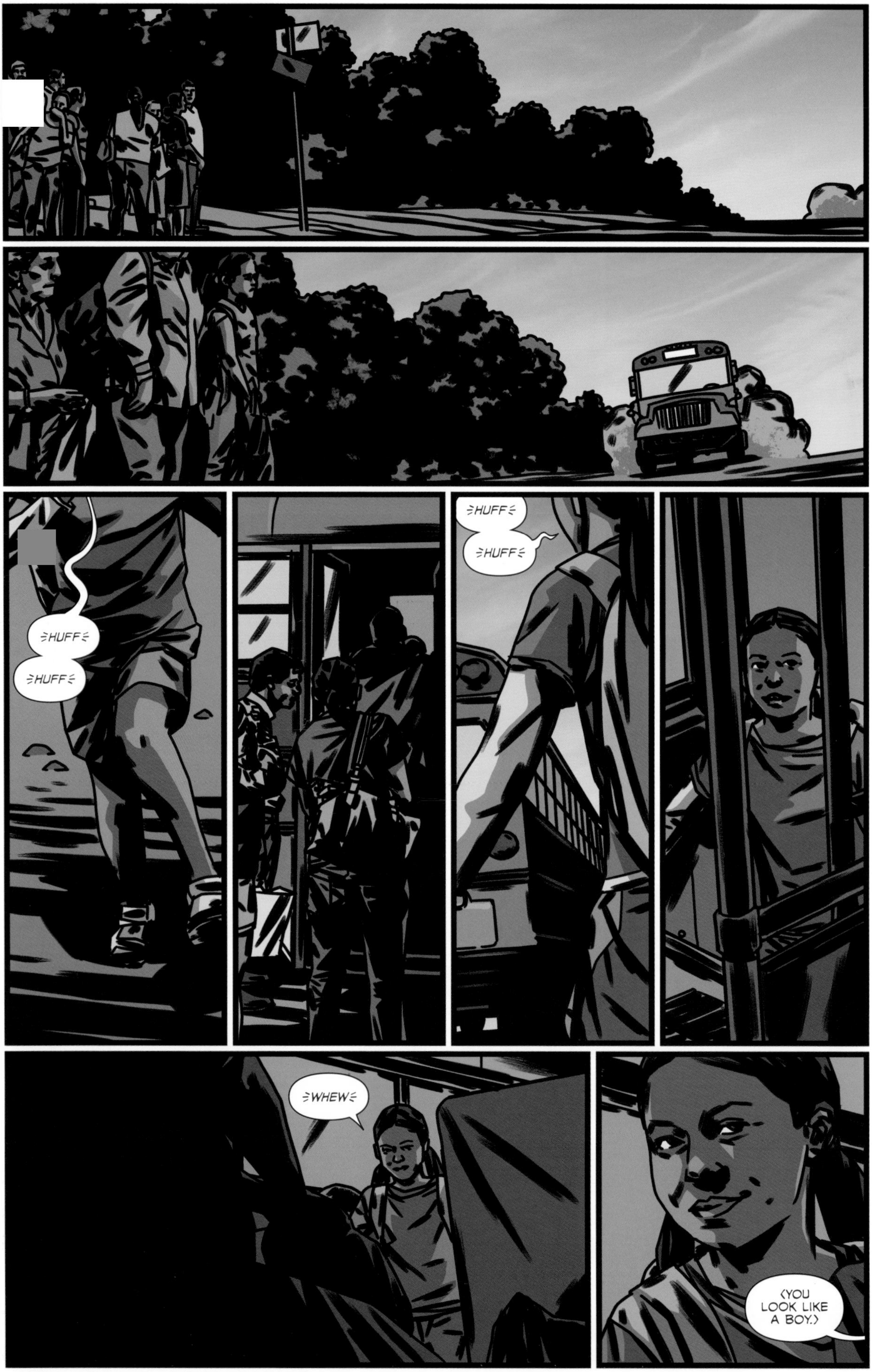
HUFF
HUFF
HUFF
HUFF
WHEW
‹YOU LOOK LIKE A BOY.›

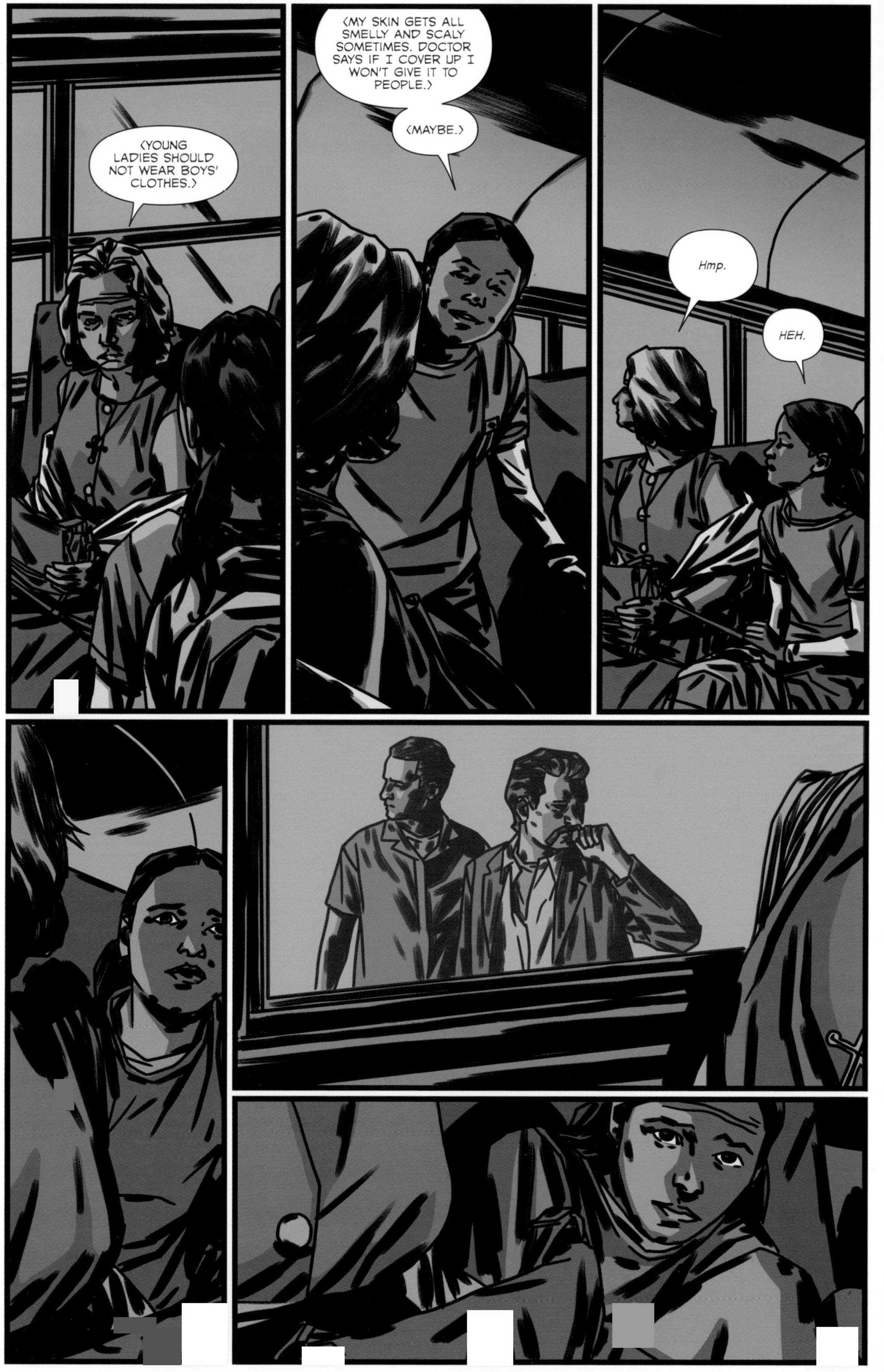
⟨YOUNG LADIES SHOULD NOT WEAR BOYS' CLOTHES.⟩
⟨MY SKIN GETS ALL SMELLY AND SCALY SOMETIMES. DOCTOR SAYS IF I COVER UP I WON'T GIVE IT TO PEOPLE.⟩
⟨MAYBE.⟩
Hmp.
HEH.

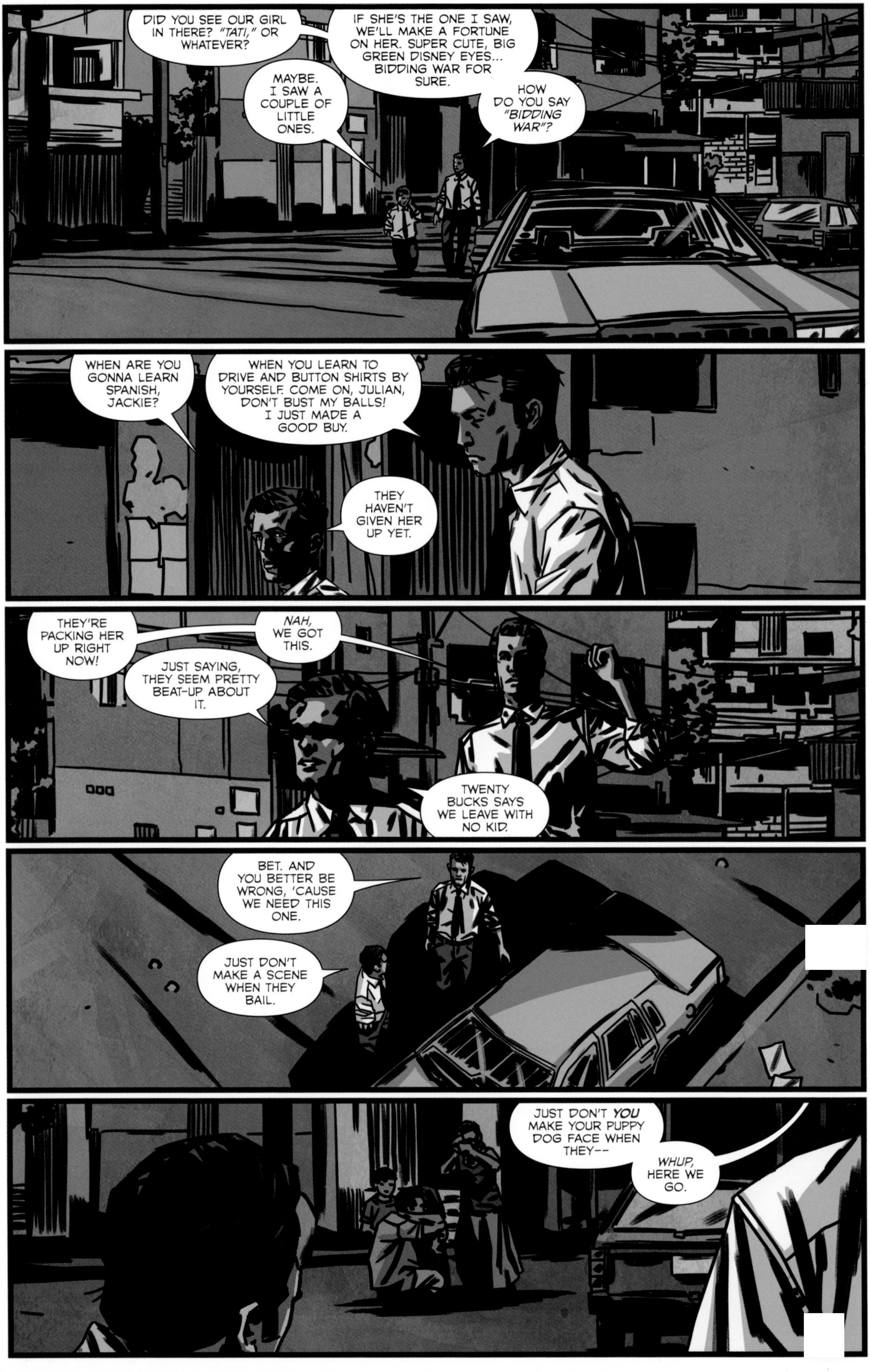
DID YOU SEE OUR GIRL IN THERE? "TATI," OR WHATEVER?
MAYBE. I SAW A COUPLE OF LITTLE ONES.
IF SHE'S THE ONE I SAW, WE'LL MAKE A FORTUNE ON HER. SUPER CUTE, BIG GREEN DISNEY EYES... BIDDING WAR FOR SURE.
HOW DO YOU SAY "BIDDING WAR"?
WHEN ARE YOU GONNA LEARN SPANISH, JACKIE?
WHEN YOU LEARN TO DRIVE AND BUTTON SHIRTS BY YOURSELF. COME ON, JULIAN, DON'T BUST MY BALLS! I JUST MADE A GOOD BUY.
THEY HAVEN'T GIVEN HER UP YET.
THEY'RE PACKING HER UP RIGHT NOW!
NAH, WE GOT THIS.
JUST SAYING, THEY SEEM PRETTY BEAT-UP ABOUT IT.
TWENTY BUCKS SAYS WE LEAVE WITH NO KID.
BET. AND YOU BETTER BE WRONG, 'CAUSE WE NEED THIS ONE.
JUST DON'T MAKE A SCENE WHEN THEY BAIL.
JUST DON'T YOU MAKE YOUR PUPPY DOG FACE WHEN THEY--
WHUP, HERE WE GO.

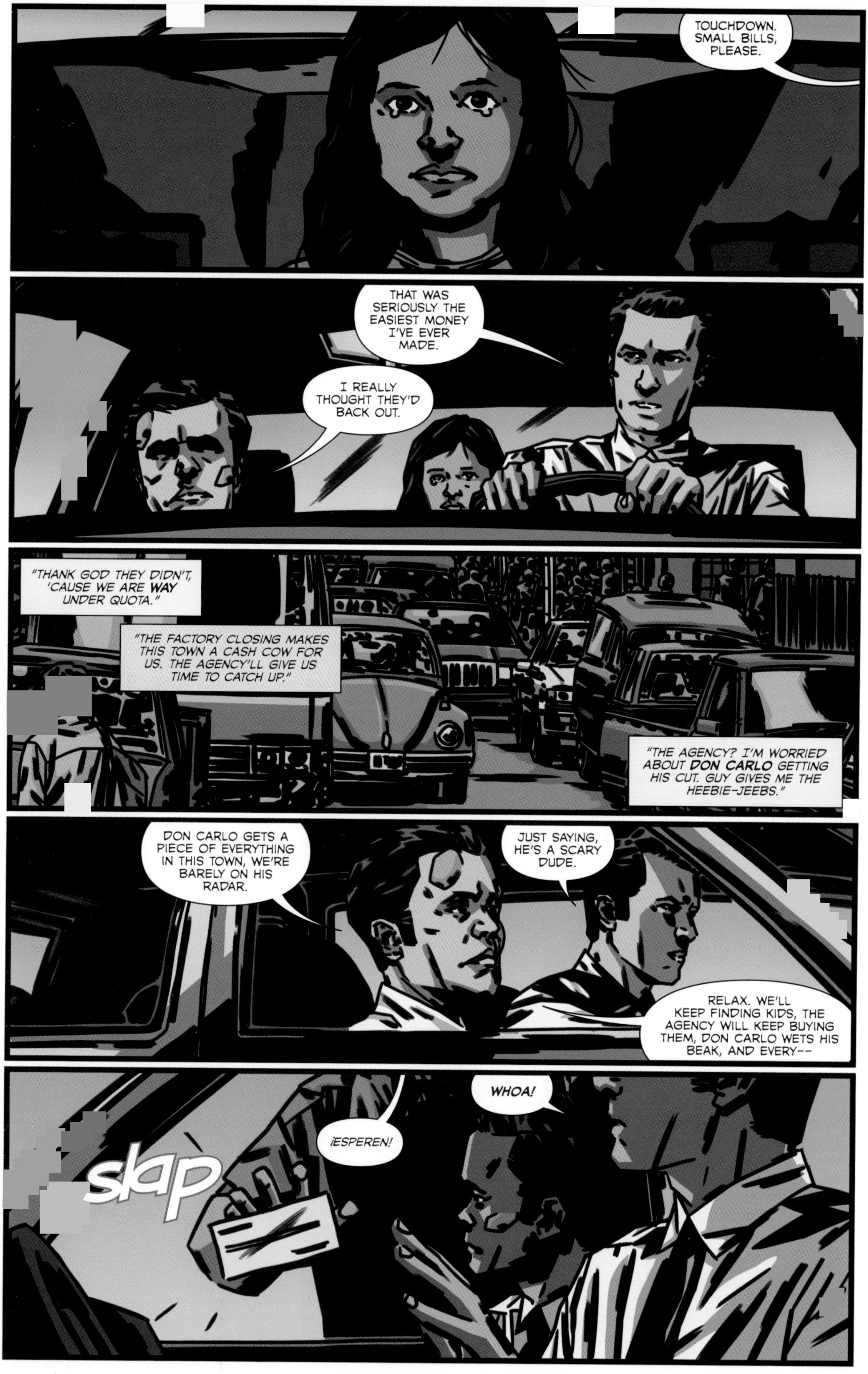
TOUCHDOWN. SMALL BILLS, PLEASE.
THAT WAS SERIOUSLY THE EASIEST MONEY I'VE EVER MADE.
I REALLY THOUGHT THEY'D BACK OUT.
"THANK GOD THEY DIDN'T, 'CAUSE WE ARE WAY UNDER QUOTA."
"THE FACTORY CLOSING MAKES THIS TOWN A CASH COW FOR US. THE AGENCY'LL GIVE US TIME TO CATCH UP."
"THE AGENCY? I'M WORRIED ABOUT DON CARLO GETTING HIS CUT. GUY GIVES ME THE HEEBIE-JEEBS."
DON CARLO GETS A PIECE OF EVERYTHING IN THIS TOWN, WE'RE BARELY ON HIS RADAR.
JUST SAYING, HE'S A SCARY DUDE.
RELAX. WE'LL KEEP FINDING KIDS, THE AGENCY WILL KEEP BUYING THEM, DON CARLO WETS HIS BEAK, AND EVERY--
slap
¡ESPEREN!
WHOA!

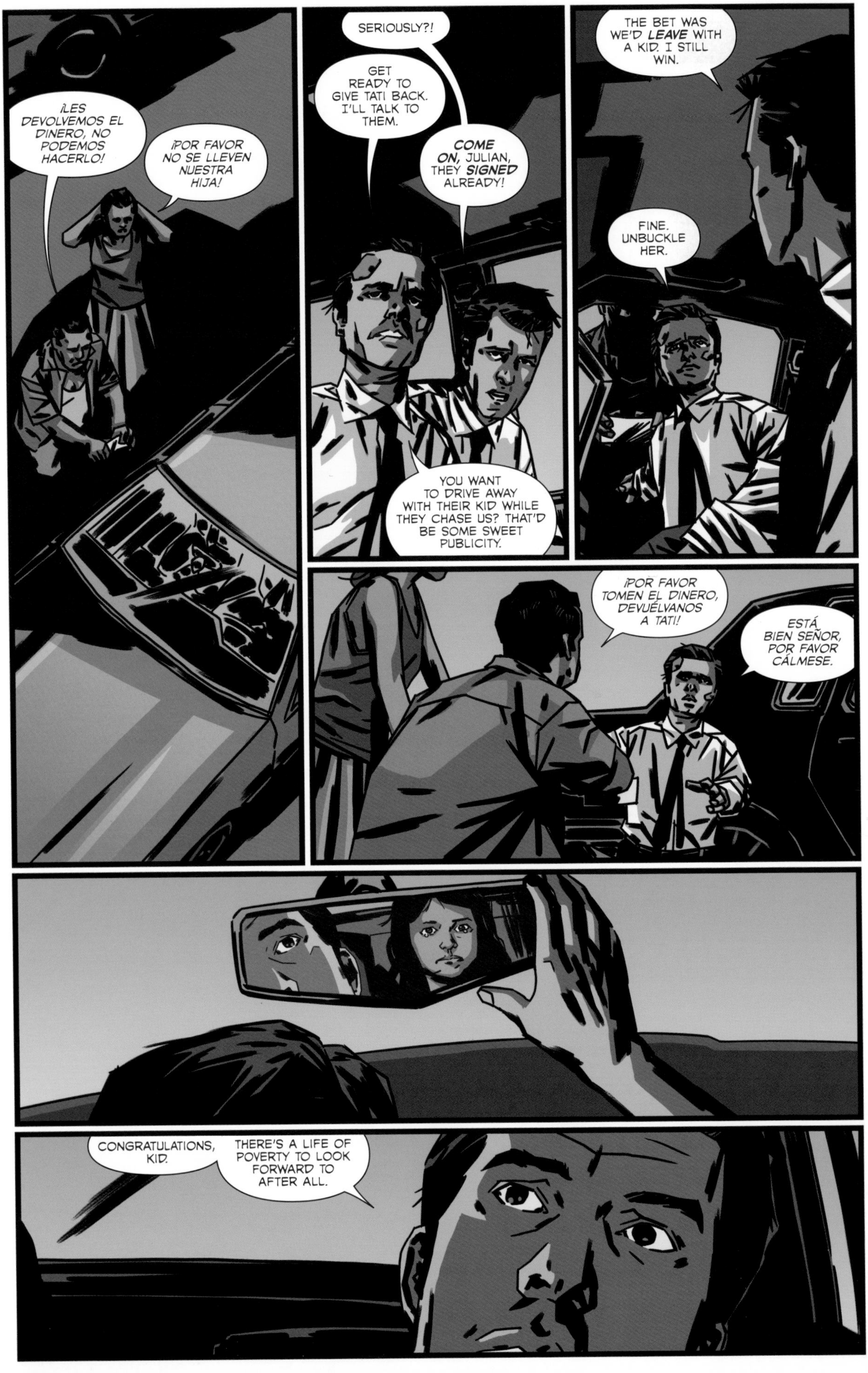
¡LES DEVOLVEMOS EL DINERO, NO PODEMOS HACERLO!
¡POR FAVOR NO SE LLEVEN NUESTRA HIJA!
SERIOUSLY?!
GET READY TO GIVE TATI BACK. I'LL TALK TO THEM.
COME ON, JULIAN, THEY SIGNED ALREADY!
YOU WANT TO DRIVE AWAY WITH THEIR KID WHILE THEY CHASE US? THAT'D BE SOME SWEET PUBLICITY.
THE BET WAS WE'D LEAVE WITH A KID. I STILL WIN.
FINE. UNBUCKLE HER.
¡POR FAVOR TOMEN EL DINERO, DEVUÉLVANOS A TATI!
ESTÁ BIEN SEÑOR, POR FAVOR CÁLMESE.
CONGRATULATIONS, KID.
THERE'S A LIFE OF POVERTY TO LOOK FORWARD TO AFTER ALL.

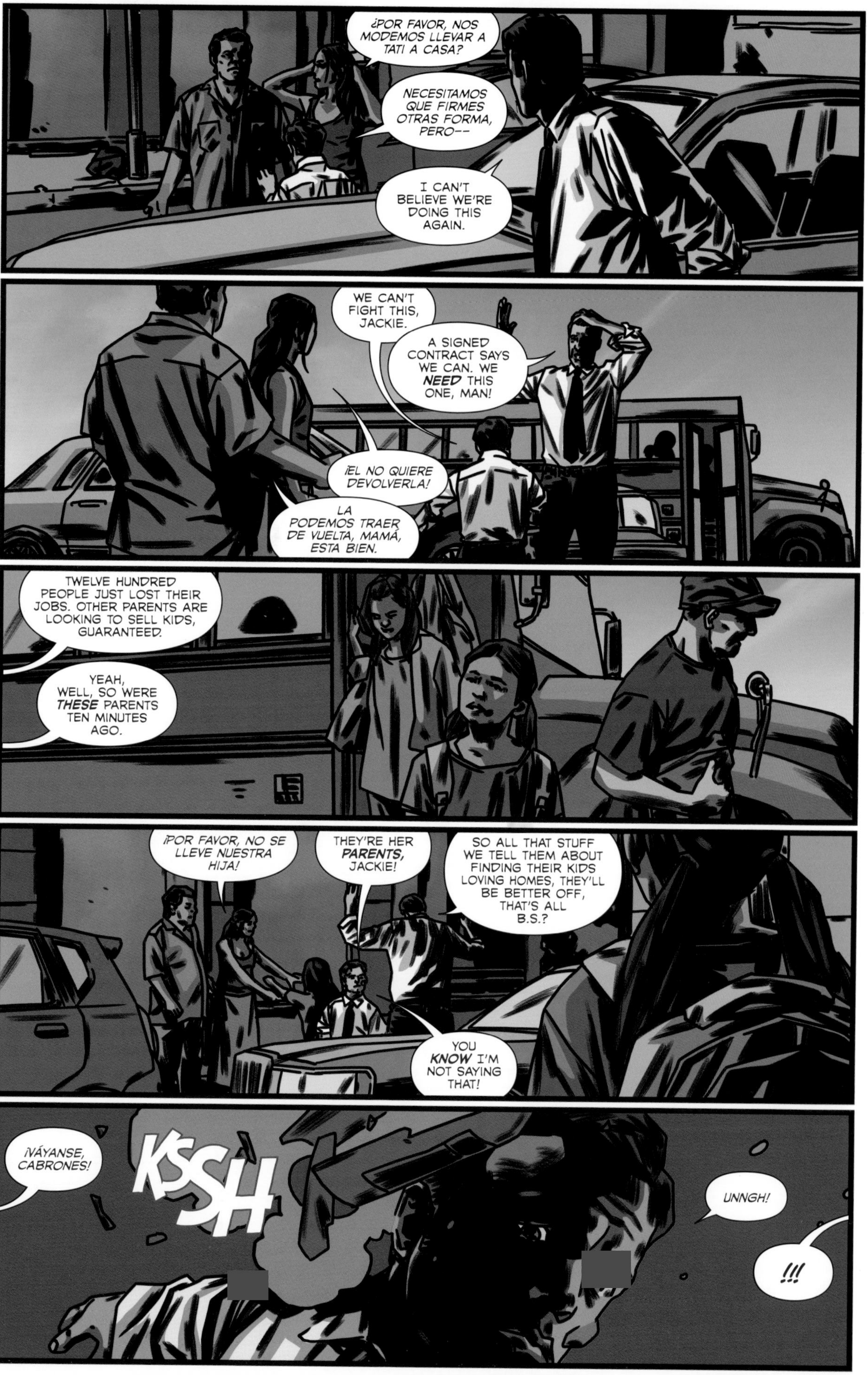
¿POR FAVOR, NOS MODEMOS LLEVAR A TATI A CASA?
NECESITAMOS QUE FIRMES OTRAS FORMA, PERO--
I CAN'T BELIEVE WE'RE DOING THIS AGAIN.
WE CAN'T FIGHT THIS, JACKIE.
A SIGNED CONTRACT SAYS WE CAN. WE NEED THIS ONE, MAN!
¡EL NO QUIERE DEVOLVERLA!
LA PODEMOS TRAER DE VUELTA, MAMÁ, ESTA BIEN.
TWELVE HUNDRED PEOPLE JUST LOST THEIR JOBS. OTHER PARENTS ARE LOOKING TO SELL KIDS, GUARANTEED.
YEAH, WELL, SO WERE THESE PARENTS TEN MINUTES AGO.
¡POR FAVOR, NO SE LLEVE NUESTRA HIJA!
THEY'RE HER PARENTS, JACKIE!
SO ALL THAT STUFF WE TELL THEM ABOUT FINDING THEIR KIDS LOVING HOMES, THEY'LL BE BETTER OFF, THAT'S ALL B.S.?
YOU KNOW I'M NOT SAYING THAT!
¡VÁYANSE, CABRONES!
KSSH
UNNGH!
!!!

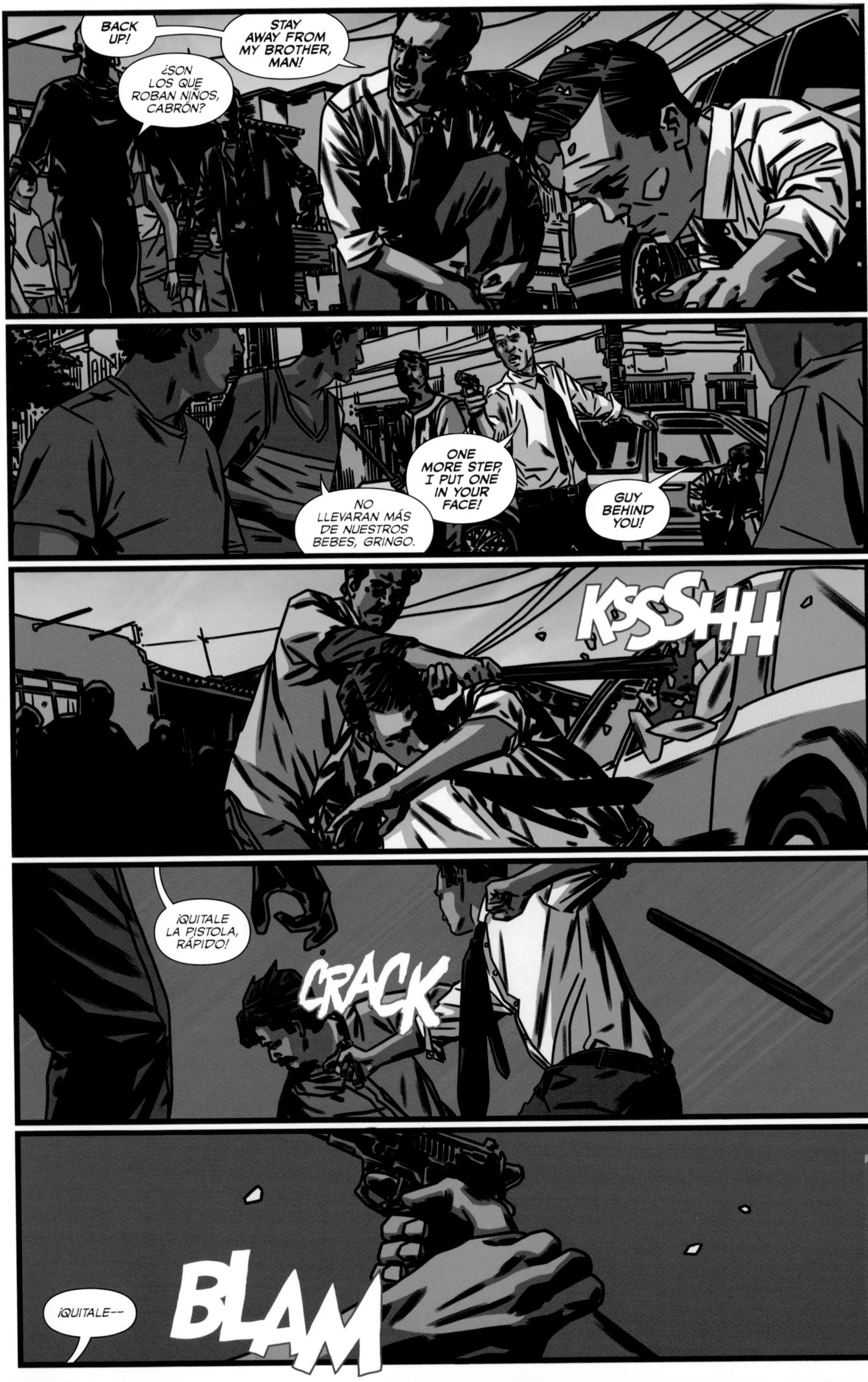
BACK UP!
STAY AWAY FROM MY BROTHER, MAN!
¿SON LOS QUE ROBAN NIÑOS, CABRÓN?
NO LLEVARAN MÁS DE NUESTROS BEBES, GRINGO.
ONE MORE STEP, I PUT ONE IN YOUR FACE!
GUY BEHIND YOU!
KSSSHHH
¡QUITALE LA PISTOLA, RÁPIDO!
CRACK
¡QUITALE--
BLAM

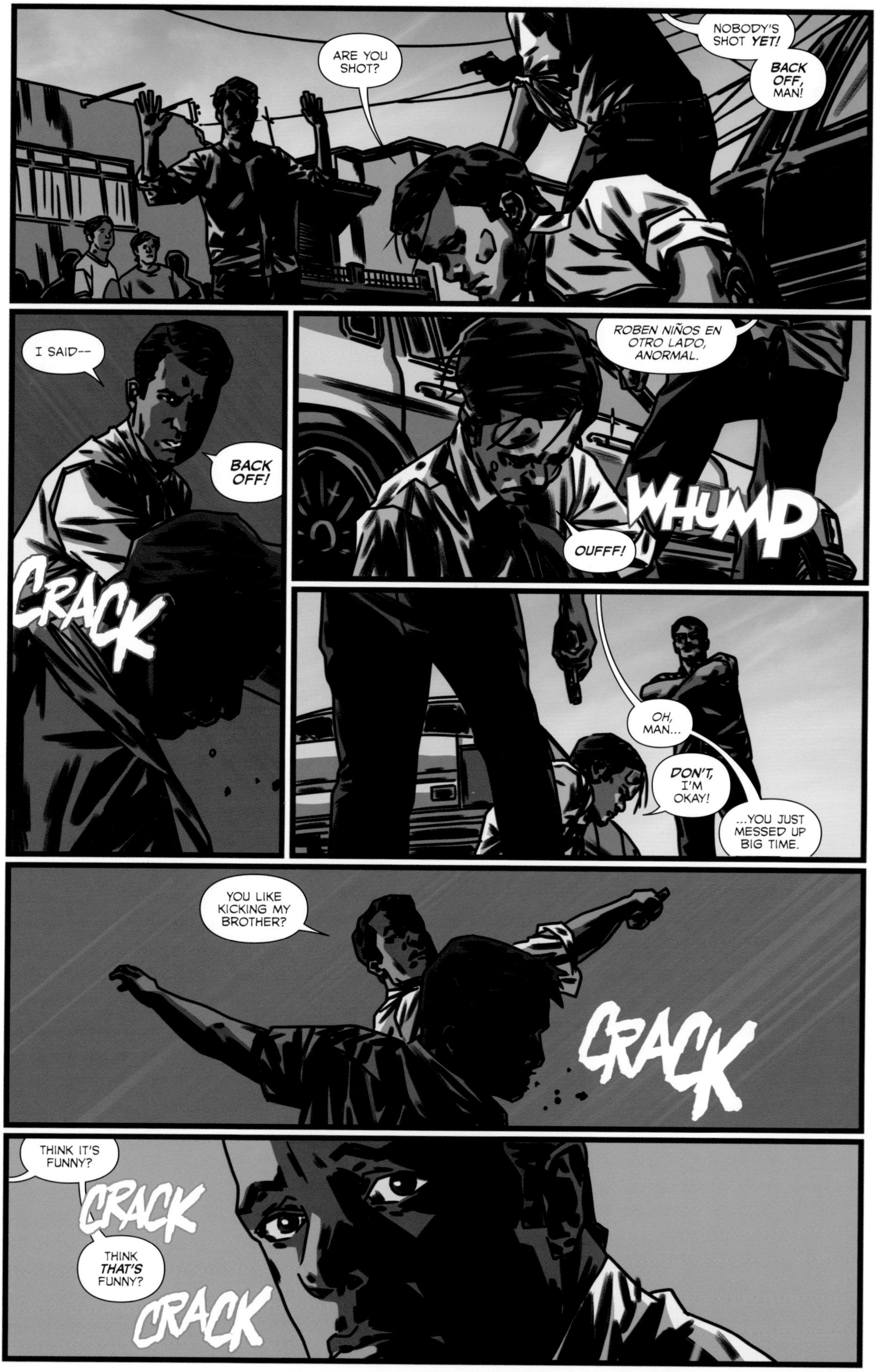
ARE YOU SHOT?
NOBODY'S SHOT *YET!*
BACK OFF, MAN!
I SAID--
BACK OFF!
CRACK
ROBEN NIÑOS EN OTRO LADO, ANORMAL.
WHUMP
OUFFF!
OH, MAN...
DON'T, I'M OKAY!
...YOU JUST MESSED UP BIG TIME.
YOU LIKE KICKING MY BROTHER?
CRACK
THINK IT'S FUNNY?
CRACK
THINK *THAT'S* FUNNY?
CRACK

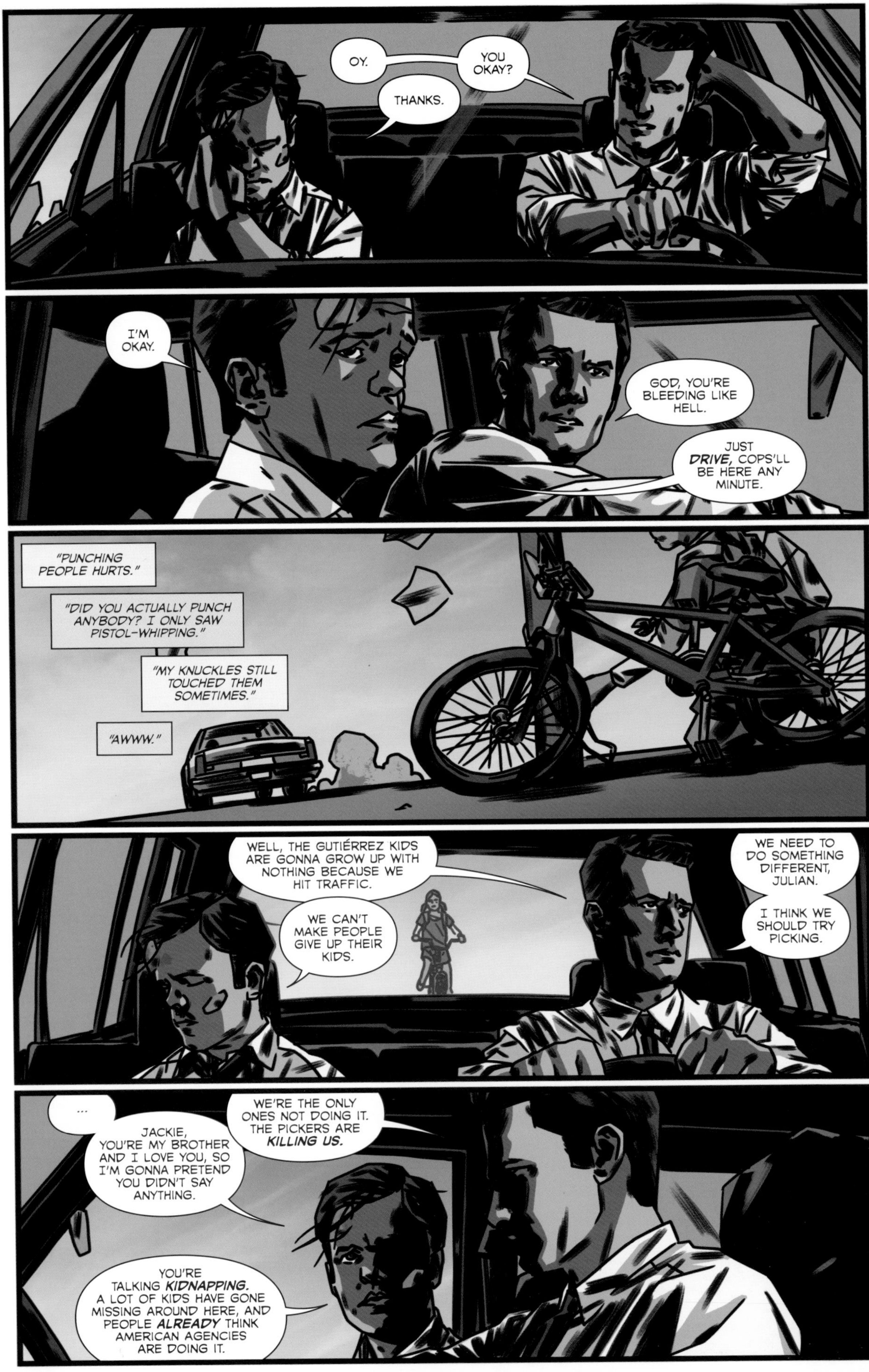
OY.
THANKS.
YOU OKAY?
I'M OKAY.
GOD, YOU'RE BLEEDING LIKE HELL.
JUST DRIVE, COPS'LL BE HERE ANY MINUTE.
"PUNCHING PEOPLE HURTS."
"DID YOU ACTUALLY PUNCH ANYBODY? I ONLY SAW PISTOL-WHIPPING."
"MY KNUCKLES STILL TOUCHED THEM SOMETIMES."
"AWWW."
WELL, THE GUTIÉRREZ KIDS ARE GONNA GROW UP WITH NOTHING BECAUSE WE HIT TRAFFIC.
WE CAN'T MAKE PEOPLE GIVE UP THEIR KIDS.
WE NEED TO DO SOMETHING DIFFERENT, JULIAN.
I THINK WE SHOULD TRY PICKING.
...
WE'RE THE ONLY ONES NOT DOING IT. THE PICKERS ARE KILLING US.
JACKIE, YOU'RE MY BROTHER AND I LOVE YOU, SO I'M GONNA PRETEND YOU DIDN'T SAY ANYTHING.
YOU'RE TALKING KIDNAPPING. A LOT OF KIDS HAVE GONE MISSING AROUND HERE, AND PEOPLE ALREADY THINK AMERICAN AGENCIES ARE DOING IT.

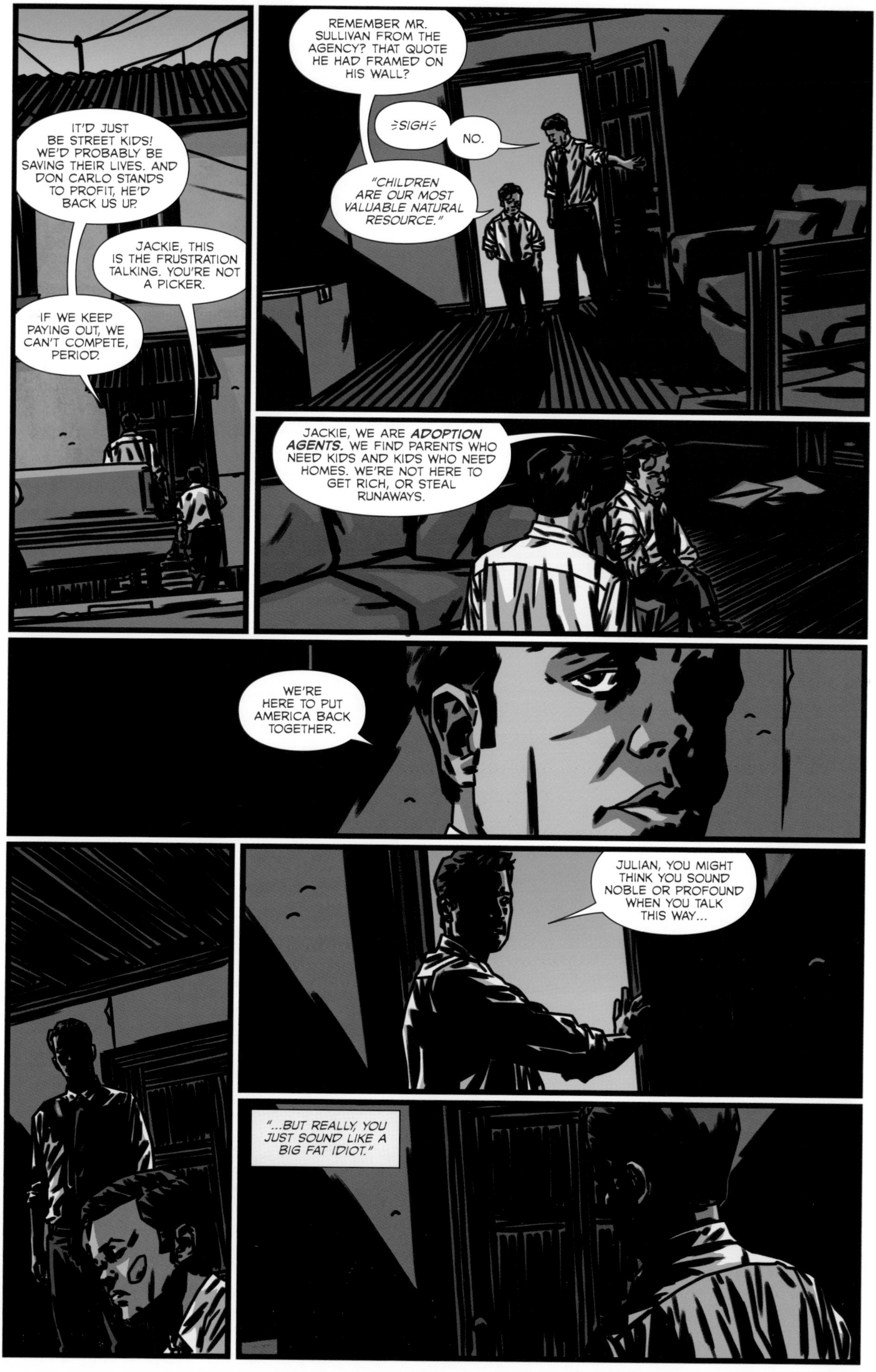
IT'D JUST BE STREET KIDS! WE'D PROBABLY BE SAVING THEIR LIVES. AND DON CARLO STANDS TO PROFIT, HE'D BACK US UP.
JACKIE, THIS IS THE FRUSTRATION TALKING. YOU'RE NOT A PICKER.
IF WE KEEP PAYING OUT, WE CAN'T COMPETE, PERIOD.
REMEMBER MR. SULLIVAN FROM THE AGENCY? THAT QUOTE HE HAD FRAMED ON HIS WALL?
SIGH
NO.
"CHILDREN ARE OUR MOST VALUABLE NATURAL RESOURCE."
JACKIE, WE ARE ADOPTION AGENTS. WE FIND PARENTS WHO NEED KIDS AND KIDS WHO NEED HOMES. WE'RE NOT HERE TO GET RICH, OR STEAL RUNAWAYS.
WE'RE HERE TO PUT AMERICA BACK TOGETHER.
JULIAN, YOU MIGHT THINK YOU SOUND NOBLE OR PROFOUND WHEN YOU TALK THIS WAY...
"...BUT REALLY, YOU JUST SOUND LIKE A BIG FAT IDIOT."

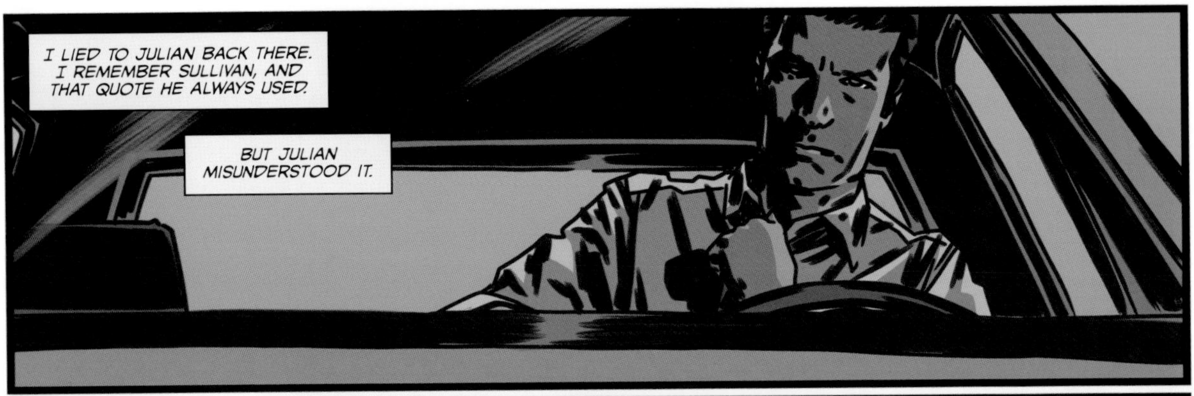
I LIED TO JULIAN BACK THERE. I REMEMBER SULLIVAN, AND THAT QUOTE HE ALWAYS USED.
BUT JULIAN MISUNDERSTOOD IT.
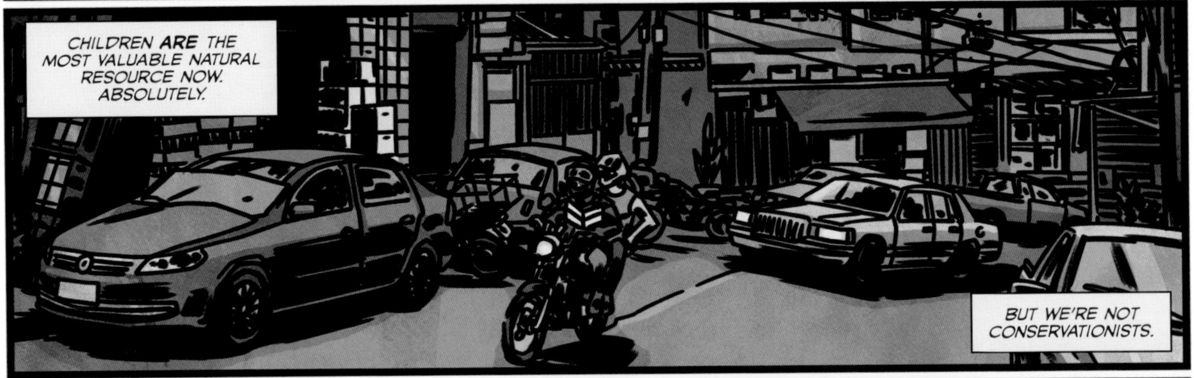
CHILDREN **ARE** THE MOST VALUABLE NATURAL RESOURCE NOW. ABSOLUTELY.
BUT WE'RE NOT CONSERVATIONISTS.
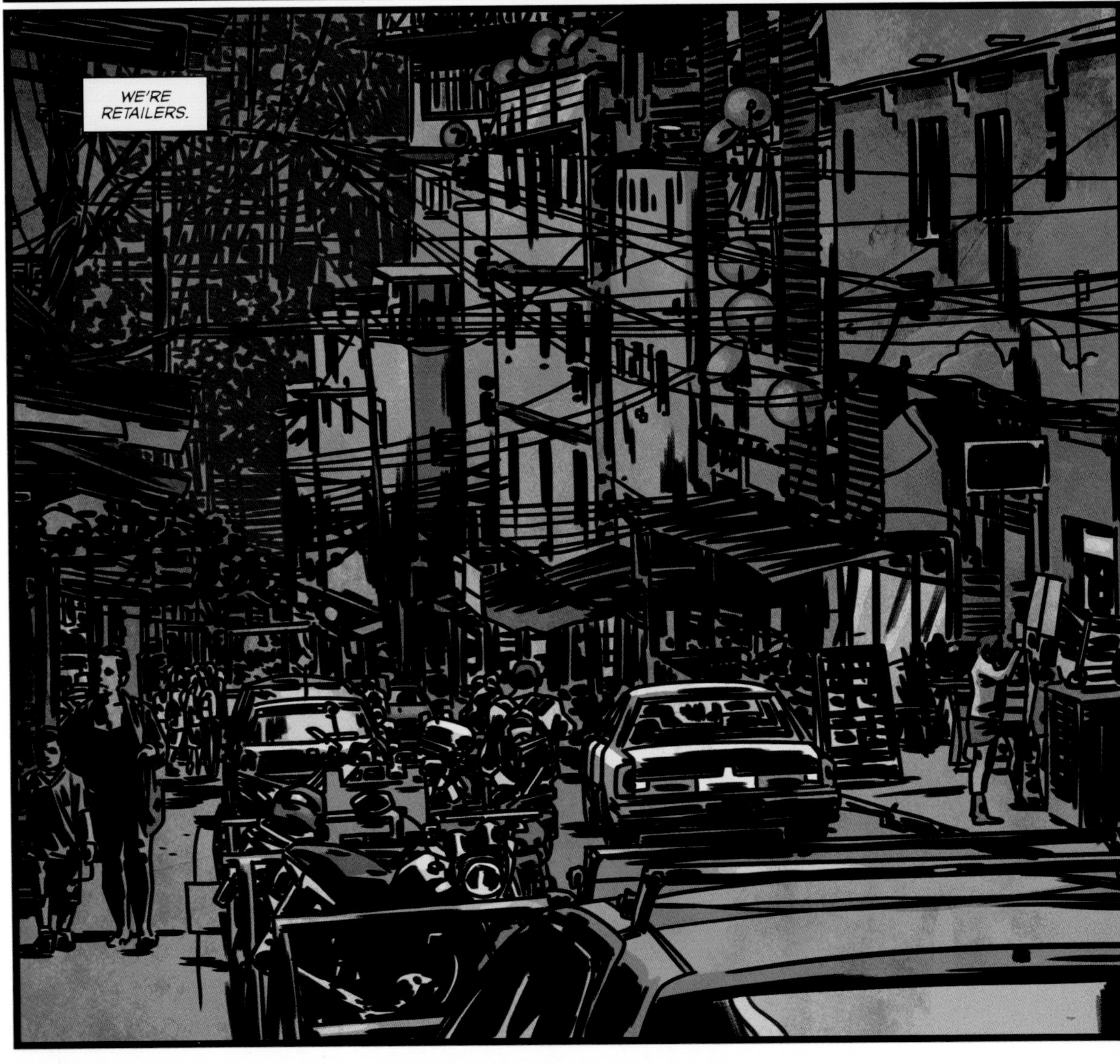
WE'RE RETAILERS.

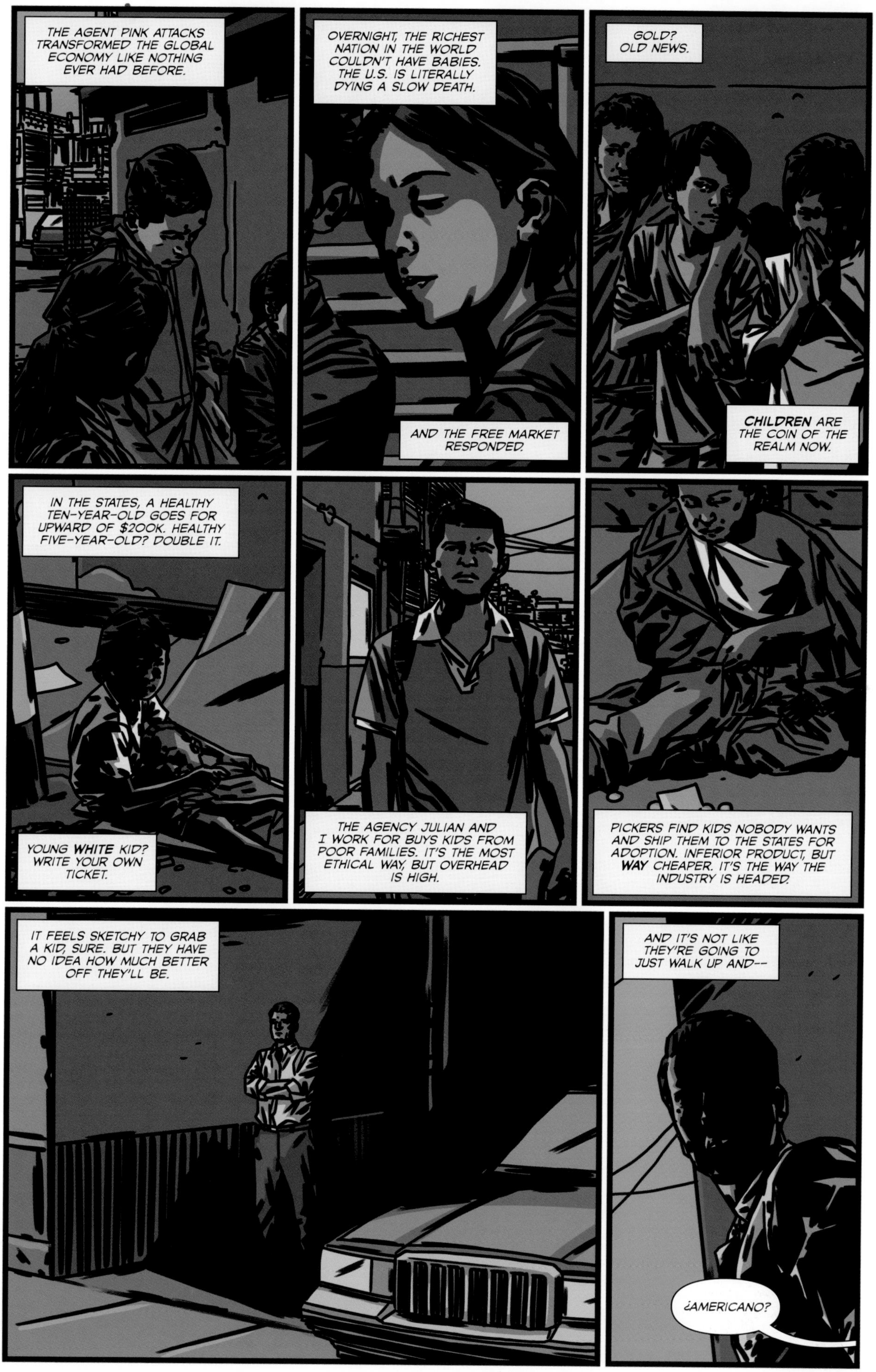
THE AGENT PINK ATTACKS TRANSFORMED THE GLOBAL ECONOMY LIKE NOTHING EVER HAD BEFORE.
OVERNIGHT, THE RICHEST NATION IN THE WORLD COULDN'T HAVE BABIES. THE U.S. IS LITERALLY DYING A SLOW DEATH.
AND THE FREE MARKET RESPONDED.
GOLD? OLD NEWS.
CHILDREN ARE THE COIN OF THE REALM NOW.
IN THE STATES, A HEALTHY TEN-YEAR-OLD GOES FOR UPWARD OF $200K. HEALTHY FIVE-YEAR-OLD? DOUBLE IT.
YOUNG WHITE KID? WRITE YOUR OWN TICKET.
THE AGENCY JULIAN AND I WORK FOR BUYS KIDS FROM POOR FAMILIES. IT'S THE MOST ETHICAL WAY, BUT OVERHEAD IS HIGH.
PICKERS FIND KIDS NOBODY WANTS AND SHIP THEM TO THE STATES FOR ADOPTION. INFERIOR PRODUCT, BUT WAY CHEAPER. IT'S THE WAY THE INDUSTRY IS HEADED.
IT FEELS SKETCHY TO GRAB A KID, SURE. BUT THEY HAVE NO IDEA HOW MUCH BETTER OFF THEY'LL BE.
AND IT'S NOT LIKE THEY'RE GOING TO JUST WALK UP AND--
¿AMERICANO?

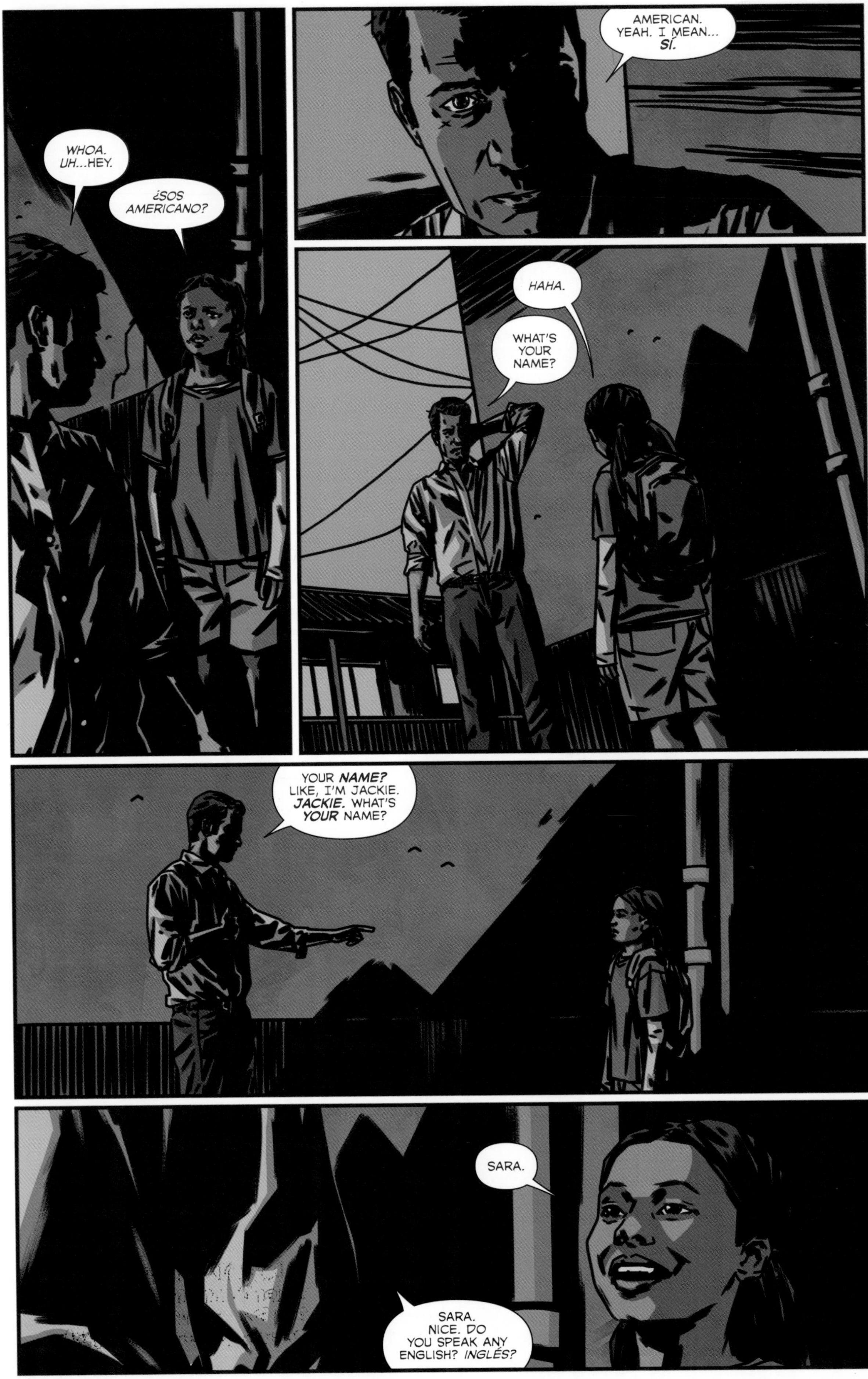
WHOA. UH...HEY.
¿SOS AMERICANO?
AMERICAN. YEAH. I MEAN... *SÍ.*
HAHA.
WHAT'S YOUR NAME?
YOUR ***NAME?*** LIKE, I'M JACKIE. ***JACKIE.*** WHAT'S ***YOUR*** NAME?
SARA.
SARA. NICE. DO YOU SPEAK ANY ENGLISH? *INGLÉS?*

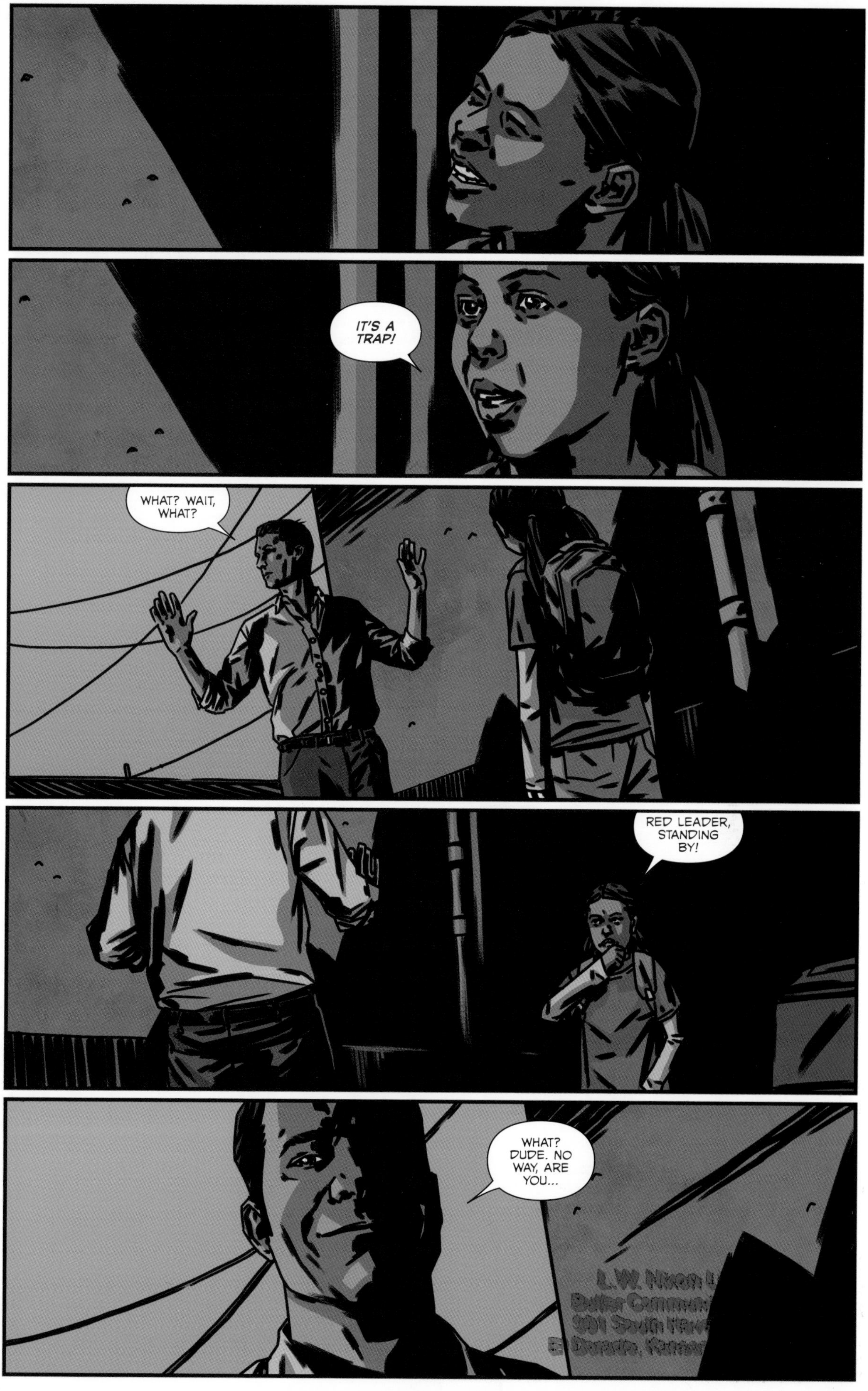
IT'S A TRAP!
WHAT? WAIT, WHAT?
RED LEADER, STANDING BY!
WHAT? DUDE. NO WAY, ARE YOU...

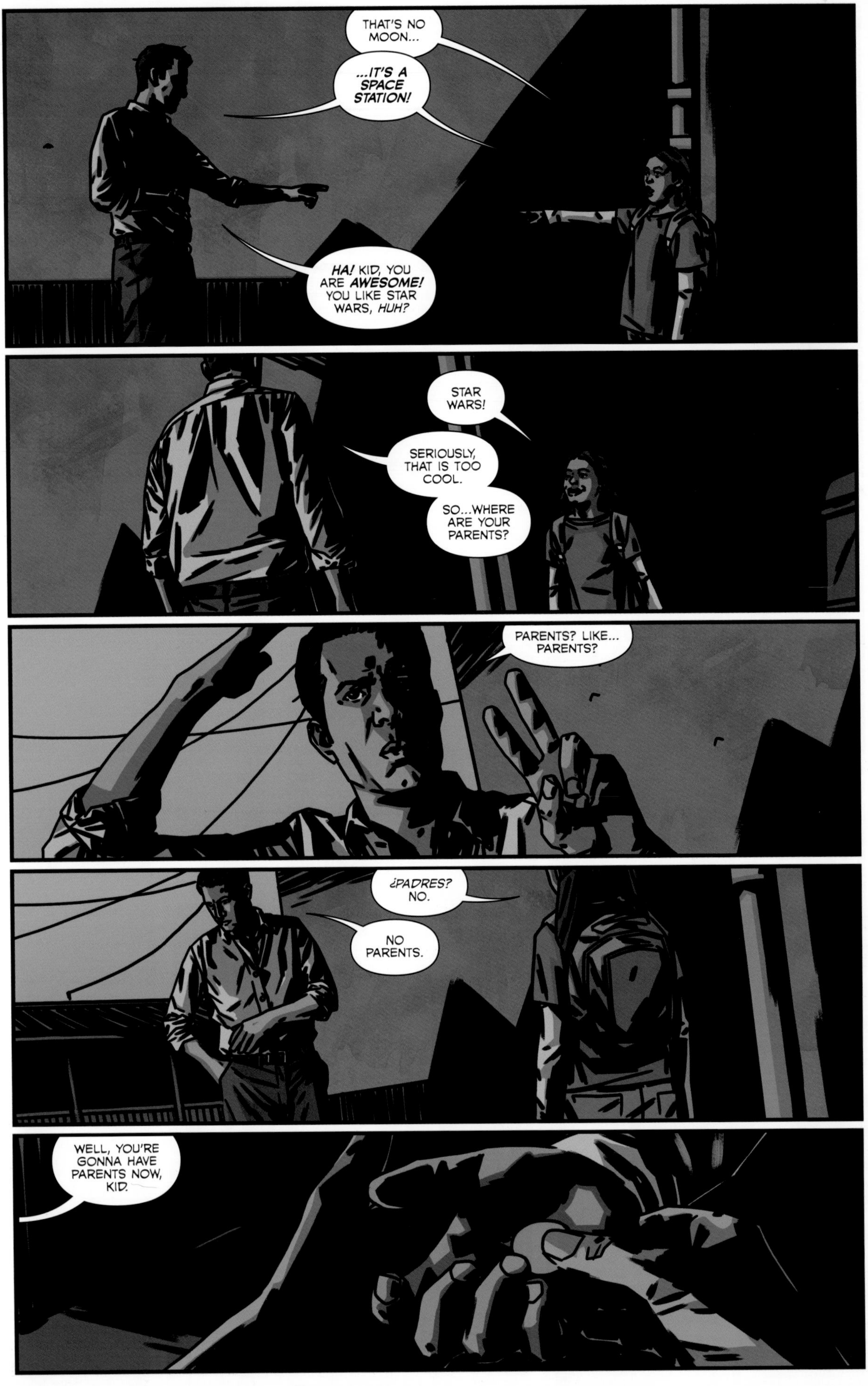
THAT'S NO MOON...
...IT'S A SPACE STATION!
HA! KID, YOU ARE AWESOME! YOU LIKE STAR WARS, HUH?
STAR WARS!
SERIOUSLY, THAT IS TOO COOL.
SO...WHERE ARE YOUR PARENTS?
PARENTS? LIKE... PARENTS?
¿PADRES? NO.
NO PARENTS.
WELL, YOU'RE GONNA HAVE PARENTS NOW, KID.

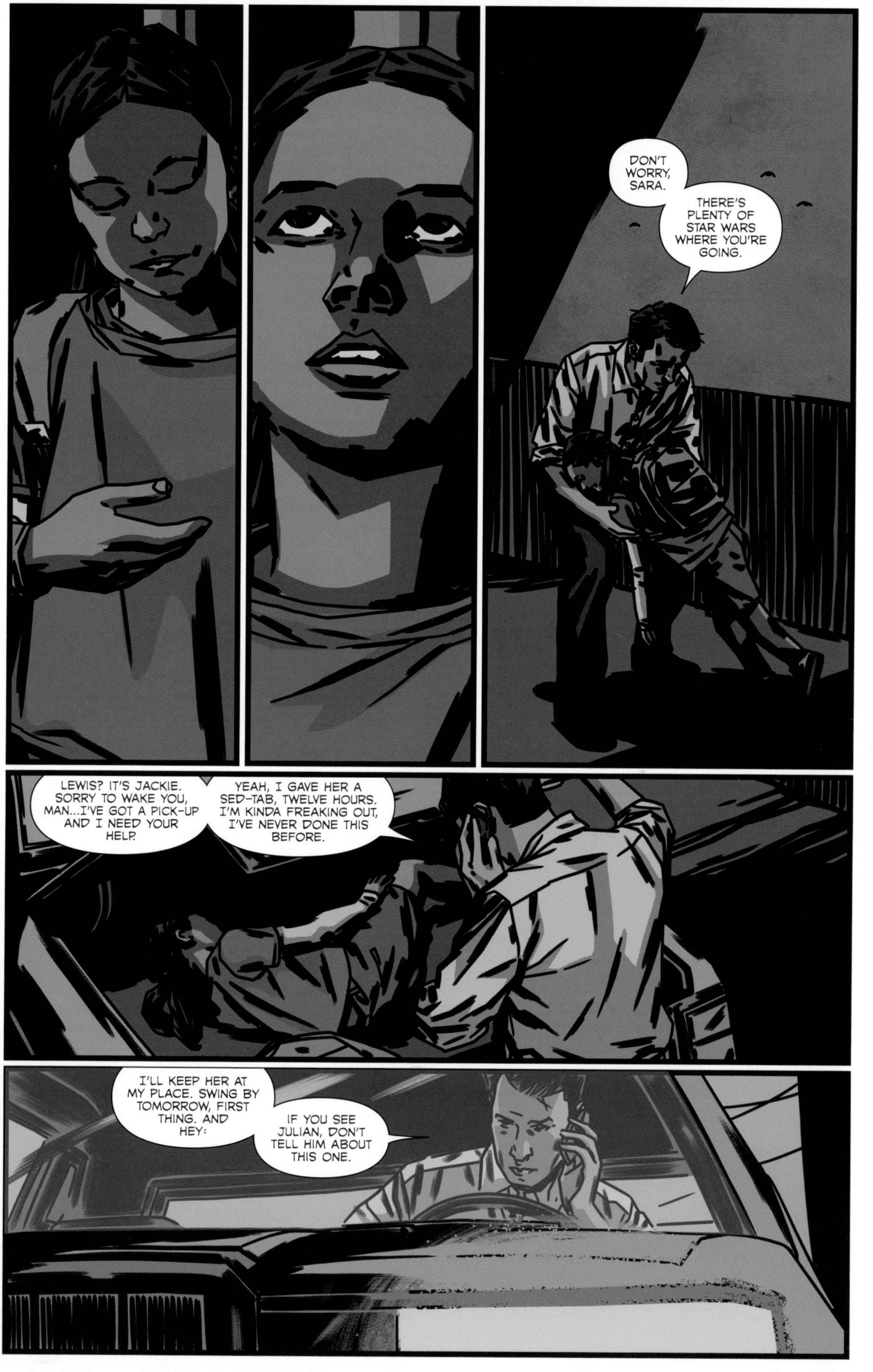
DON'T WORRY, SARA.
THERE'S PLENTY OF STAR WARS WHERE YOU'RE GOING.
LEWIS? IT'S JACKIE. SORRY TO WAKE YOU, MAN...I'VE GOT A PICK-UP AND I NEED YOUR HELP.
YEAH, I GAVE HER A SED-TAB, TWELVE HOURS. I'M KINDA FREAKING OUT, I'VE NEVER DONE THIS BEFORE.
I'LL KEEP HER AT MY PLACE. SWING BY TOMORROW, FIRST THING. AND HEY:
IF YOU SEE JULIAN, DON'T TELL HIM ABOUT THIS ONE.

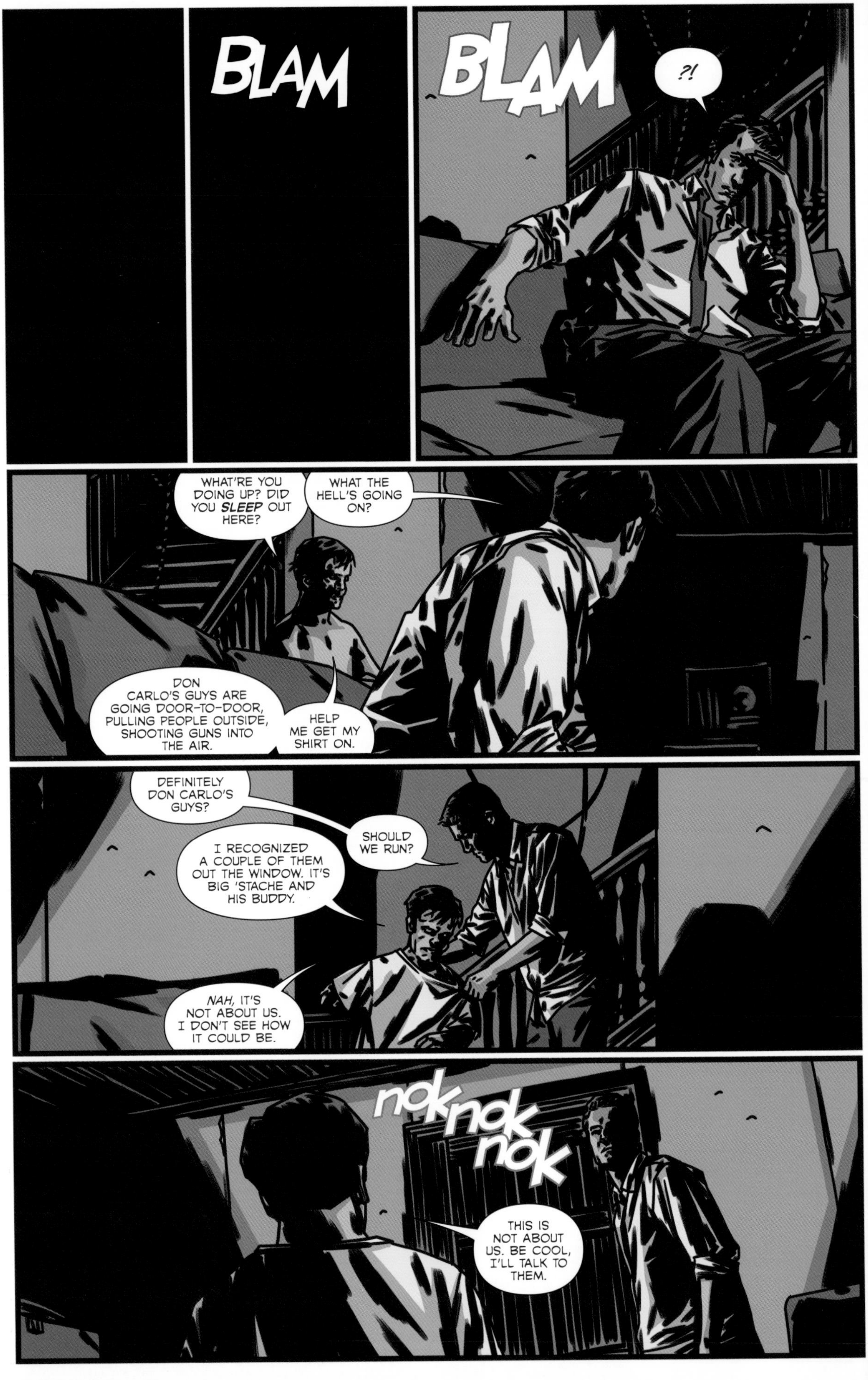
BLAM
BLAM
?!
WHAT'RE YOU DOING UP? DID YOU SLEEP OUT HERE?
WHAT THE HELL'S GOING ON?
DON CARLO'S GUYS ARE GOING DOOR-TO-DOOR, PULLING PEOPLE OUTSIDE, SHOOTING GUNS INTO THE AIR.
HELP ME GET MY SHIRT ON.
DEFINITELY DON CARLO'S GUYS?
SHOULD WE RUN?
I RECOGNIZED A COUPLE OF THEM OUT THE WINDOW. IT'S BIG 'STACHE AND HIS BUDDY.
NAH, IT'S NOT ABOUT US. I DON'T SEE HOW IT COULD BE.
noknoknok
THIS IS NOT ABOUT US. BE COOL, I'LL TALK TO THEM.

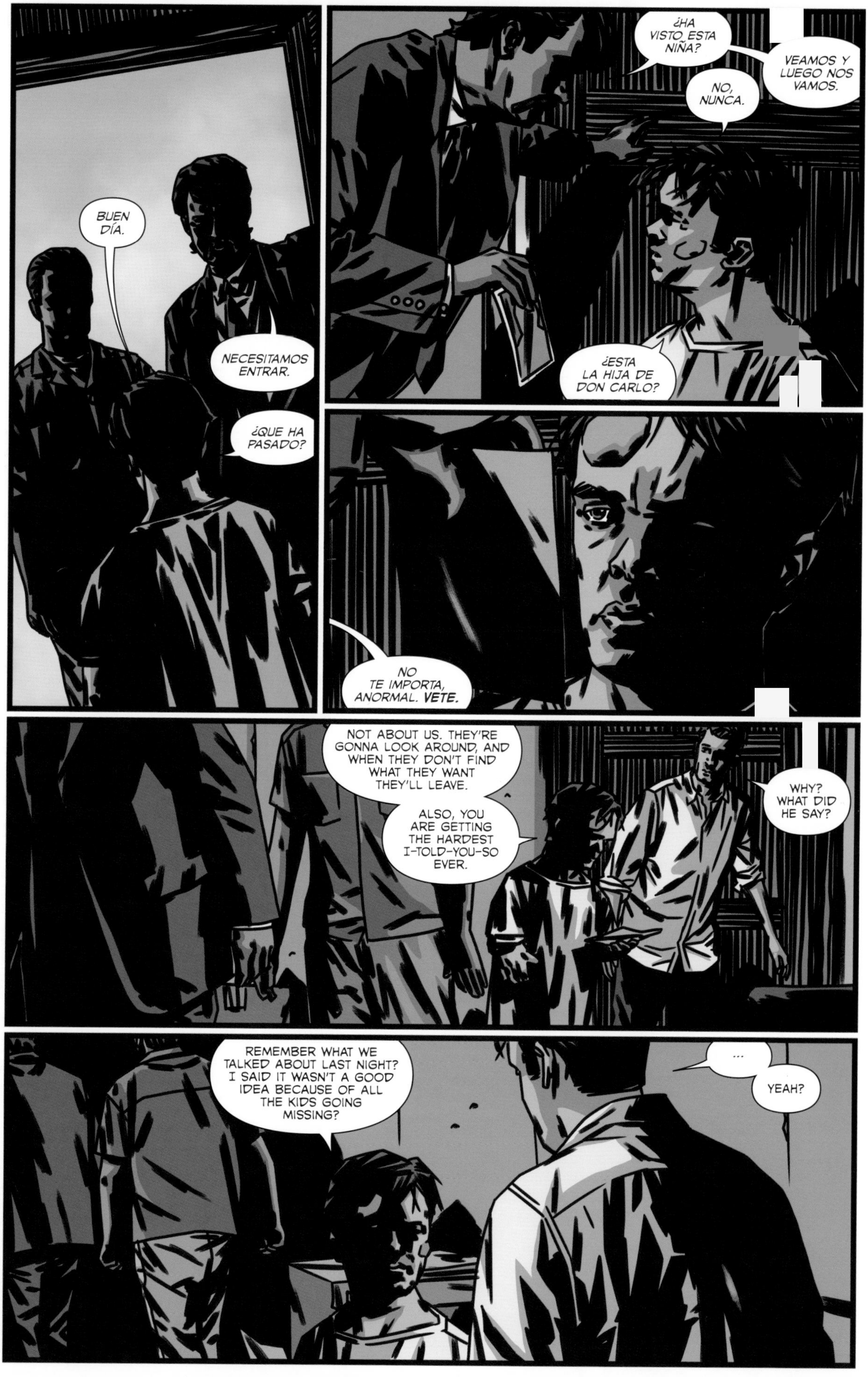
BUEN DÍA.
NECESITAMOS ENTRAR.
¿QUE HA PASADO?
¿HA VISTO ESTA NIÑA?
NO, NUNCA.
VEAMOS Y LUEGO NOS VAMOS.
¿ESTA LA HIJA DE DON CARLO?
NO TE IMPORTA, ANORMAL. **VETE.**
WHY? WHAT DID HE SAY?
NOT ABOUT US. THEY'RE GONNA LOOK AROUND, AND WHEN THEY DON'T FIND WHAT THEY WANT THEY'LL LEAVE.
ALSO, YOU ARE GETTING THE HARDEST I-TOLD-YOU-SO EVER.
REMEMBER WHAT WE TALKED ABOUT LAST NIGHT? I SAID IT WASN'T A GOOD IDEA BECAUSE OF ALL THE KIDS GOING MISSING?
...
YEAH?

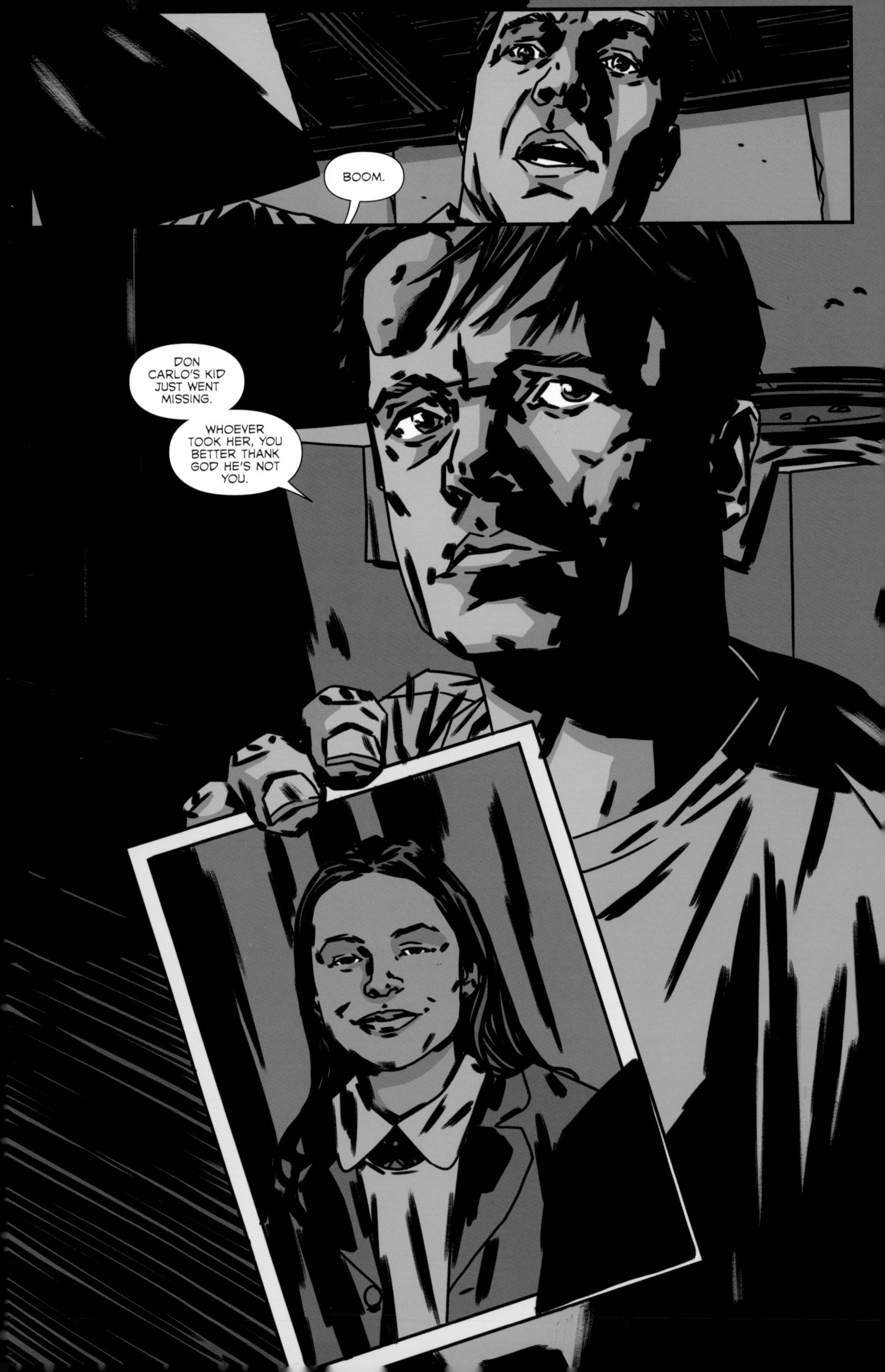
BOOM.
DON CARLO'S KID JUST WENT MISSING.
WHOEVER TOOK HER, YOU BETTER THANK GOD HE'S NOT YOU.

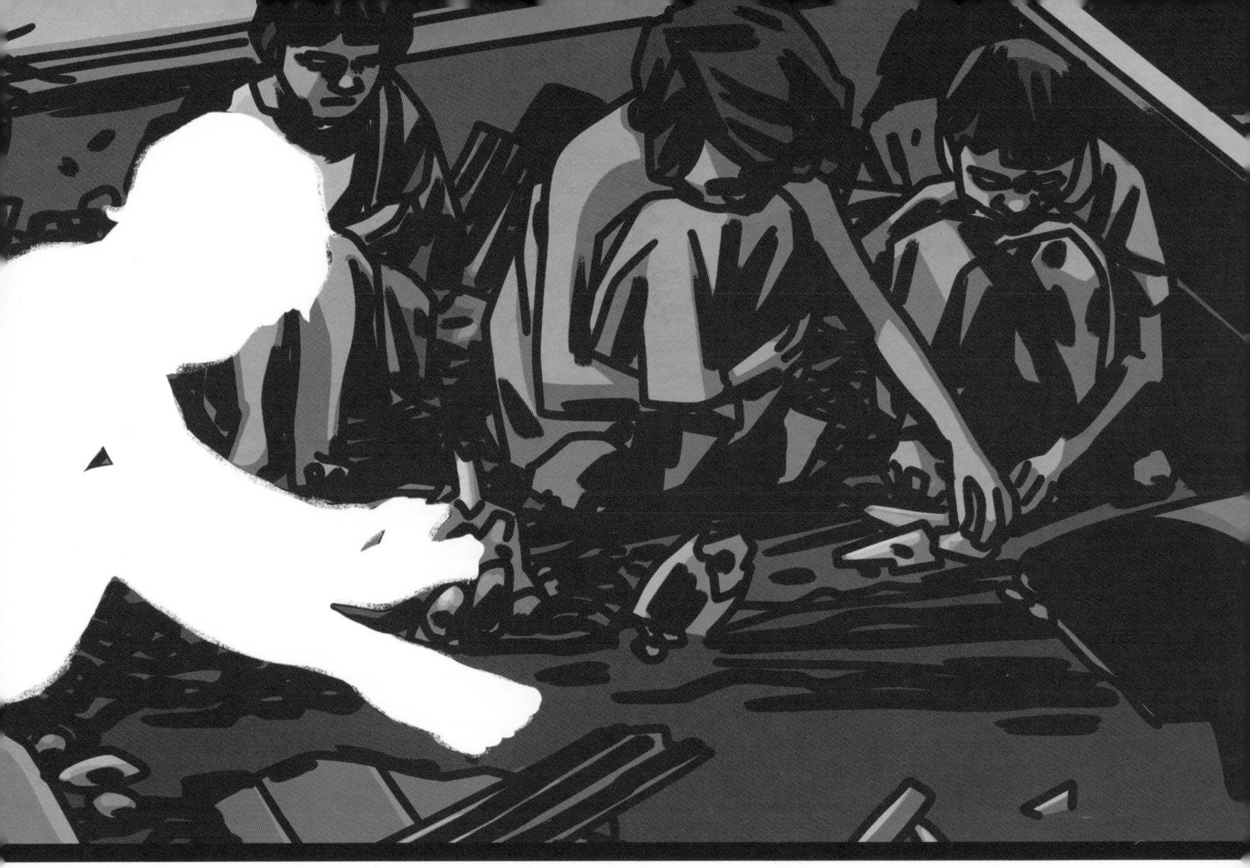

TWO

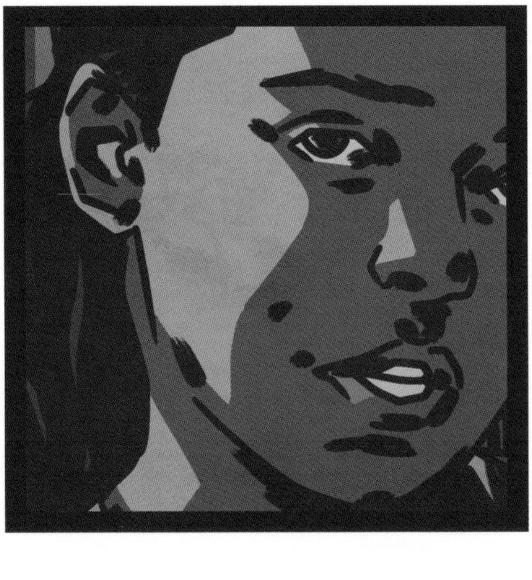

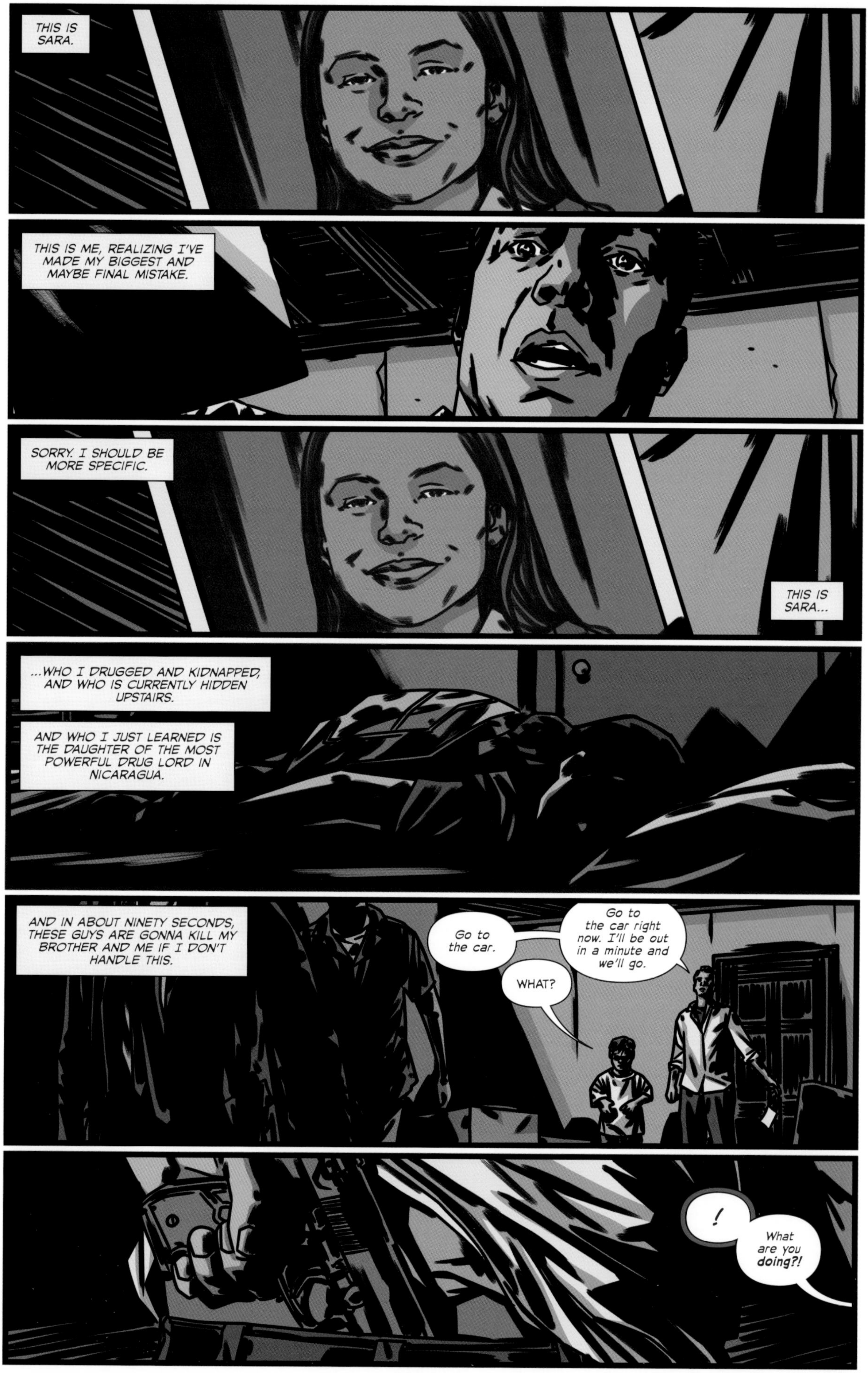
THIS IS SARA.
THIS IS ME, REALIZING I'VE MADE MY BIGGEST AND MAYBE FINAL MISTAKE.
SORRY. I SHOULD BE MORE SPECIFIC.
THIS IS SARA...
...WHO I DRUGGED AND KIDNAPPED, AND WHO IS CURRENTLY HIDDEN UPSTAIRS.
AND WHO I JUST LEARNED IS THE DAUGHTER OF THE MOST POWERFUL DRUG LORD IN NICARAGUA.
AND IN ABOUT NINETY SECONDS, THESE GUYS ARE GONNA KILL MY BROTHER AND ME IF I DON'T HANDLE THIS.
Go to the car.
WHAT?
Go to the car right now. I'll be out in a minute and we'll go.
!
What are you **doing?!**

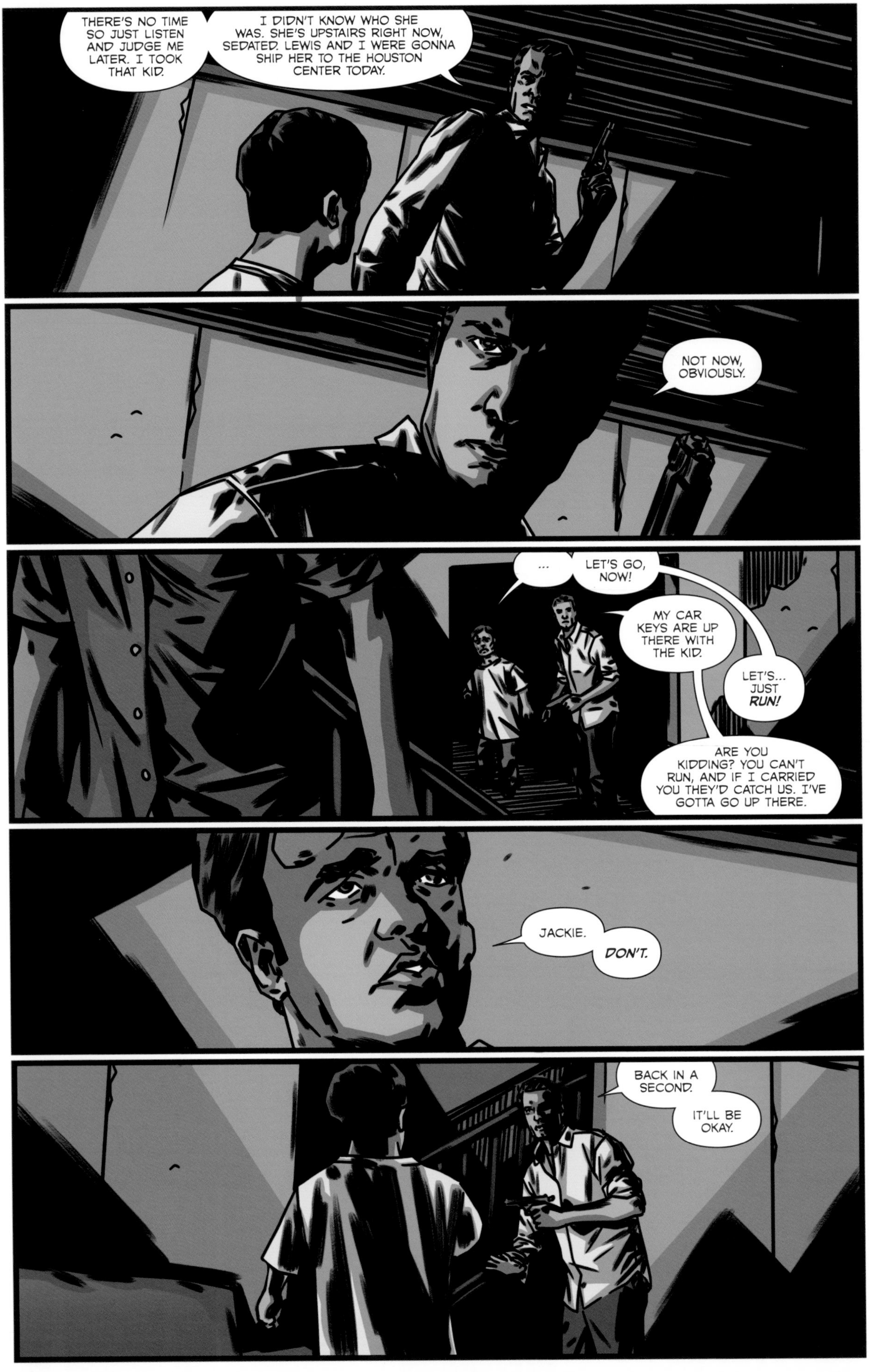
THERE'S NO TIME SO JUST LISTEN AND JUDGE ME LATER. I TOOK THAT KID.
I DIDN'T KNOW WHO SHE WAS. SHE'S UPSTAIRS RIGHT NOW, SEDATED. LEWIS AND I WERE GONNA SHIP HER TO THE HOUSTON CENTER TODAY.
NOT NOW, OBVIOUSLY.
...
LET'S GO, NOW!
MY CAR KEYS ARE UP THERE WITH THE KID.
LET'S... JUST *RUN!*
ARE YOU KIDDING? YOU CAN'T RUN, AND IF I CARRIED YOU THEY'D CATCH US. I'VE GOTTA GO UP THERE.
JACKIE.
DON'T.
BACK IN A SECOND.
IT'LL BE OKAY.

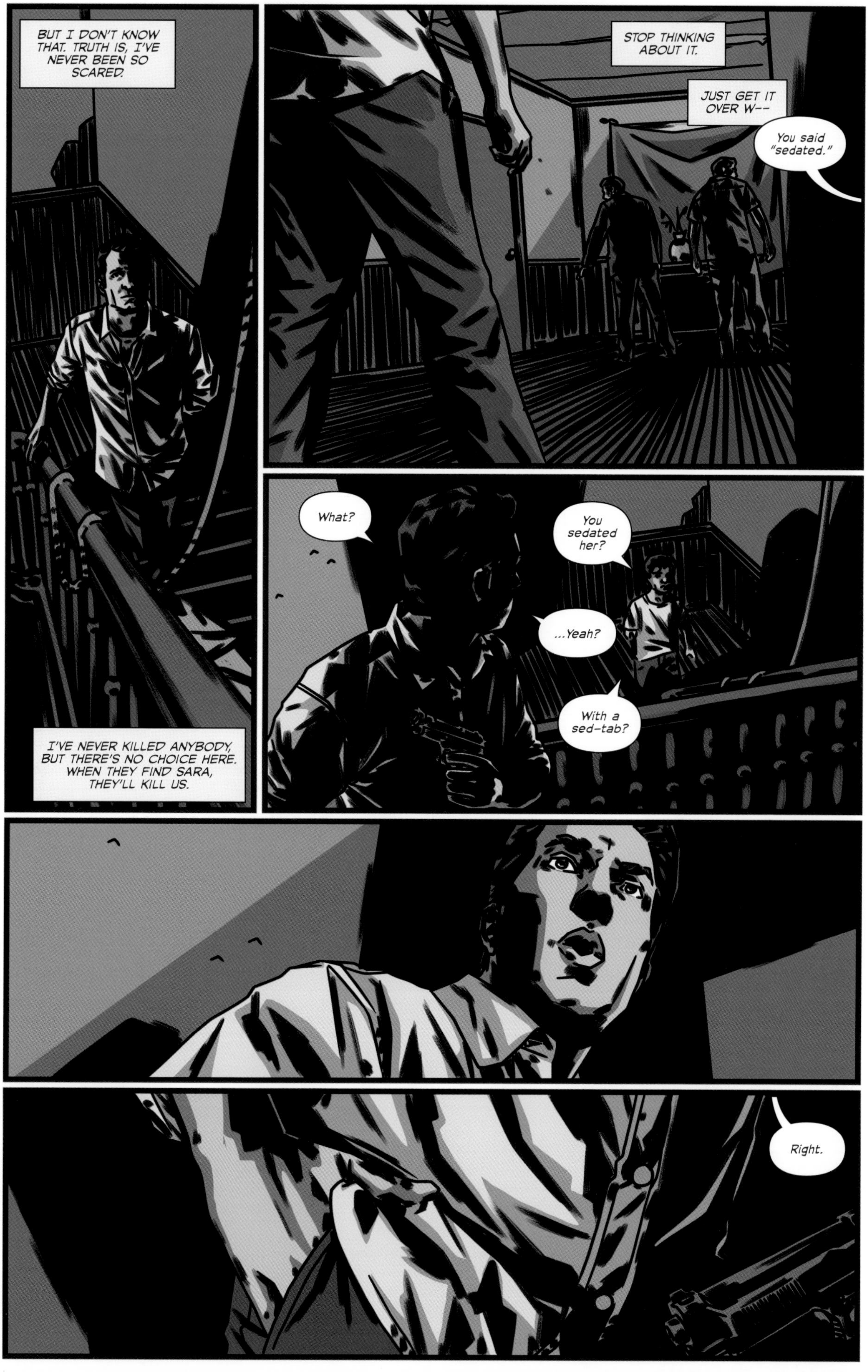
BUT I DON'T KNOW THAT. TRUTH IS, I'VE NEVER BEEN SO SCARED.
I'VE NEVER KILLED ANYBODY, BUT THERE'S NO CHOICE HERE. WHEN THEY FIND SARA, THEY'LL KILL US.
STOP THINKING ABOUT IT.
JUST GET IT OVER W--
You said "sedated."
What?
You sedated her?
...Yeah?
With a sed-tab?
Right.

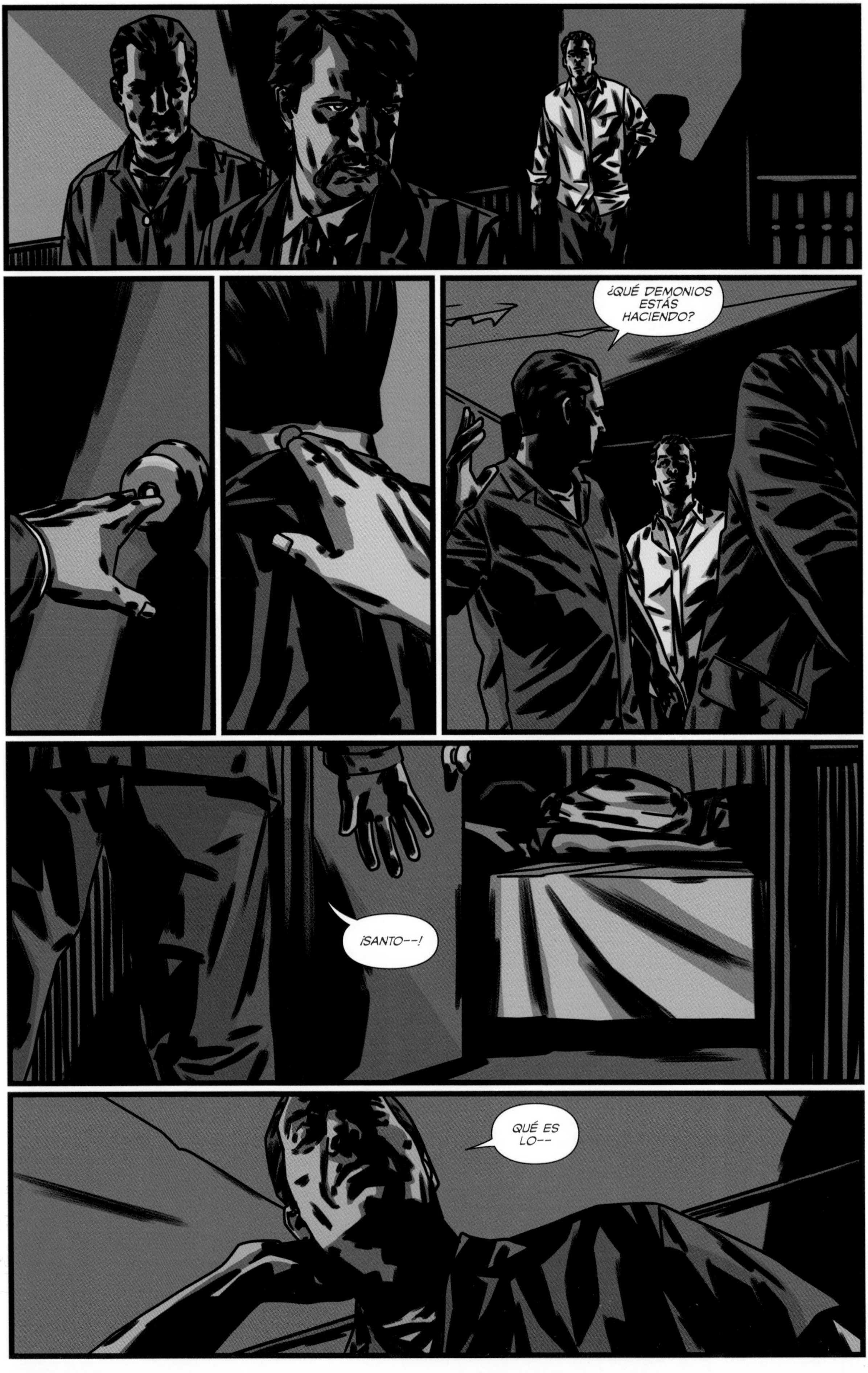
¿QUÉ DEMONIOS ESTÁS HACIENDO?
¡SANTO--!
QUÉ ES LO--

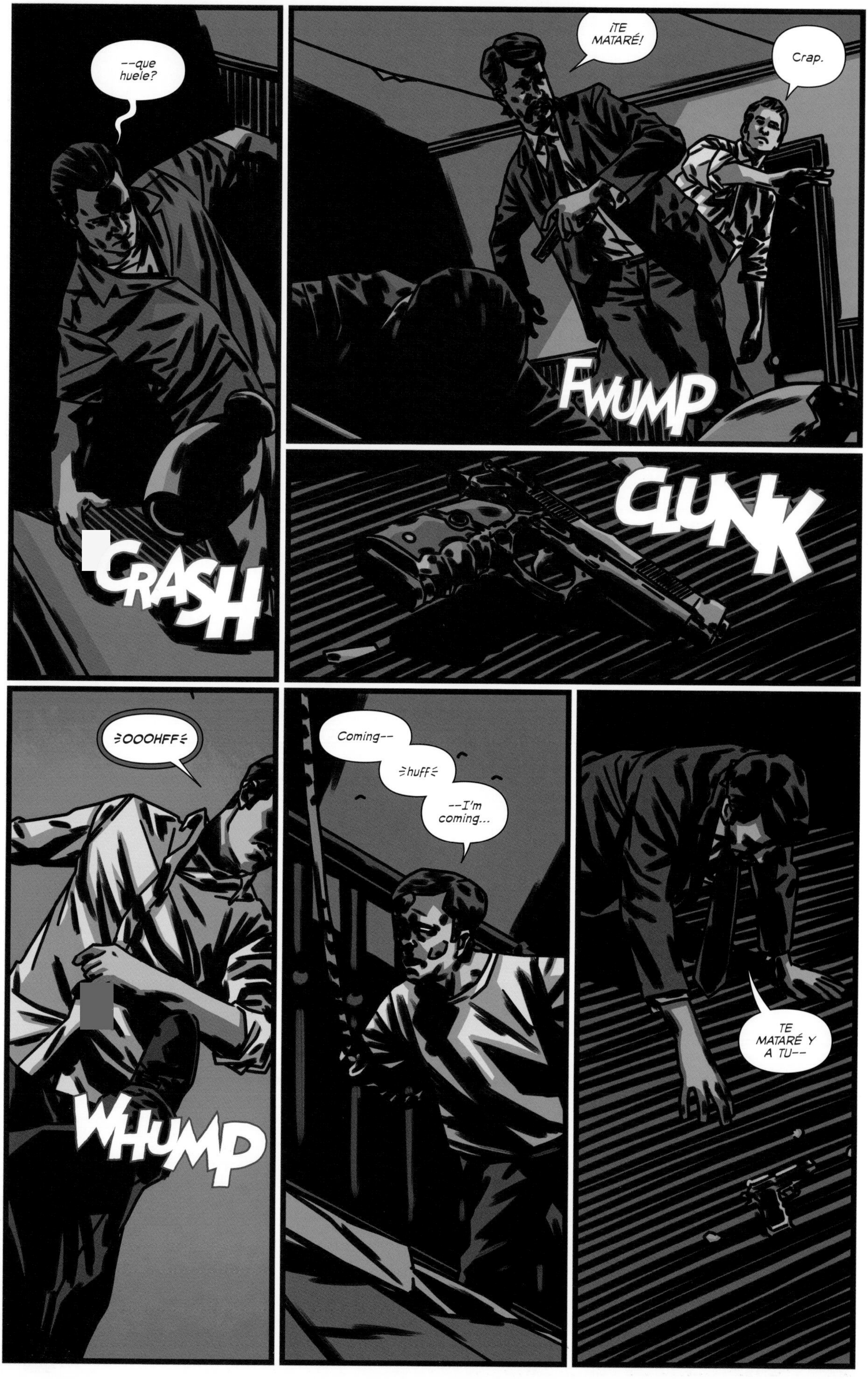

--que huele?
CRASH
¡TE MATARÉ!
Crap.
FWUMP
CLUNK
OOOHFF
WHUMP
Coming--
huff
--I'm coming...
TE MATARÉ Y A TU--

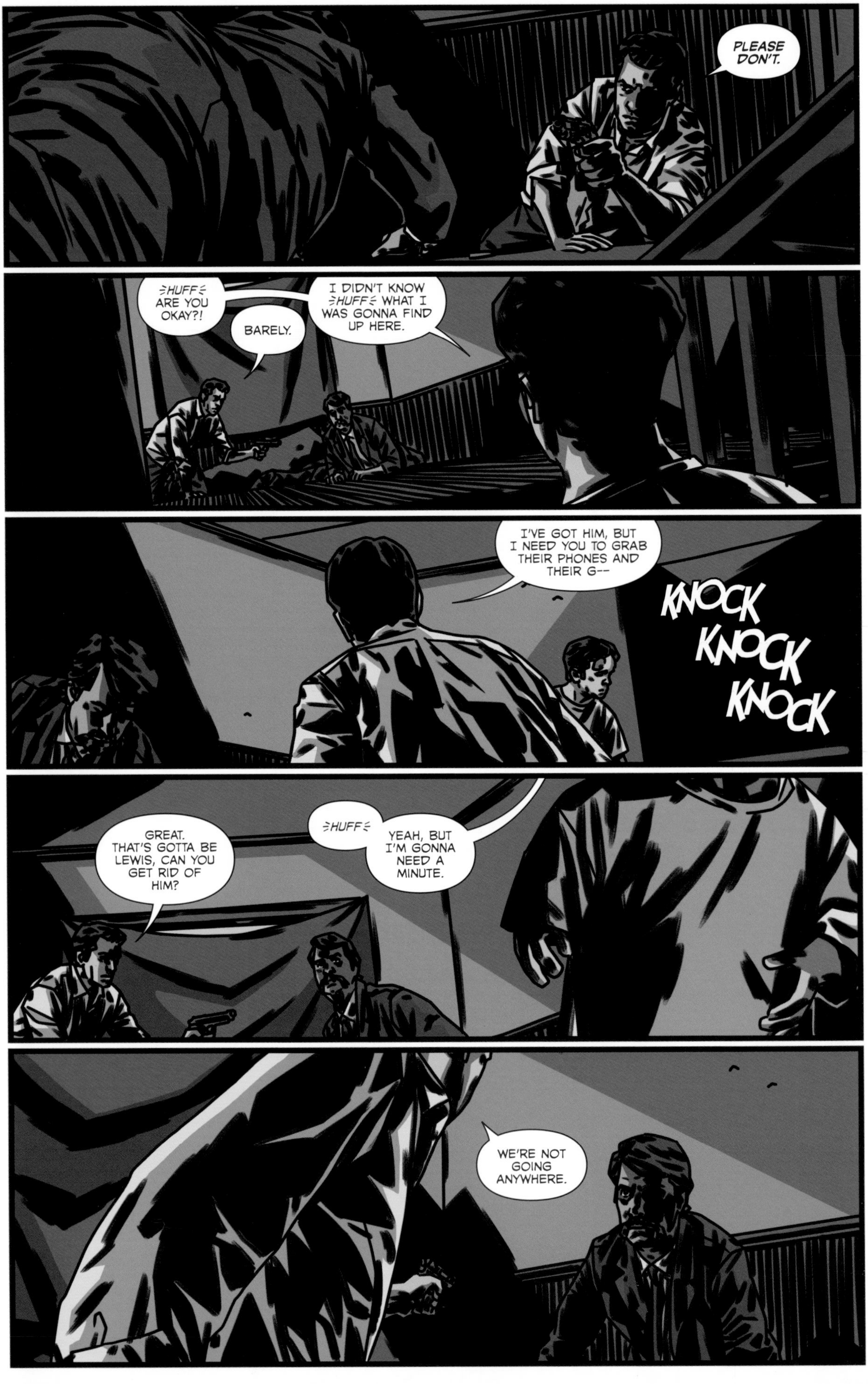
PLEASE DON'T.
≡HUFF≡ ARE YOU OKAY?!
BARELY.
I DIDN'T KNOW ≡HUFF≡ WHAT I WAS GONNA FIND UP HERE.
I'VE GOT HIM, BUT I NEED YOU TO GRAB THEIR PHONES AND THEIR G--
KNOCK KNOCK KNOCK
GREAT. THAT'S GOTTA BE LEWIS, CAN YOU GET RID OF HIM?
≡HUFF≡
YEAH, BUT I'M GONNA NEED A MINUTE.
WE'RE NOT GOING ANYWHERE.

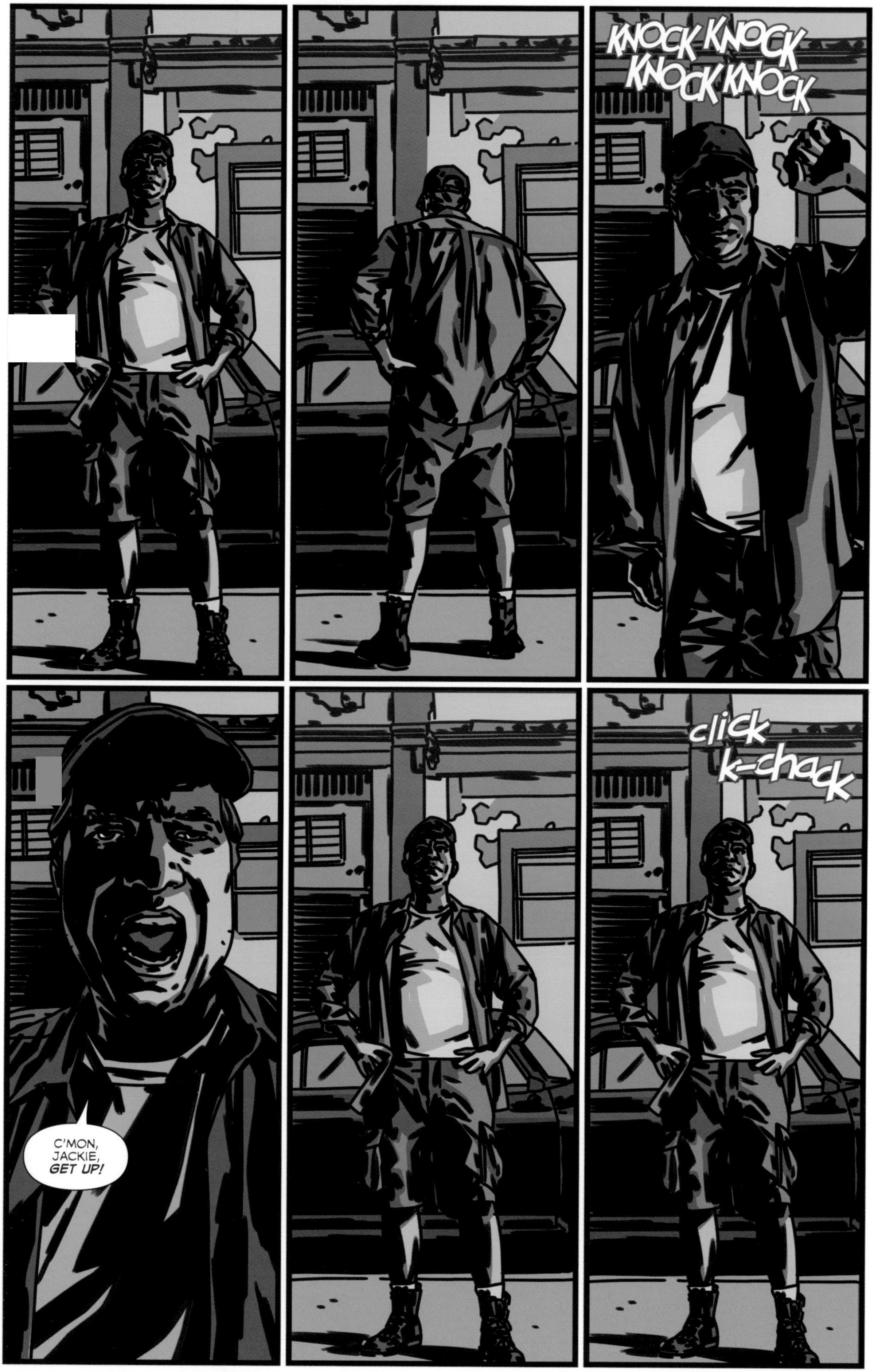
KNOCK KNOCK KNOCK KNOCK
C'MON, JACKIE, GET UP!
click k-chack

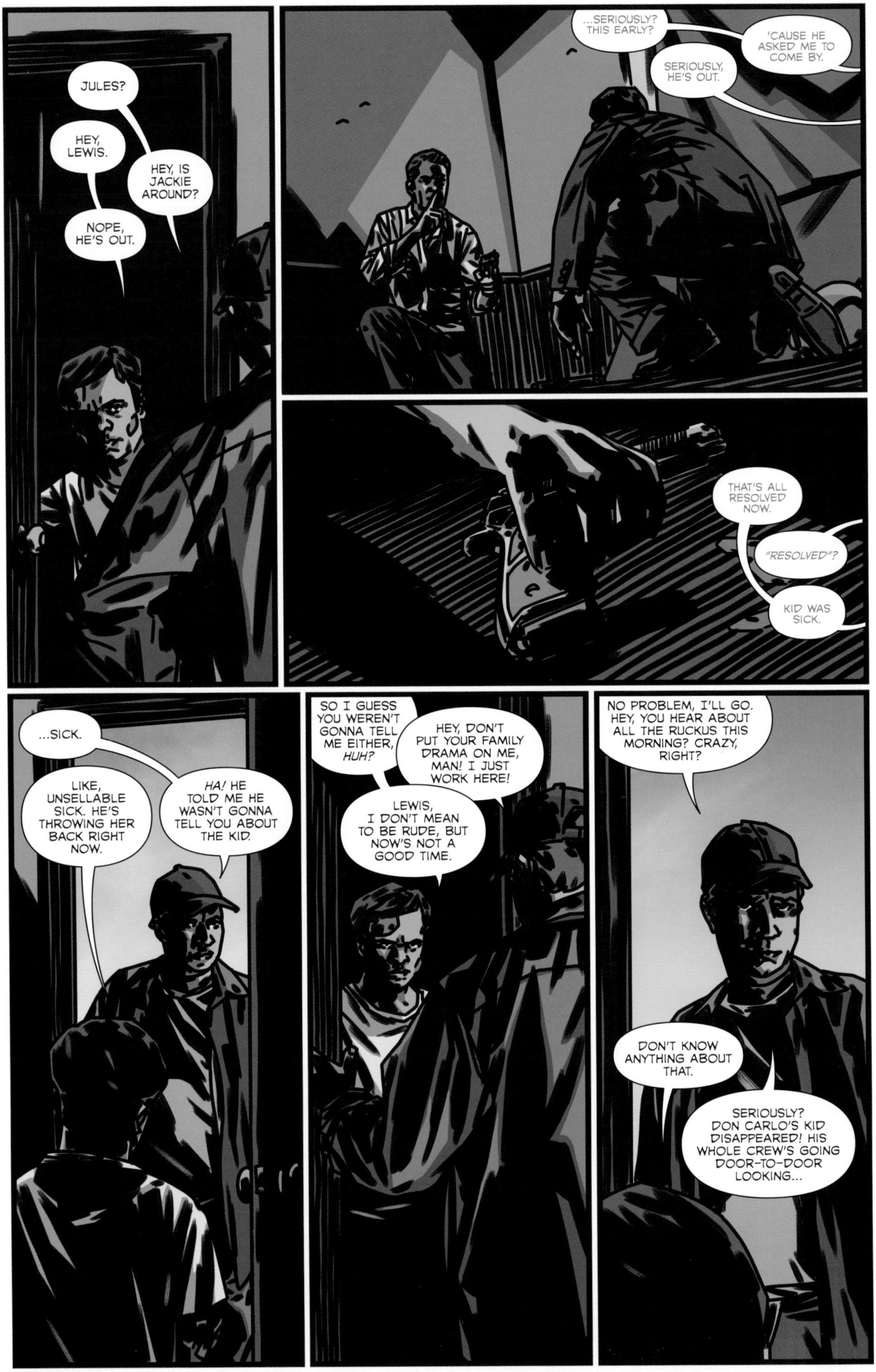
JULES?
HEY, LEWIS.
HEY, IS JACKIE AROUND?
NOPE, HE'S OUT.
...SERIOUSLY? THIS EARLY?
'CAUSE HE ASKED ME TO COME BY.
SERIOUSLY, HE'S OUT.
THAT'S ALL RESOLVED NOW.
"RESOLVED"?
KID WAS SICK.
...SICK.
LIKE, UNSELLABLE SICK. HE'S THROWING HER BACK RIGHT NOW.
HA! HE TOLD ME HE WASN'T GONNA TELL YOU ABOUT THE KID.
SO I GUESS YOU WEREN'T GONNA TELL ME EITHER, HUH?
HEY, DON'T PUT YOUR FAMILY DRAMA ON ME, MAN! I JUST WORK HERE!
LEWIS, I DON'T MEAN TO BE RUDE, BUT NOW'S NOT A GOOD TIME.
NO PROBLEM, I'LL GO. HEY, YOU HEAR ABOUT ALL THE RUCKUS THIS MORNING? CRAZY, RIGHT?
DON'T KNOW ANYTHING ABOUT THAT.
SERIOUSLY? DON CARLO'S KID DISAPPEARED! HIS WHOLE CREW'S GOING DOOR-TO-DOOR LOOKING...

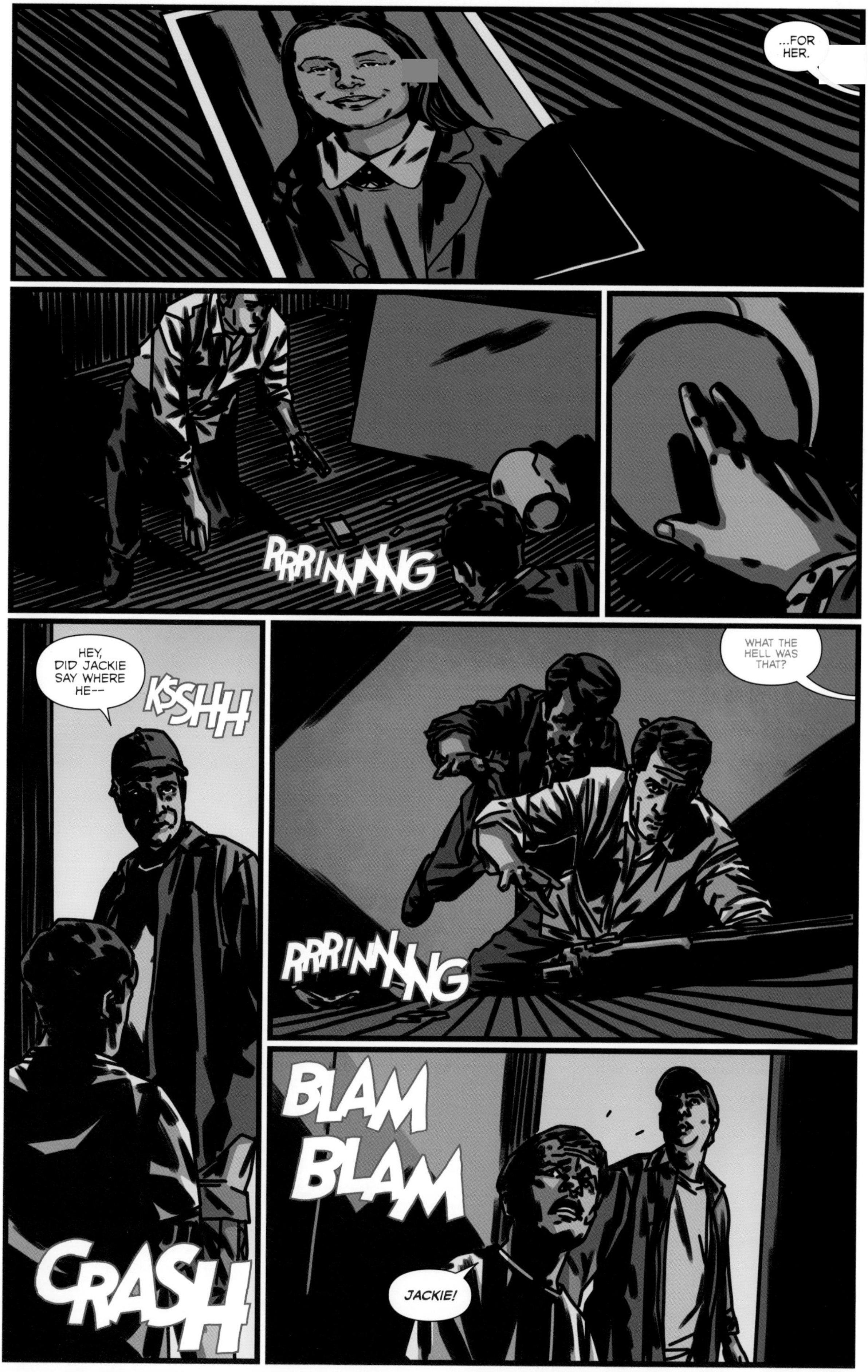
...FOR HER.
RRRINNNNG
HEY, DID JACKIE SAY WHERE HE--
KSSHH
WHAT THE HELL WAS THAT?
RRRINNNNG
CRASH
BLAM
BLAM
JACKIE!

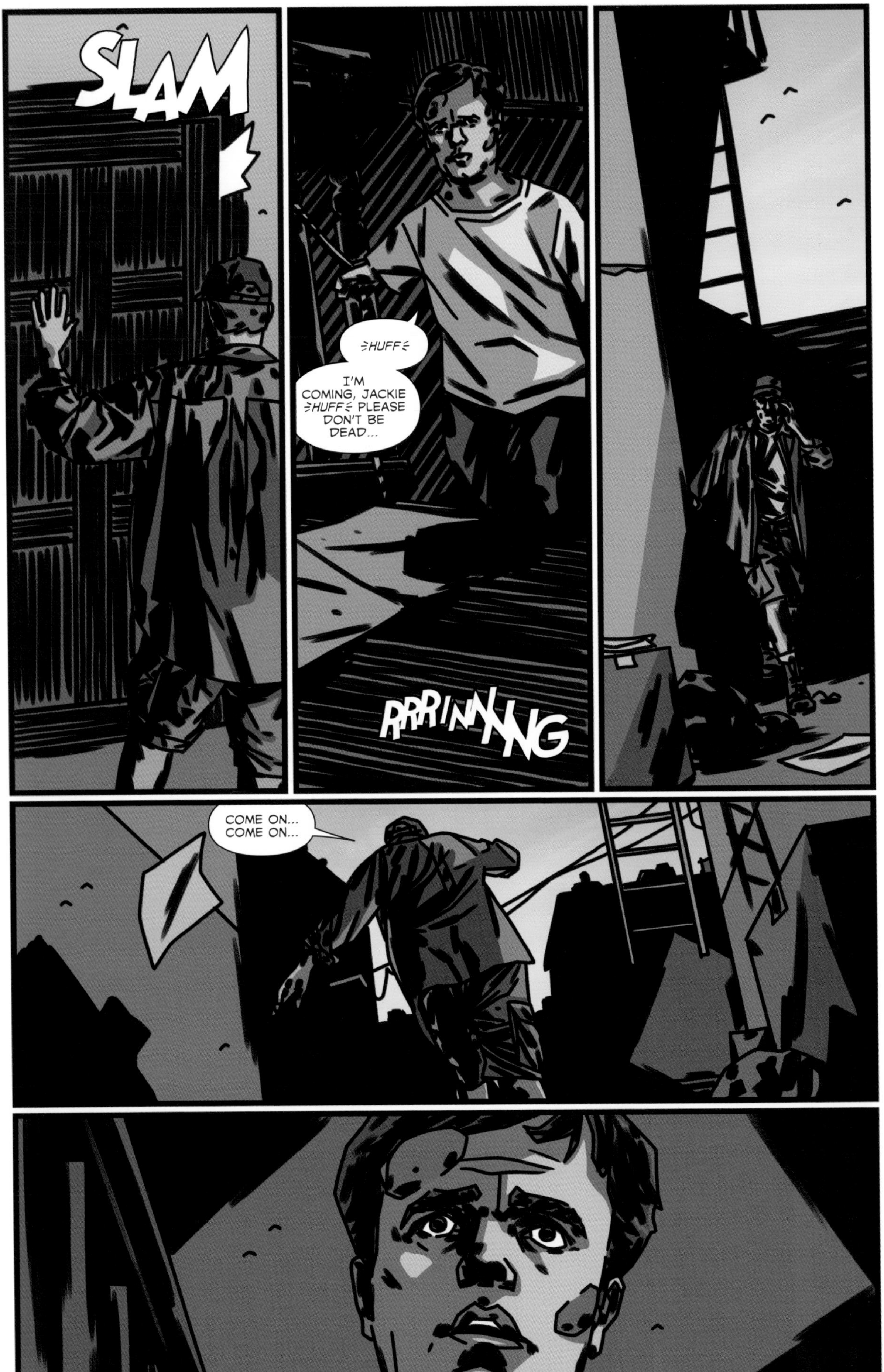
SLAM
HUFF
I'M COMING, JACKIE HUFF PLEASE DON'T BE DEAD...
RRRINNNNG
COME ON... COME ON...

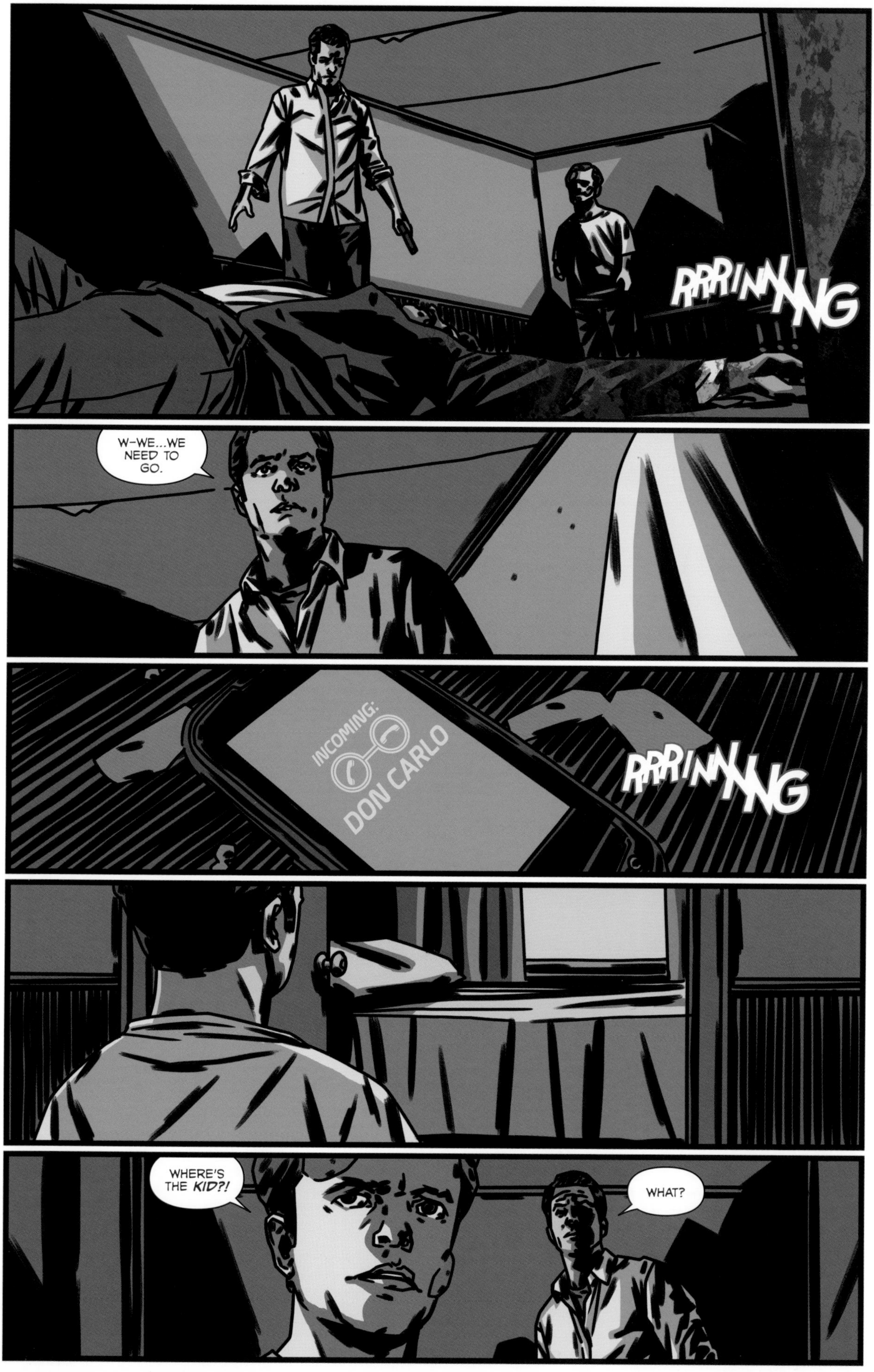
RRRINNNNG
W-WE...WE NEED TO GO.
INCOMING:
DON CARLO
RRRINNNNG
WHERE'S THE *KID?!*
WHAT?

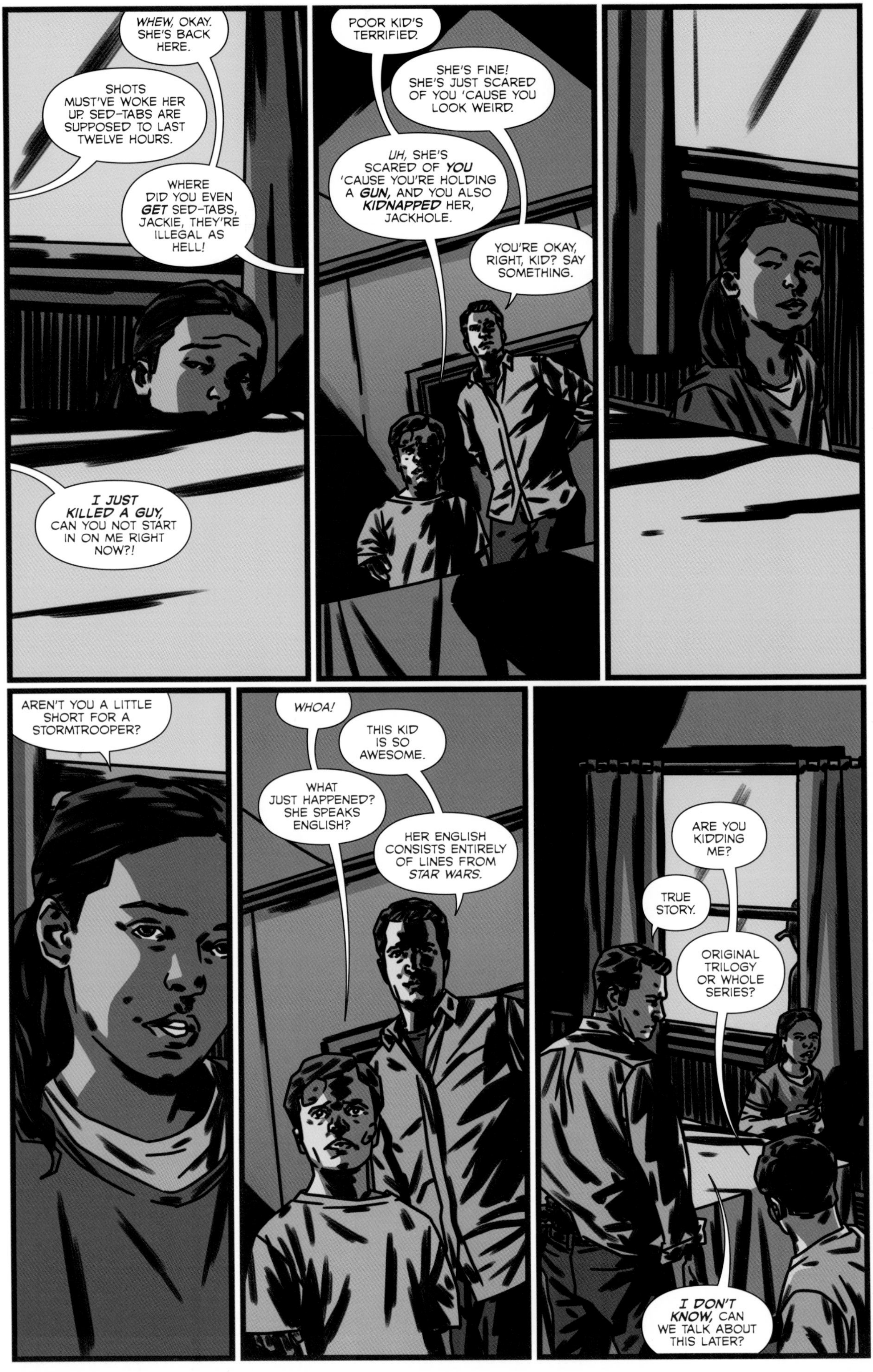
WHEW, OKAY. SHE'S BACK HERE.
SHOTS MUST'VE WOKE HER UP. SED-TABS ARE SUPPOSED TO LAST TWELVE HOURS.
WHERE DID YOU EVEN GET SED-TABS, JACKIE, THEY'RE ILLEGAL AS HELL!
I JUST KILLED A GUY, CAN YOU NOT START IN ON ME RIGHT NOW?!
POOR KID'S TERRIFIED.
SHE'S FINE! SHE'S JUST SCARED OF YOU 'CAUSE YOU LOOK WEIRD.
UH, SHE'S SCARED OF YOU 'CAUSE YOU'RE HOLDING A GUN, AND YOU ALSO KIDNAPPED HER, JACKHOLE.
YOU'RE OKAY, RIGHT, KID? SAY SOMETHING.
AREN'T YOU A LITTLE SHORT FOR A STORMTROOPER?
WHOA!
THIS KID IS SO AWESOME.
WHAT JUST HAPPENED? SHE SPEAKS ENGLISH?
HER ENGLISH CONSISTS ENTIRELY OF LINES FROM STAR WARS.
ARE YOU KIDDING ME?
TRUE STORY.
ORIGINAL TRILOGY OR WHOLE SERIES?
I DON'T KNOW, CAN WE TALK ABOUT THIS LATER?

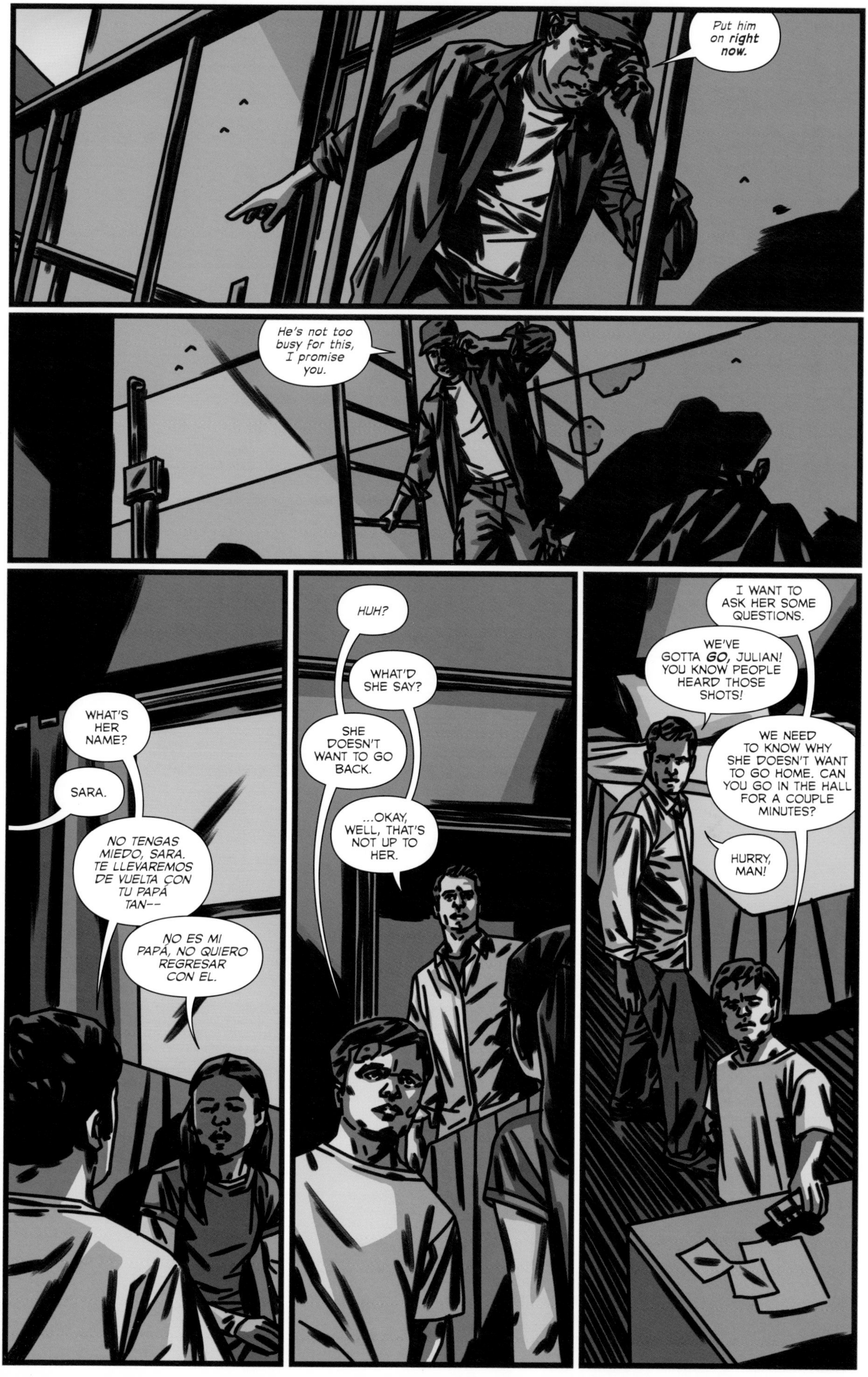
Put him on right now.
He's not too busy for this, I promise you.
WHAT'S HER NAME?
SARA.
NO TENGAS MIEDO, SARA. TE LLEVAREMOS DE VUELTA CON TU PAPÁ TAN--
NO ES MI PAPÁ, NO QUIERO REGRESAR CON EL.
HUH?
WHAT'D SHE SAY?
SHE DOESN'T WANT TO GO BACK.
...OKAY, WELL, THAT'S NOT UP TO HER.
I WANT TO ASK HER SOME QUESTIONS.
WE'VE GOTTA GO, JULIAN! YOU KNOW PEOPLE HEARD THOSE SHOTS!
WE NEED TO KNOW WHY SHE DOESN'T WANT TO GO HOME. CAN YOU GO IN THE HALL FOR A COUPLE MINUTES?
HURRY, MAN!

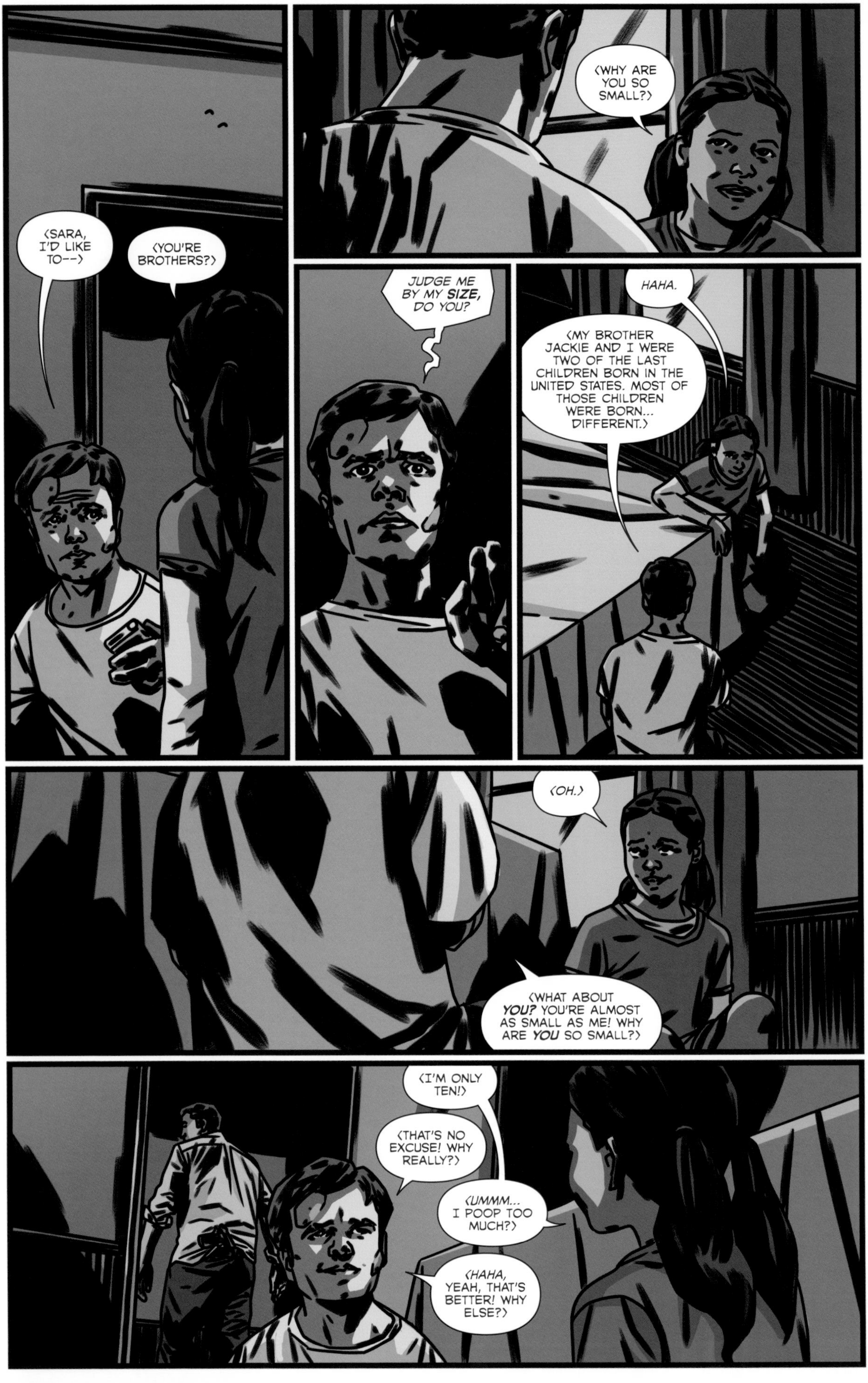
<SARA, I'D LIKE TO-->
<YOU'RE BROTHERS?>
<WHY ARE YOU SO SMALL?>
JUDGE ME BY MY **SIZE,** DO YOU?
HAHA.
<MY BROTHER JACKIE AND I WERE TWO OF THE LAST CHILDREN BORN IN THE UNITED STATES. MOST OF THOSE CHILDREN WERE BORN... DIFFERENT.>
<OH.>
<WHAT ABOUT ***YOU?*** YOU'RE ALMOST AS SMALL AS ME! WHY ARE ***YOU*** SO SMALL?>
<I'M ONLY TEN!>
<THAT'S NO EXCUSE! WHY REALLY?>
<UMMM... I POOP TOO MUCH?>
<HAHA, YEAH, THAT'S BETTER! WHY ELSE?>

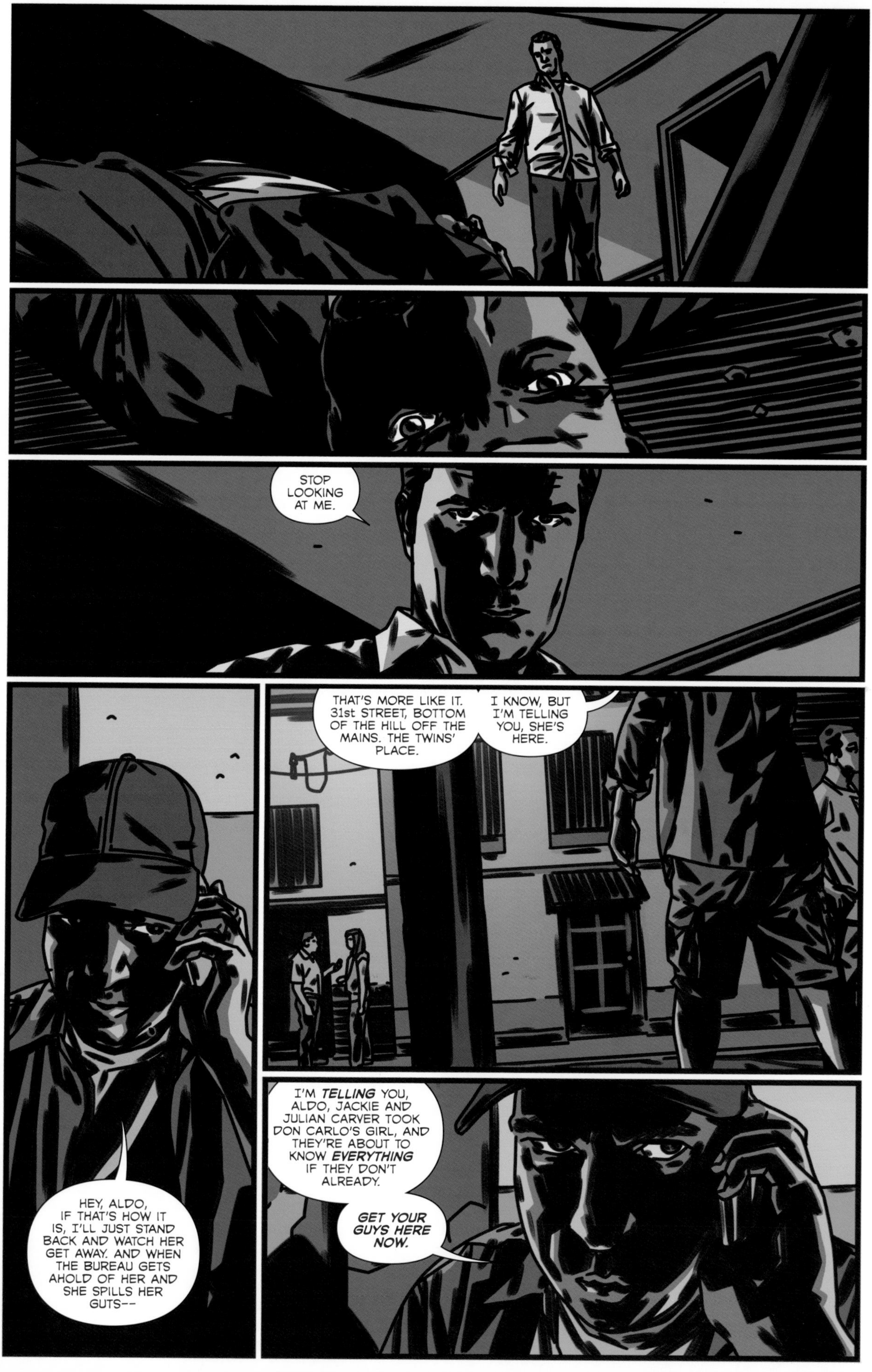
STOP LOOKING AT ME.
THAT'S MORE LIKE IT. 31st STREET, BOTTOM OF THE HILL OFF THE MAINS. THE TWINS' PLACE.
I KNOW, BUT I'M TELLING YOU, SHE'S HERE.
HEY, ALDO, IF THAT'S HOW IT IS, I'LL JUST STAND BACK AND WATCH HER GET AWAY. AND WHEN THE BUREAU GETS AHOLD OF HER AND SHE SPILLS HER GUTS--
I'M ***TELLING*** YOU, ALDO, JACKIE AND JULIAN CARVER TOOK DON CARLO'S GIRL, AND THEY'RE ABOUT TO KNOW ***EVERYTHING*** IF THEY DON'T ALREADY.
GET YOUR GUYS HERE NOW.

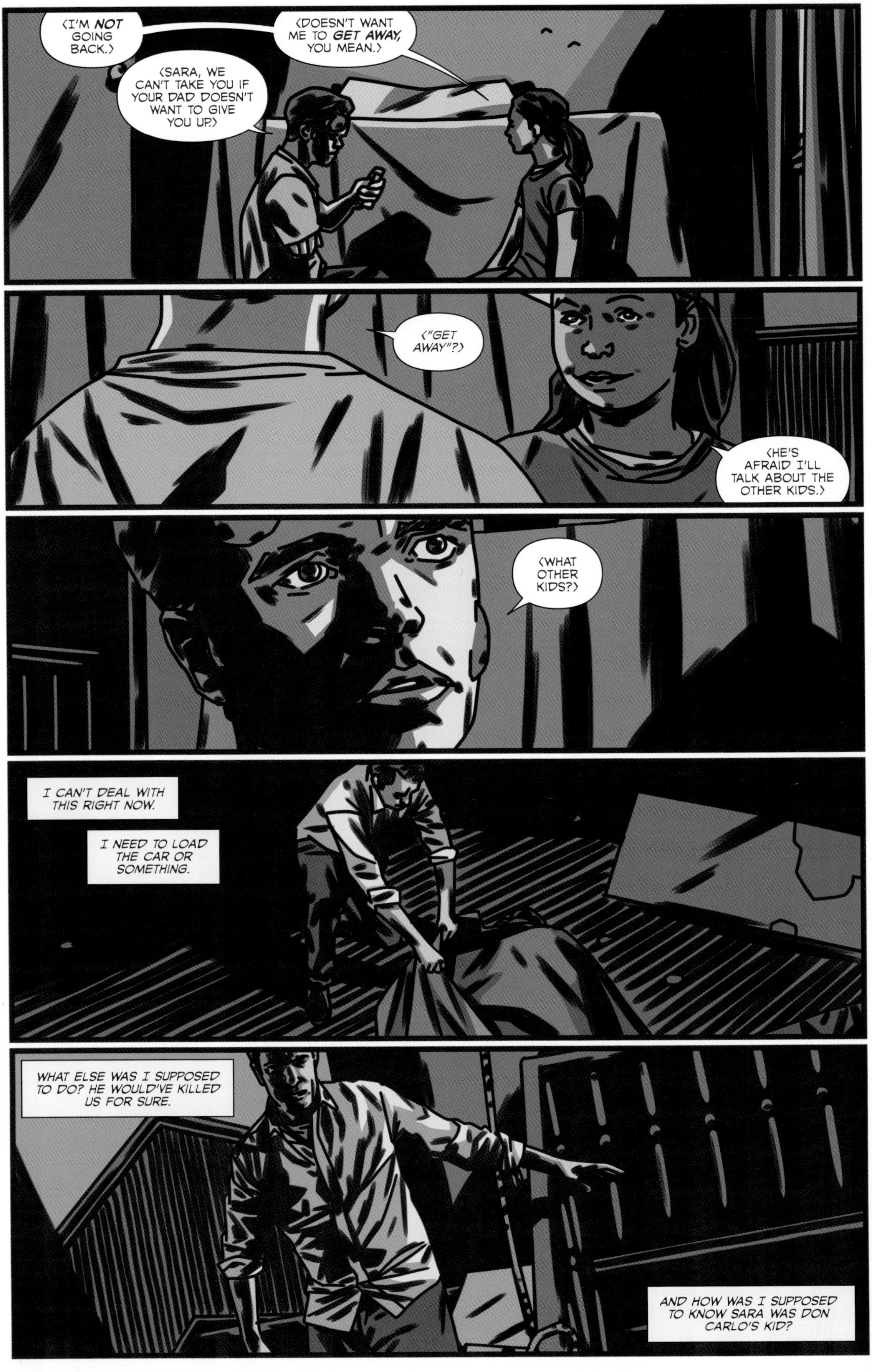
⟨I'M **NOT** GOING BACK.⟩
⟨SARA, WE CAN'T TAKE YOU IF YOUR DAD DOESN'T WANT TO GIVE YOU UP.⟩
⟨DOESN'T WANT ME TO ***GET AWAY,*** YOU MEAN.⟩
⟨*"GET AWAY"?*⟩
⟨HE'S AFRAID I'LL TALK ABOUT THE OTHER KIDS.⟩
⟨WHAT OTHER KIDS?⟩
I CAN'T DEAL WITH THIS RIGHT NOW.
I NEED TO LOAD THE CAR OR SOMETHING.
WHAT ELSE WAS I SUPPOSED TO DO? HE WOULD'VE KILLED US FOR SURE.
AND HOW WAS I SUPPOSED TO KNOW SARA WAS DON CARLO'S KID?

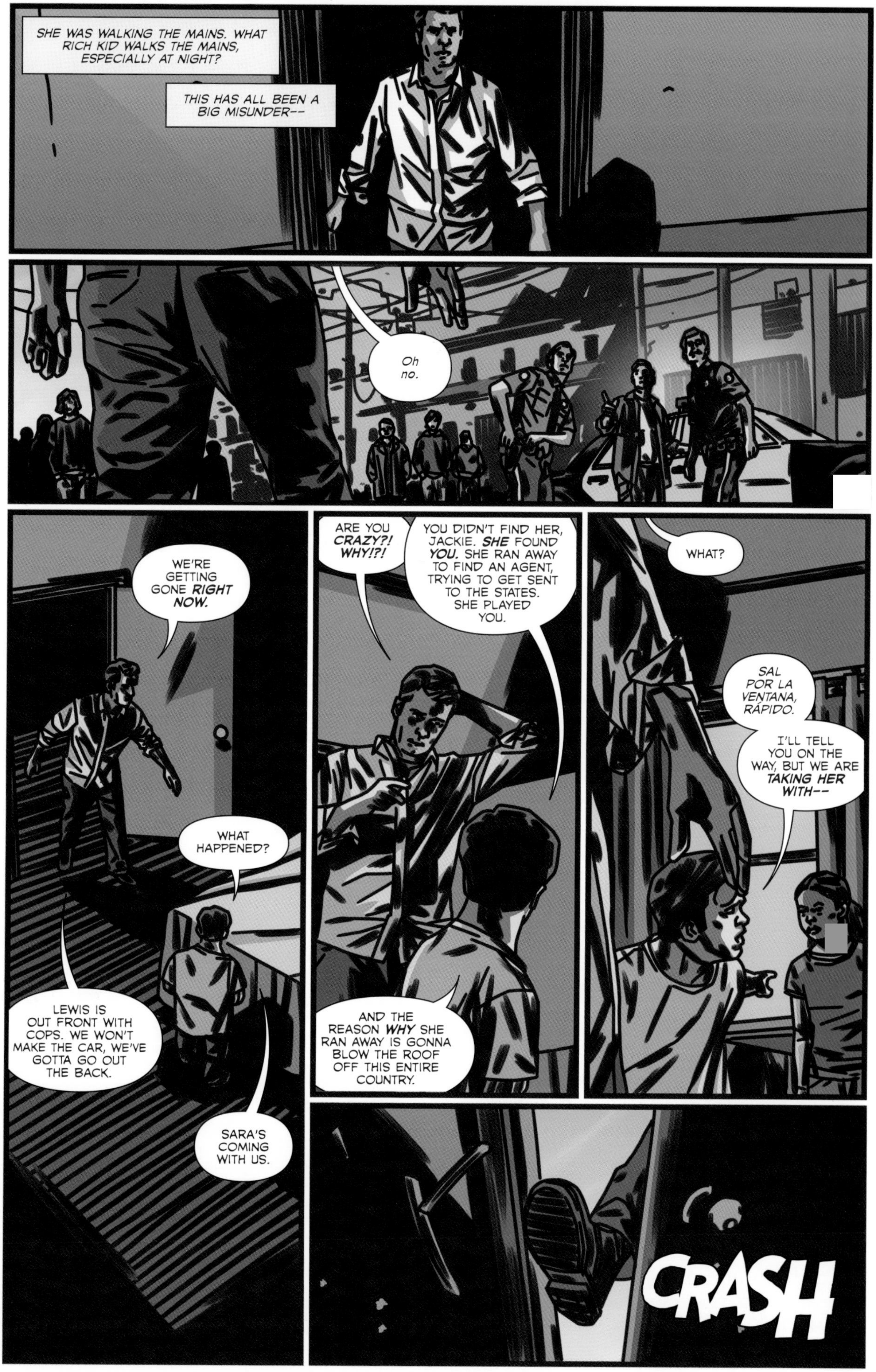
SHE WAS WALKING THE MAINS. WHAT RICH KID WALKS THE MAINS, ESPECIALLY AT NIGHT?
THIS HAS ALL BEEN A BIG MISUNDER--
Oh no.
WE'RE GETTING GONE RIGHT NOW.
WHAT HAPPENED?
LEWIS IS OUT FRONT WITH COPS. WE WON'T MAKE THE CAR, WE'VE GOTTA GO OUT THE BACK.
SARA'S COMING WITH US.
ARE YOU CRAZY?! WHY!?!
YOU DIDN'T FIND HER, JACKIE. SHE FOUND YOU. SHE RAN AWAY TO FIND AN AGENT, TRYING TO GET SENT TO THE STATES. SHE PLAYED YOU.
AND THE REASON WHY SHE RAN AWAY IS GONNA BLOW THE ROOF OFF THIS ENTIRE COUNTRY.
WHAT?
SAL POR LA VENTANA, RÁPIDO.
I'LL TELL YOU ON THE WAY, BUT WE ARE TAKING HER WITH--
CRASH

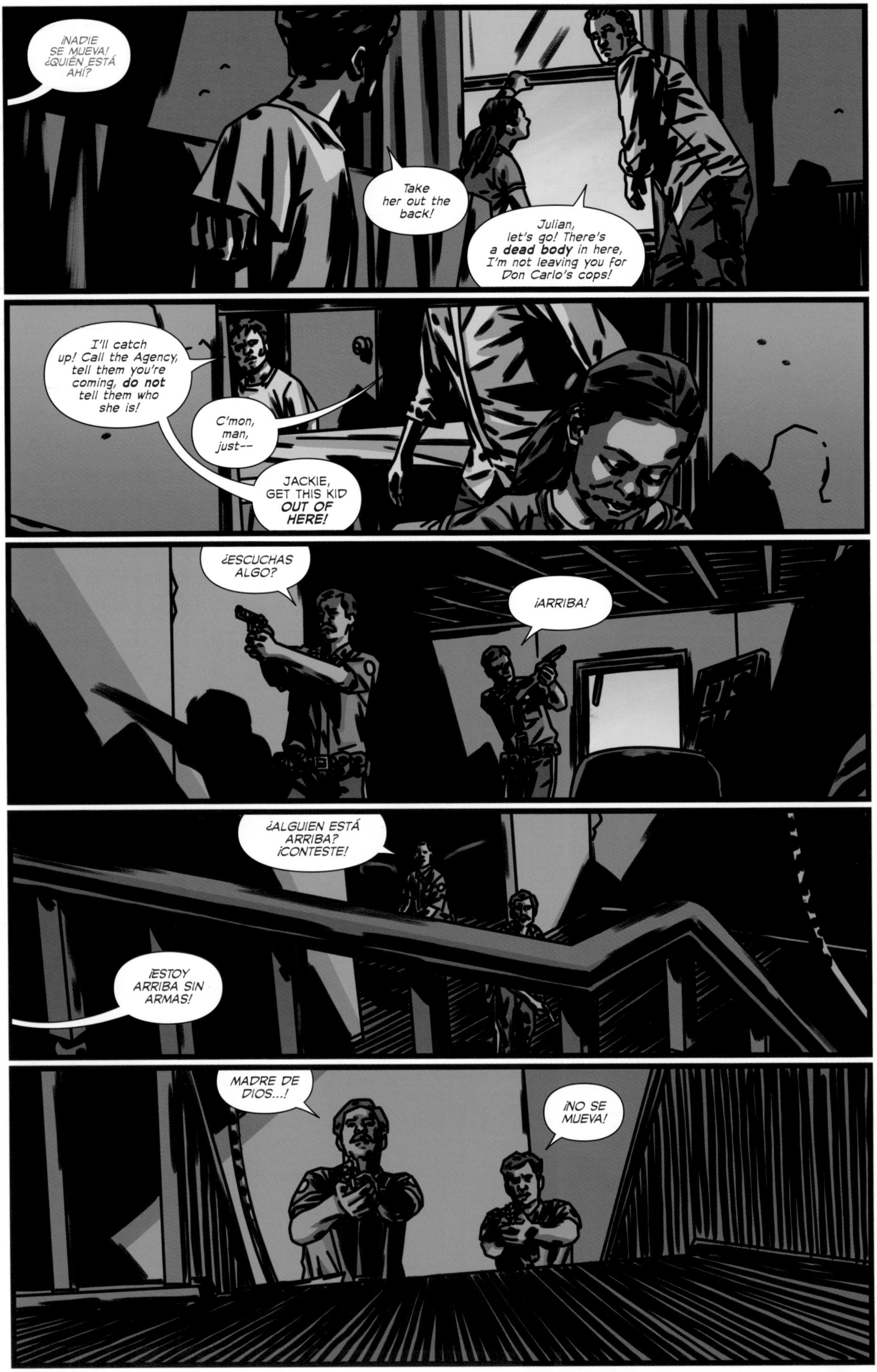
¡NADIE SE MUEVA! ¿QUIÉN ESTÁ AHÍ?
Take her out the back!
Julian, let's go! There's a **dead body** in here, I'm not leaving you for Don Carlo's cops!
I'll catch up! Call the Agency, tell them you're coming, **do not** tell them who she is!
C'mon, man, just--
JACKIE, GET THIS KID ***OUT OF HERE!***
¿ESCUCHAS ALGO?
¡ARRIBA!
¿ALGUIEN ESTÁ ARRIBA? ¡CONTESTE!
¡ESTOY ARRIBA SIN ARMAS!
MADRE DE DIOS...!
¡NO SE MUEVA!

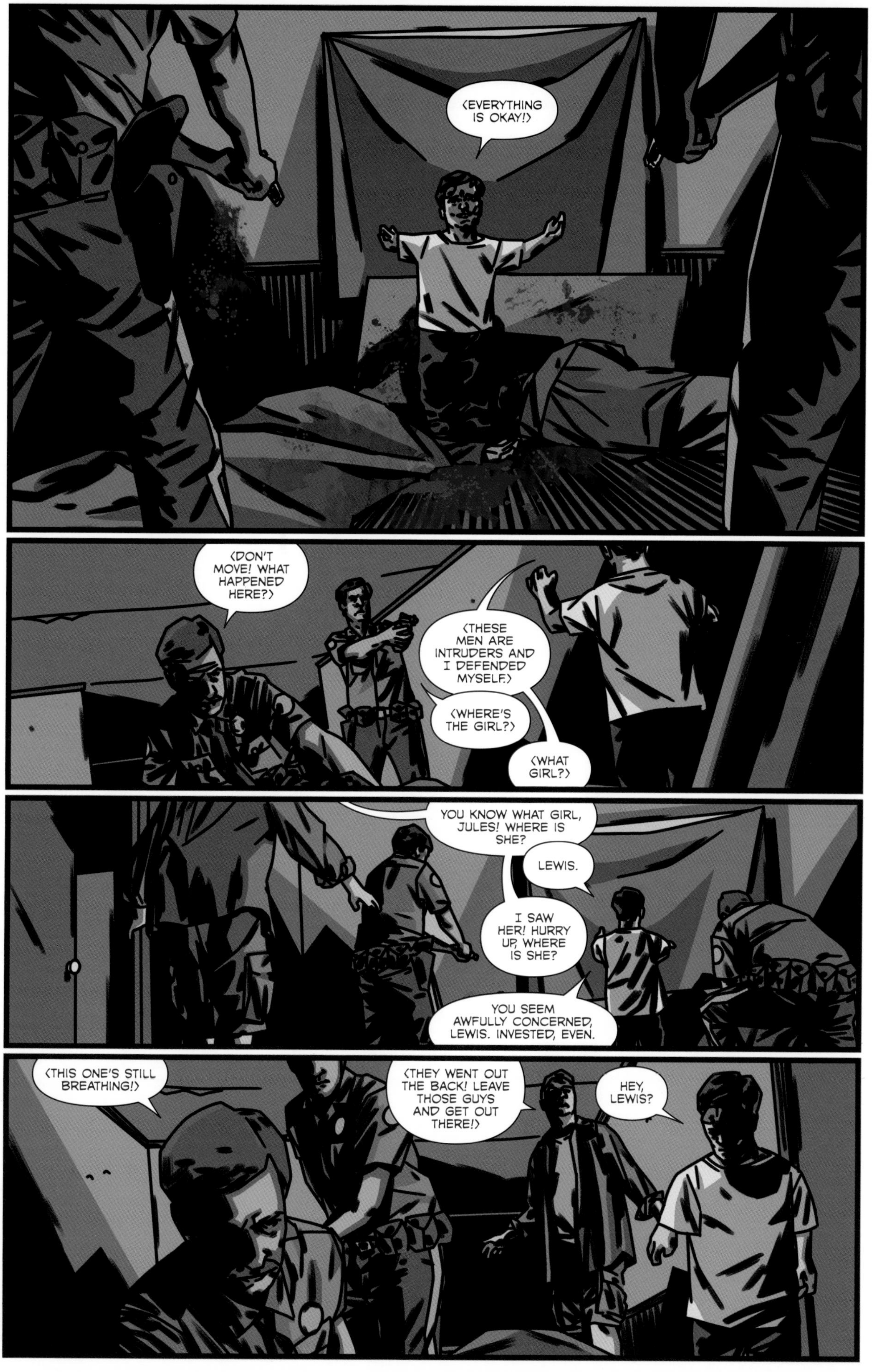
<EVERYTHING IS OKAY!>
<DON'T MOVE! WHAT HAPPENED HERE?>
<THESE MEN ARE INTRUDERS AND I DEFENDED MYSELF.>
<WHERE'S THE GIRL?>
<WHAT GIRL?>
YOU KNOW WHAT GIRL, JULES! WHERE IS SHE?
LEWIS.
I SAW HER! HURRY UP, WHERE IS SHE?
YOU SEEM AWFULLY CONCERNED, LEWIS. INVESTED, EVEN.
<THIS ONE'S STILL BREATHING!>
<THEY WENT OUT THE BACK! LEAVE THOSE GUYS AND GET OUT THERE!>
HEY, LEWIS?

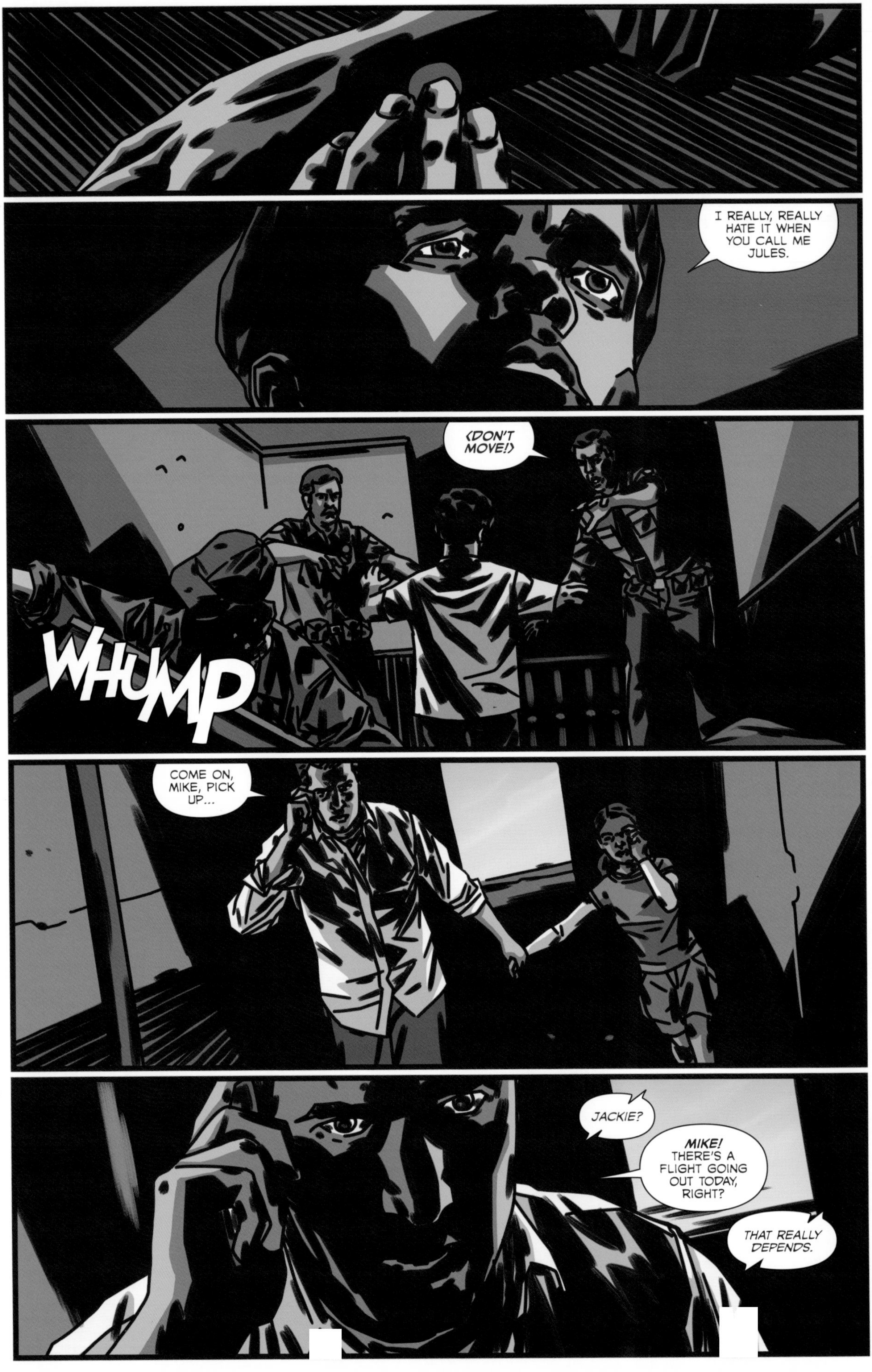
I REALLY, REALLY HATE IT WHEN YOU CALL ME JULES.
‹DON'T MOVE!›
WHUMP
COME ON, MIKE, PICK UP...
JACKIE?
MIKE! THERE'S A FLIGHT GOING OUT TODAY, RIGHT?
THAT REALLY DEPENDS.

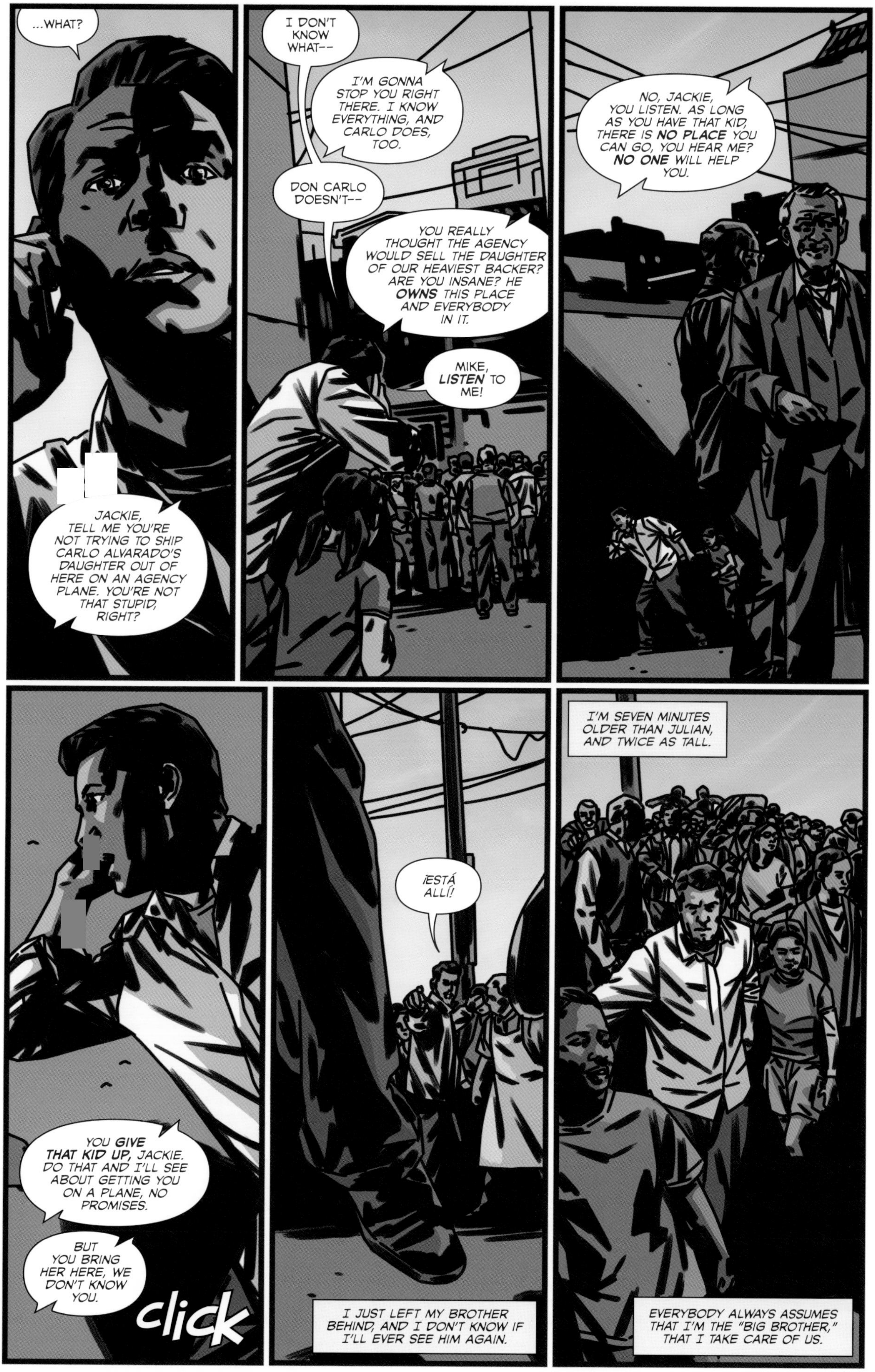
...WHAT?
JACKIE, TELL ME YOU'RE NOT TRYING TO SHIP CARLO ALVARADO'S DAUGHTER OUT OF HERE ON AN AGENCY PLANE. YOU'RE NOT THAT STUPID, RIGHT?
I DON'T KNOW WHAT--
I'M GONNA STOP YOU RIGHT THERE. I KNOW EVERYTHING, AND CARLO DOES, TOO.
DON CARLO DOESN'T--
YOU REALLY THOUGHT THE AGENCY WOULD SELL THE DAUGHTER OF OUR HEAVIEST BACKER? ARE YOU INSANE? HE OWNS THIS PLACE AND EVERYBODY IN IT.
MIKE, LISTEN TO ME!
NO, JACKIE, YOU LISTEN. AS LONG AS YOU HAVE THAT KID, THERE IS NO PLACE YOU CAN GO, YOU HEAR ME? NO ONE WILL HELP YOU.
YOU GIVE THAT KID UP, JACKIE. DO THAT AND I'LL SEE ABOUT GETTING YOU ON A PLANE, NO PROMISES.
BUT YOU BRING HER HERE, WE DON'T KNOW YOU.
click
¡ESTÁ ALLÍ!
I JUST LEFT MY BROTHER BEHIND, AND I DON'T KNOW IF I'LL EVER SEE HIM AGAIN.
I'M SEVEN MINUTES OLDER THAN JULIAN, AND TWICE AS TALL.
EVERYBODY ALWAYS ASSUMES THAT I'M THE "BIG BROTHER," THAT I TAKE CARE OF US.

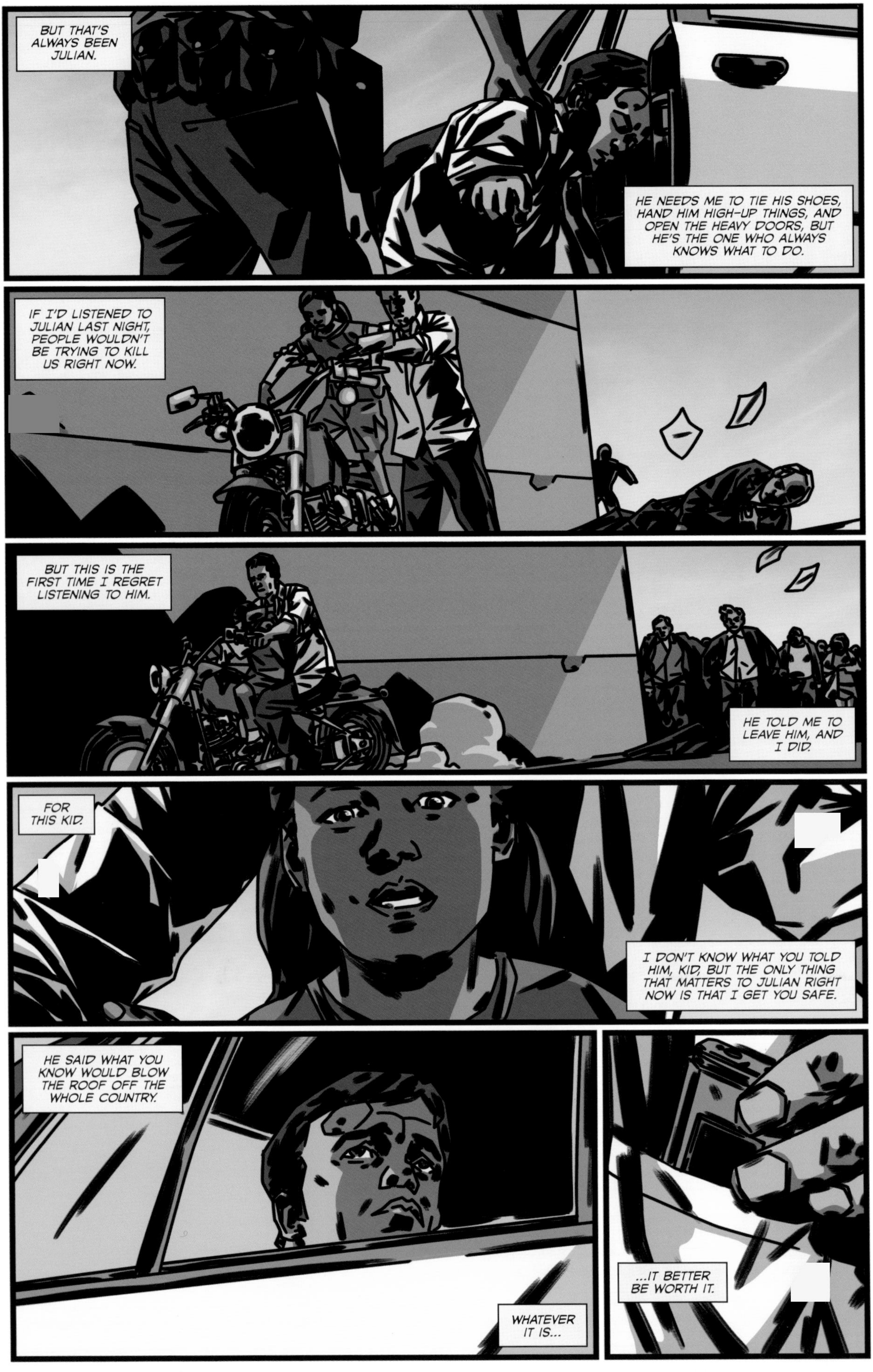
BUT THAT'S ALWAYS BEEN JULIAN.
HE NEEDS ME TO TIE HIS SHOES, HAND HIM HIGH-UP THINGS, AND OPEN THE HEAVY DOORS, BUT HE'S THE ONE WHO ALWAYS KNOWS WHAT TO DO.
IF I'D LISTENED TO JULIAN LAST NIGHT, PEOPLE WOULDN'T BE TRYING TO KILL US RIGHT NOW.
BUT THIS IS THE FIRST TIME I REGRET LISTENING TO HIM.
HE TOLD ME TO LEAVE HIM, AND I DID.
FOR THIS KID.
I DON'T KNOW WHAT YOU TOLD HIM, KID, BUT THE ONLY THING THAT MATTERS TO JULIAN RIGHT NOW IS THAT I GET YOU SAFE.
HE SAID WHAT YOU KNOW WOULD BLOW THE ROOF OFF THE WHOLE COUNTRY.
WHATEVER IT IS...
...IT BETTER BE WORTH IT.

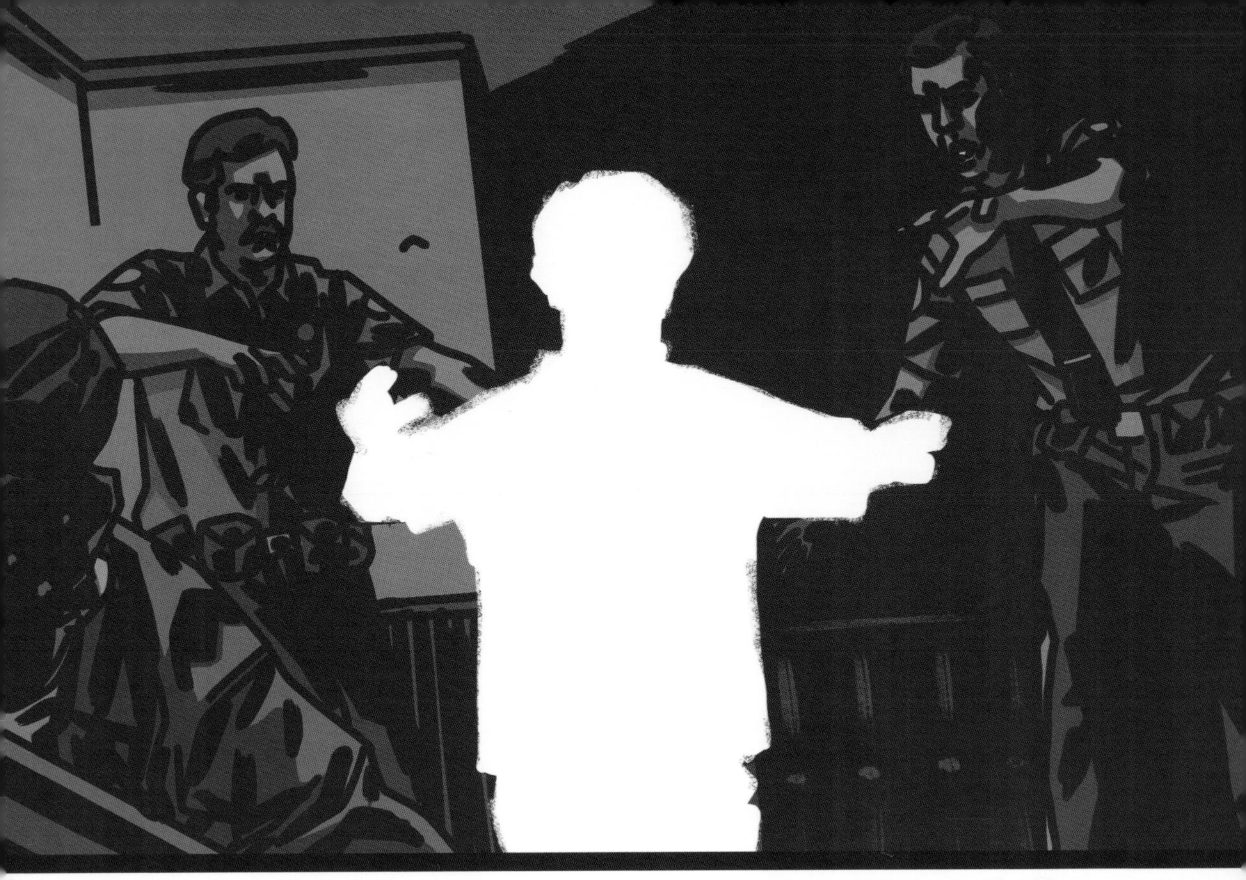

THREE

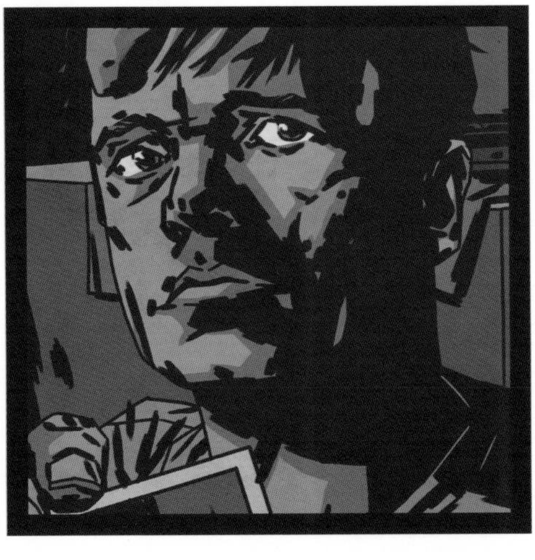

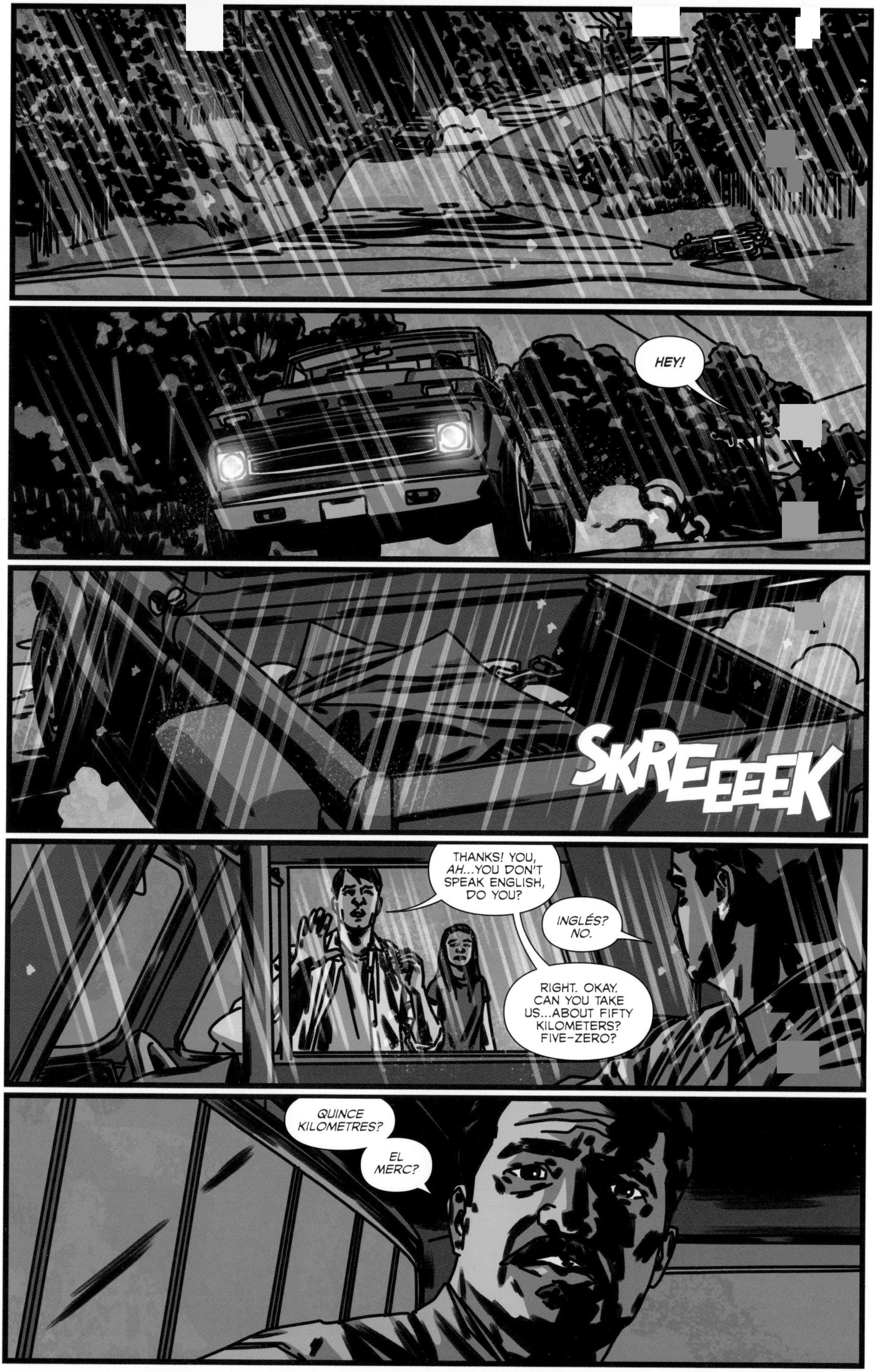
HEY!
SKREEEEK
THANKS! YOU, AH...YOU DON'T SPEAK ENGLISH, DO YOU?
INGLÉS? NO.
RIGHT. OKAY. CAN YOU TAKE US...ABOUT FIFTY KILOMETERS? FIVE-ZERO?
QUINCE KILOMETRES?
EL MERC?

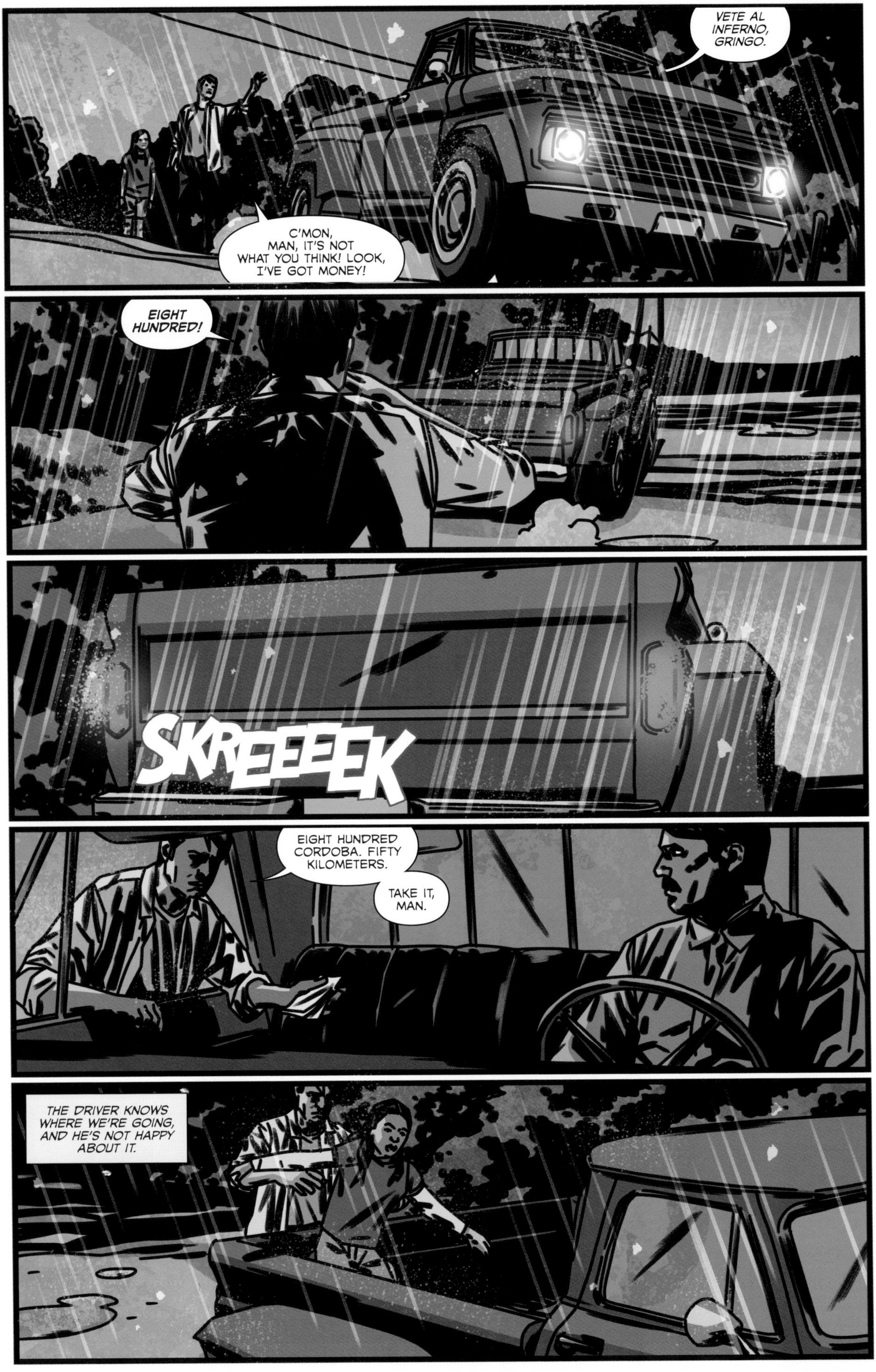
VETE AL INFERNO, GRINGO.
C'MON, MAN, IT'S NOT WHAT YOU THINK! LOOK, I'VE GOT MONEY!
EIGHT HUNDRED!
SKREEEEK
EIGHT HUNDRED CORDOBA. FIFTY KILOMETERS.
TAKE IT, MAN.
THE DRIVER KNOWS WHERE WE'RE GOING, AND HE'S NOT HAPPY ABOUT IT.

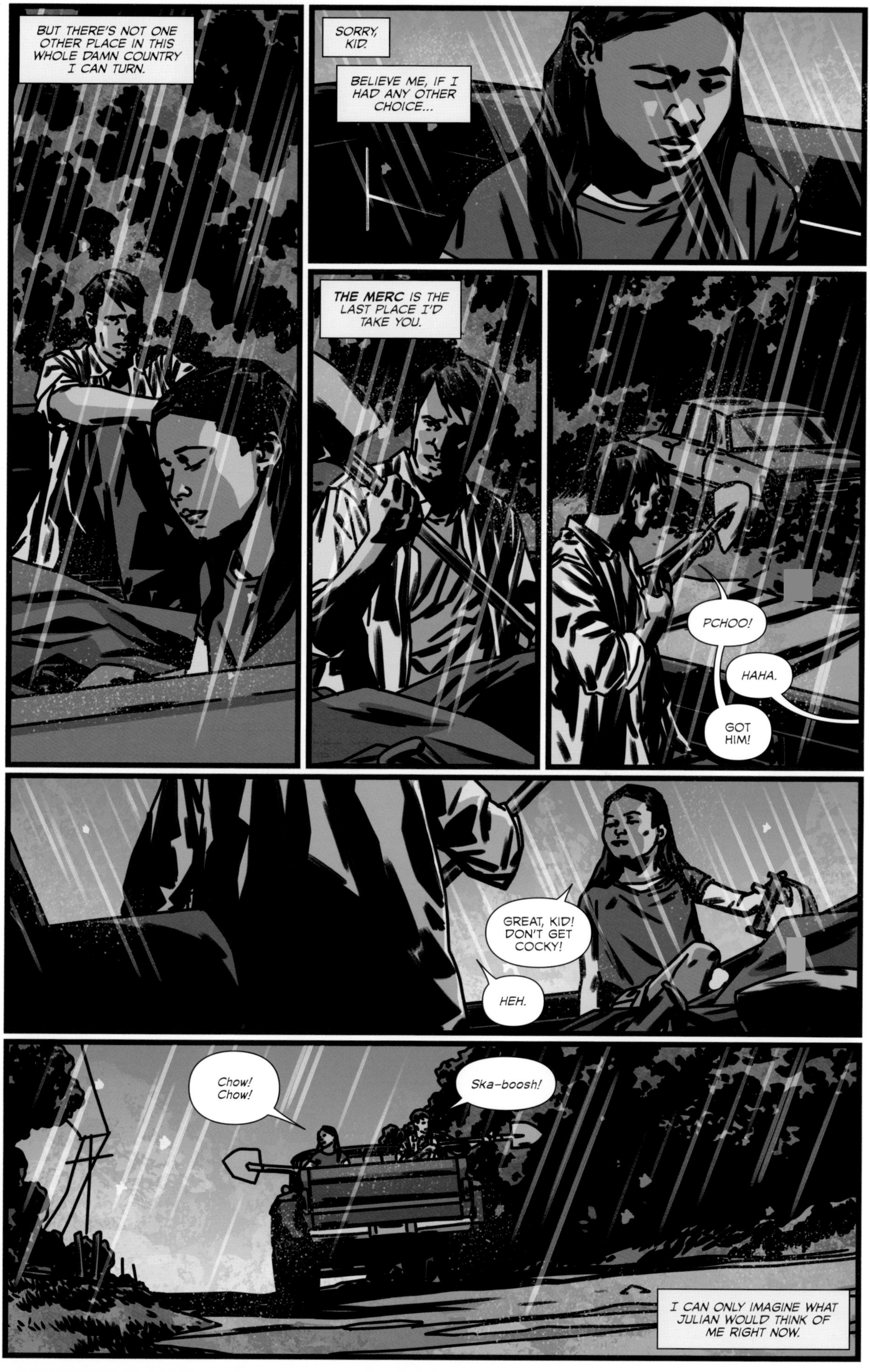
BUT THERE'S NOT ONE OTHER PLACE IN THIS WHOLE DAMN COUNTRY I CAN TURN.
SORRY, KID.
BELIEVE ME, IF I HAD ANY OTHER CHOICE...
THE MERC IS THE LAST PLACE I'D TAKE YOU.
PCHOO!
HAHA.
GOT HIM!
GREAT, KID! DON'T GET COCKY!
HEH.
Chow! Chow!
Ska-boosh!
I CAN ONLY IMAGINE WHAT JULIAN WOULD THINK OF ME RIGHT NOW.

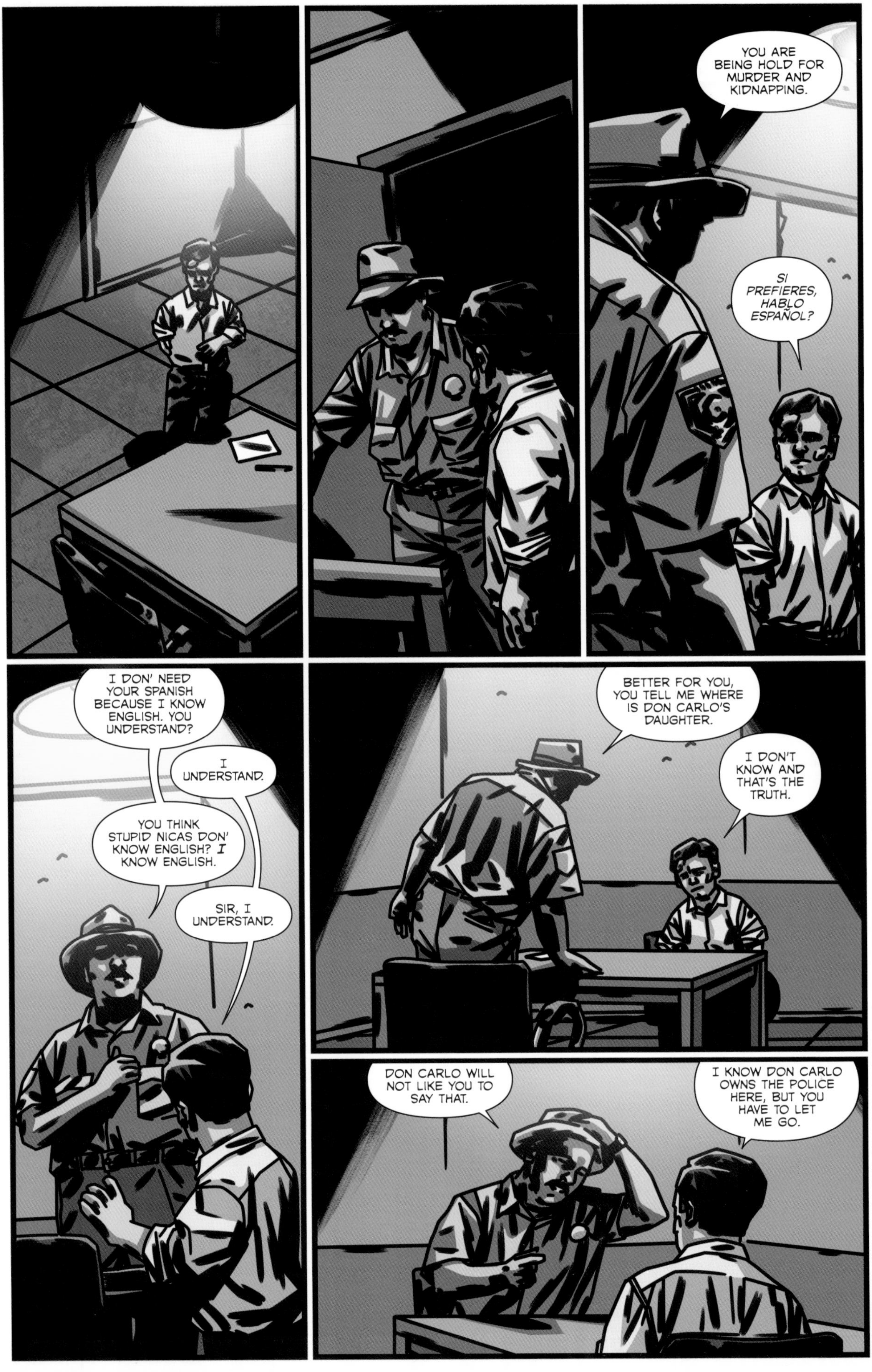
YOU ARE BEING HOLD FOR MURDER AND KIDNAPPING.
SI PREFIERES, HABLO ESPAÑOL?
I DON' NEED YOUR SPANISH BECAUSE I KNOW ENGLISH. YOU UNDERSTAND?
I UNDERSTAND.
YOU THINK STUPID NICAS DON' KNOW ENGLISH? *I* KNOW ENGLISH.
SIR, I UNDERSTAND.
BETTER FOR YOU, YOU TELL ME WHERE IS DON CARLO'S DAUGHTER.
I DON'T KNOW AND THAT'S THE TRUTH.
DON CARLO WILL NOT LIKE YOU TO SAY THAT.
I KNOW DON CARLO OWNS THE POLICE HERE, BUT YOU HAVE TO LET ME GO.

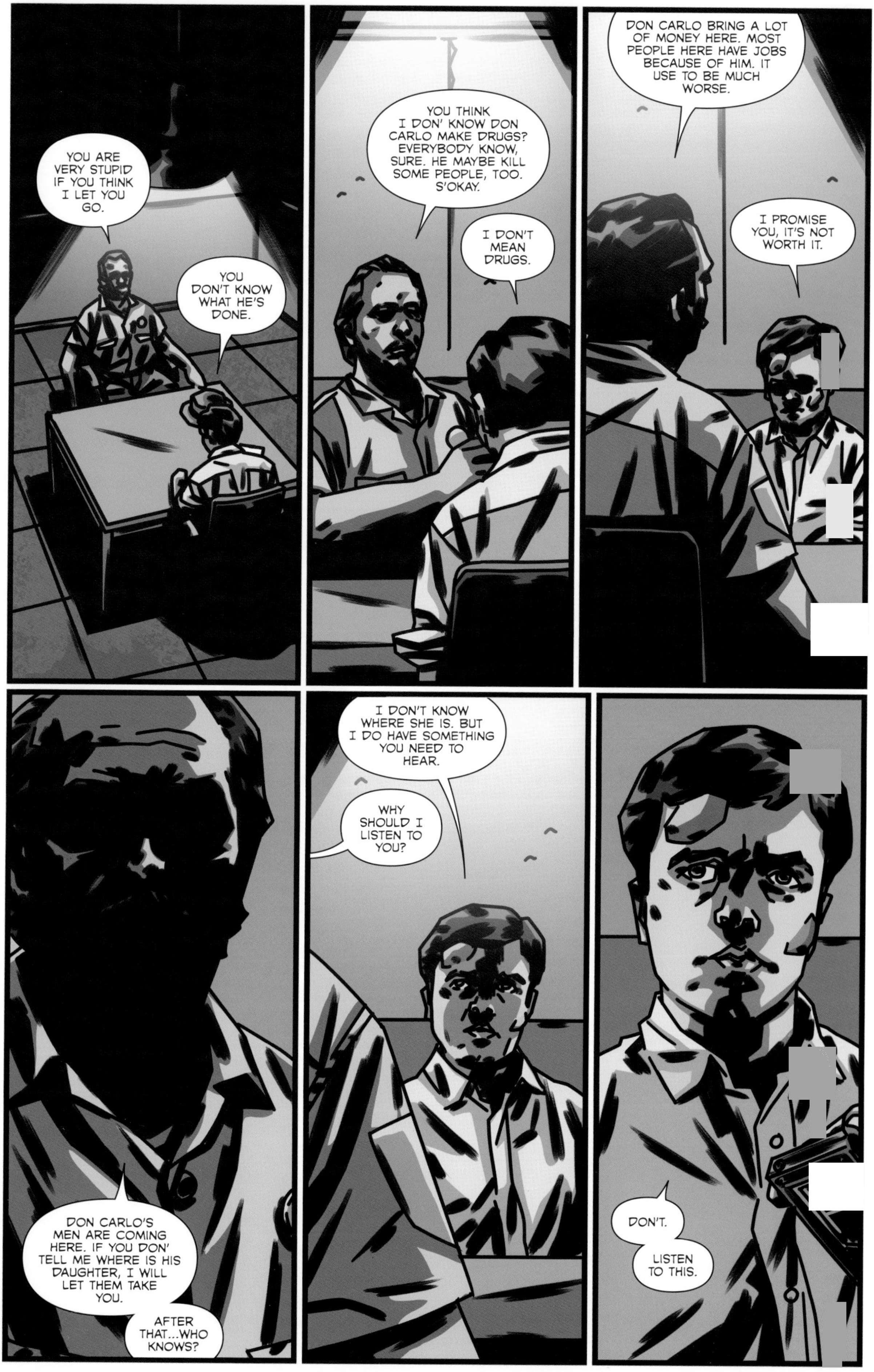
YOU ARE VERY STUPID IF YOU THINK I LET YOU GO.
YOU DON'T KNOW WHAT HE'S DONE.
YOU THINK I DON' KNOW DON CARLO MAKE DRUGS? EVERYBODY KNOW, SURE. HE MAYBE KILL SOME PEOPLE, TOO. S'OKAY.
I DON'T MEAN DRUGS.
DON CARLO BRING A LOT OF MONEY HERE. MOST PEOPLE HERE HAVE JOBS BECAUSE OF HIM. IT USE TO BE MUCH WORSE.
I PROMISE YOU, IT'S NOT WORTH IT.
DON CARLO'S MEN ARE COMING HERE. IF YOU DON' TELL ME WHERE IS HIS DAUGHTER, I WILL LET THEM TAKE YOU.
AFTER THAT...WHO KNOWS?
I DON'T KNOW WHERE SHE IS. BUT I DO HAVE SOMETHING YOU NEED TO HEAR.
WHY SHOULD I LISTEN TO YOU?
DON'T.
LISTEN TO THIS.

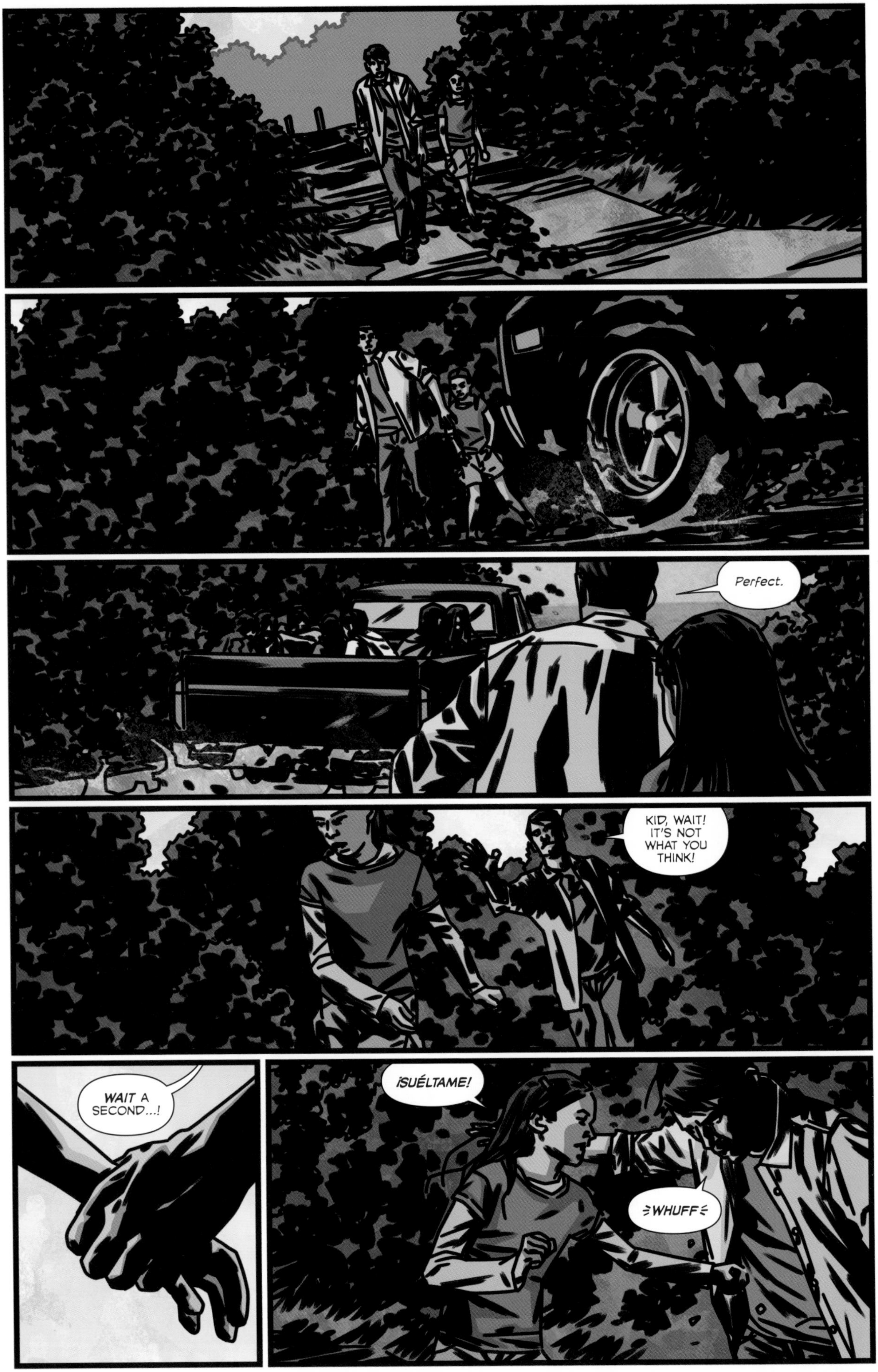
Perfect.
KID, WAIT! IT'S NOT WHAT YOU THINK!
WAIT A SECOND...!
¡SUÉLTAME!
WHUFF

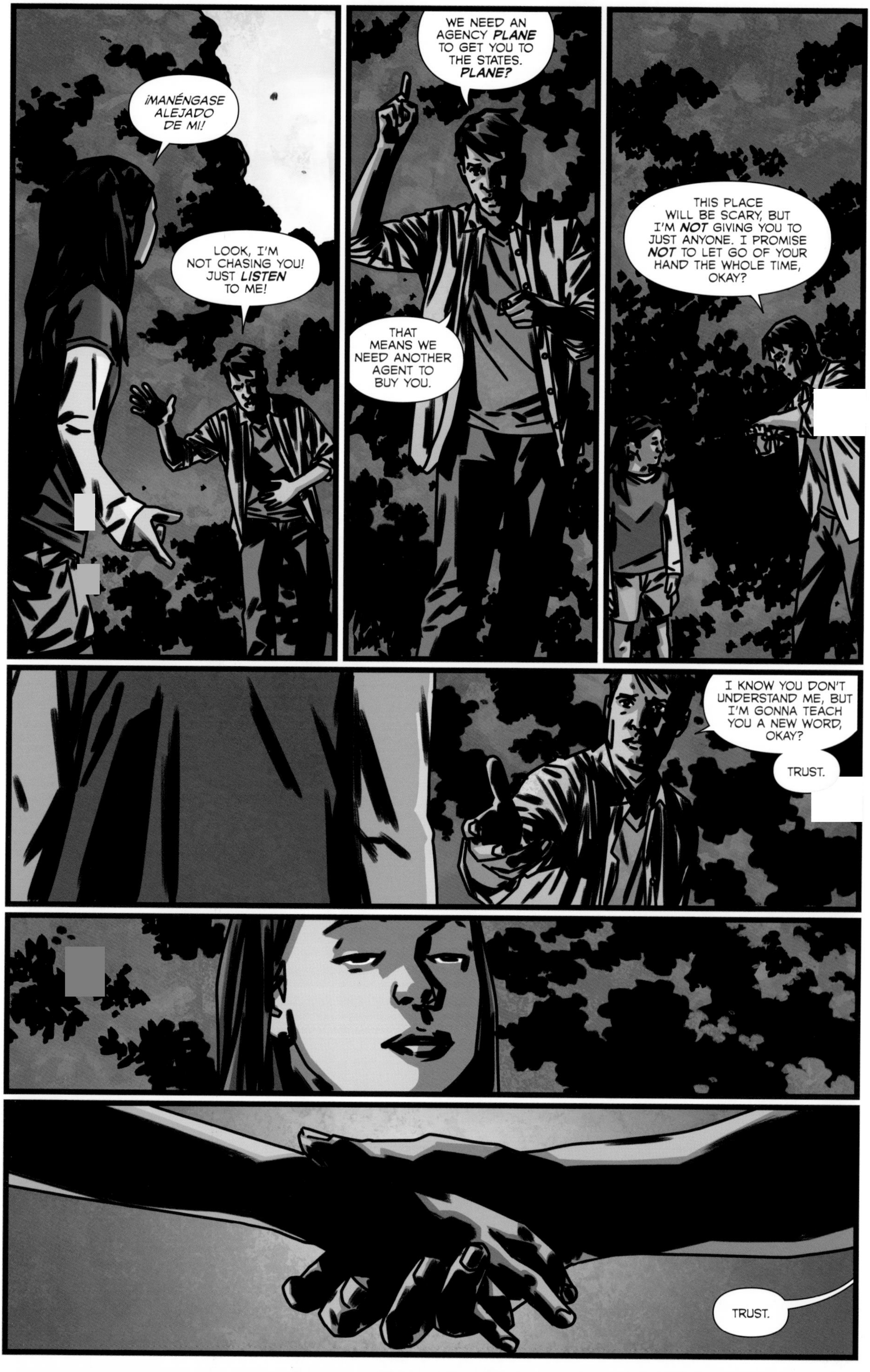
¡MANÉNGASE ALEJADO DE MI!
LOOK, I'M NOT CHASING YOU! JUST LISTEN TO ME!
WE NEED AN AGENCY PLANE TO GET YOU TO THE STATES. PLANE?
THAT MEANS WE NEED ANOTHER AGENT TO BUY YOU.
THIS PLACE WILL BE SCARY, BUT I'M NOT GIVING YOU TO JUST ANYONE. I PROMISE NOT TO LET GO OF YOUR HAND THE WHOLE TIME, OKAY?
I KNOW YOU DON'T UNDERSTAND ME, BUT I'M GONNA TEACH YOU A NEW WORD, OKAY?
TRUST.
TRUST.

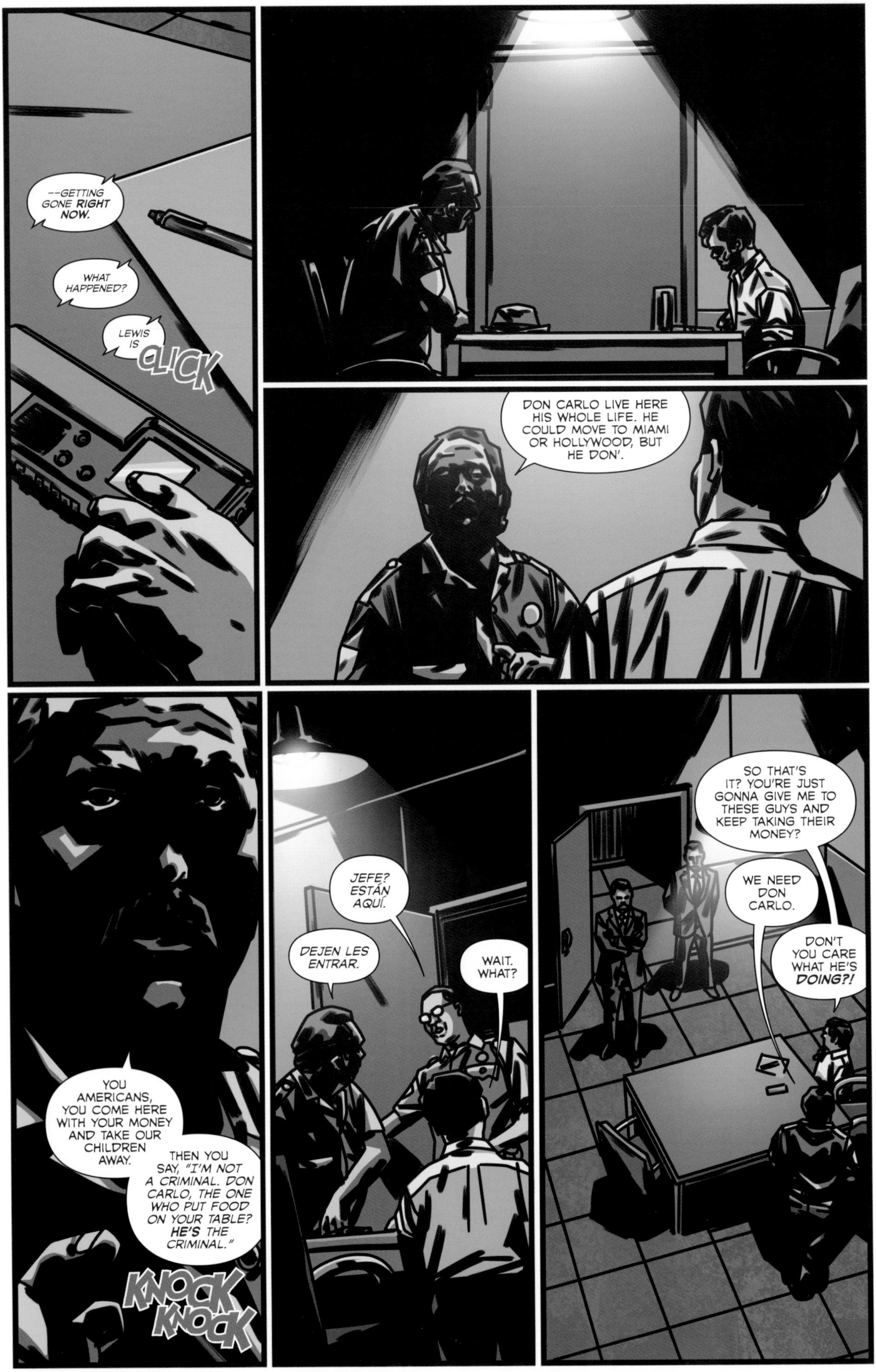
--GETTING GONE RIGHT NOW.
WHAT HAPPENED?
LEWIS IS
CLICK
DON CARLO LIVE HERE HIS WHOLE LIFE. HE COULD MOVE TO MIAMI OR HOLLYWOOD, BUT HE DON'.
YOU AMERICANS, YOU COME HERE WITH YOUR MONEY AND TAKE OUR CHILDREN AWAY.
THEN YOU SAY, "I'M NOT A CRIMINAL. DON CARLO, THE ONE WHO PUT FOOD ON YOUR TABLE? HE'S THE CRIMINAL."
KNOCK KNOCK
JEFE? ESTÁN AQUÍ.
DEJEN LES ENTRAR.
WAIT. WHAT?
SO THAT'S IT? YOU'RE JUST GONNA GIVE ME TO THESE GUYS AND KEEP TAKING THEIR MONEY?
WE NEED DON CARLO.
DON'T YOU CARE WHAT HE'S DOING?!

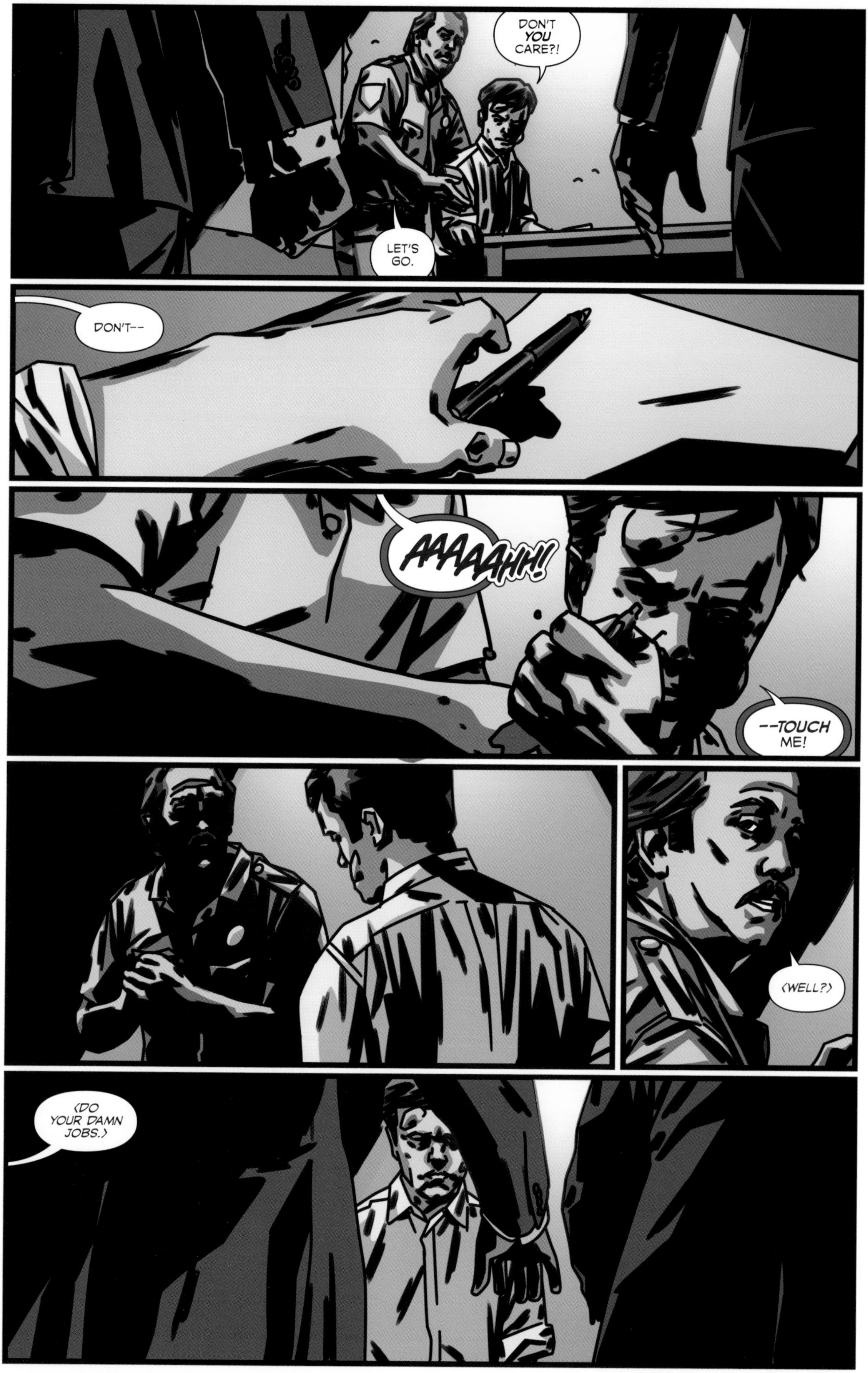
DON'T YOU CARE?!
LET'S GO.
DON'T--
AAAAAHH!!
--TOUCH ME!
⟨WELL?⟩
⟨DO YOUR DAMN JOBS.⟩

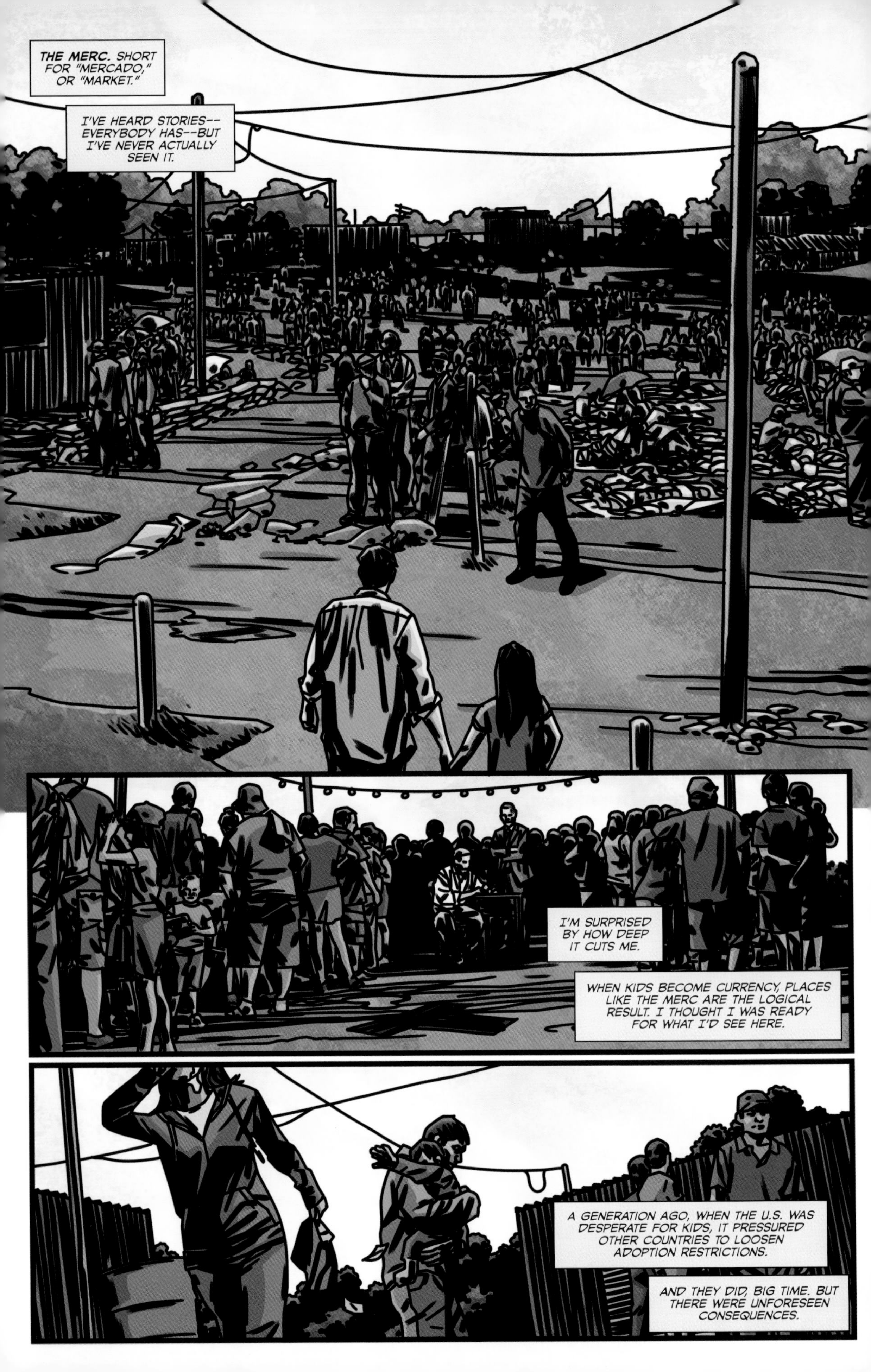
THE MERC. SHORT FOR "MERCADO," OR "MARKET."
I'VE HEARD STORIES--EVERYBODY HAS--BUT I'VE NEVER ACTUALLY SEEN IT.
I'M SURPRISED BY HOW DEEP IT CUTS ME.
WHEN KIDS BECOME CURRENCY, PLACES LIKE THE MERC ARE THE LOGICAL RESULT. I THOUGHT I WAS READY FOR WHAT I'D SEE HERE.
A GENERATION AGO, WHEN THE U.S. WAS DESPERATE FOR KIDS, IT PRESSURED OTHER COUNTRIES TO LOOSEN ADOPTION RESTRICTIONS.
AND THEY DID, BIG TIME. BUT THERE WERE UNFORESEEN CONSEQUENCES.

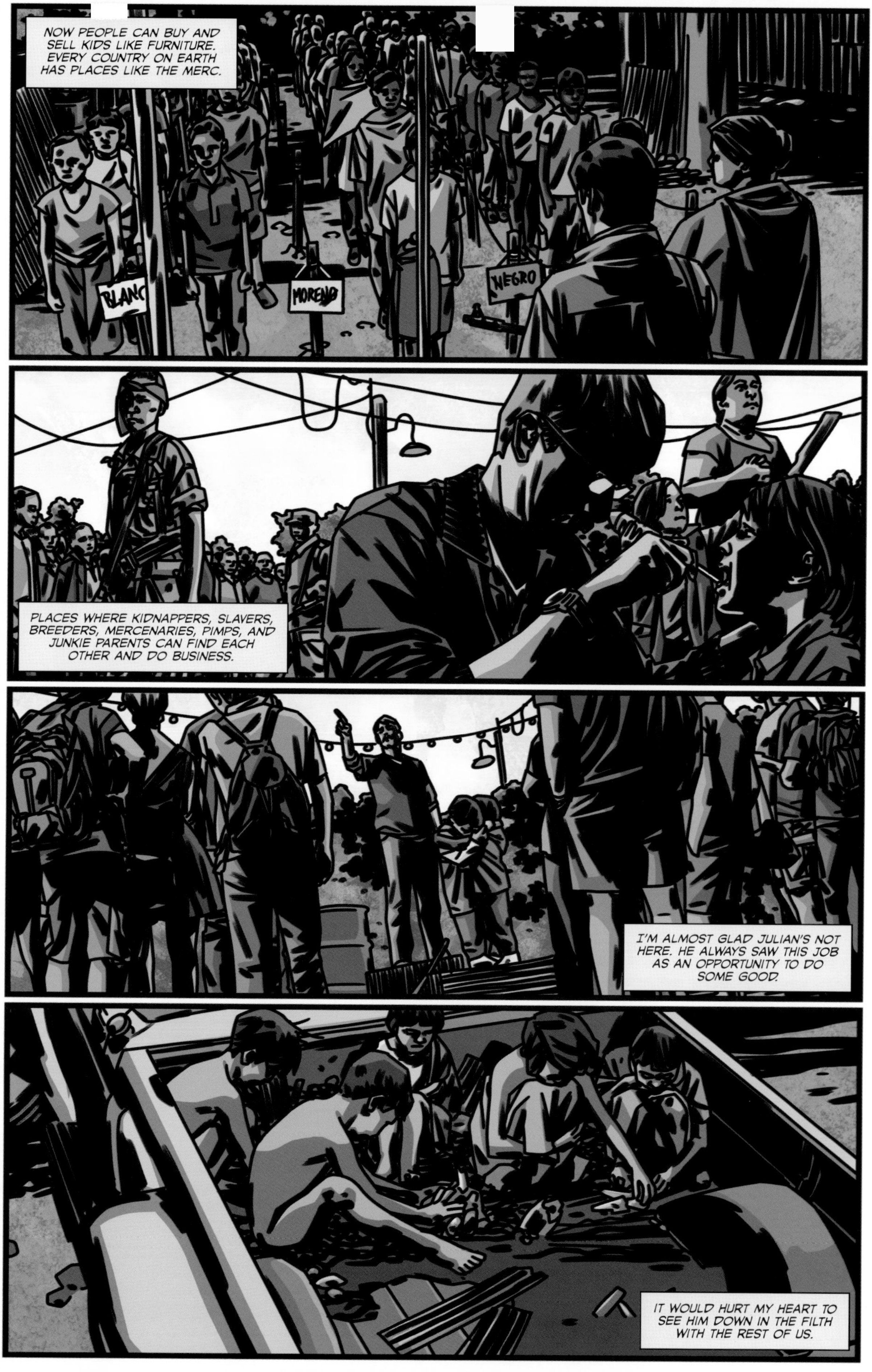
NOW PEOPLE CAN BUY AND SELL KIDS LIKE FURNITURE. EVERY COUNTRY ON EARTH HAS PLACES LIKE THE MERC.
BLANC
MORENO
NEGRO
PLACES WHERE KIDNAPPERS, SLAVERS, BREEDERS, MERCENARIES, PIMPS, AND JUNKIE PARENTS CAN FIND EACH OTHER AND DO BUSINESS.
I'M ALMOST GLAD JULIAN'S NOT HERE. HE ALWAYS SAW THIS JOB AS AN OPPORTUNITY TO DO SOME GOOD.
IT WOULD HURT MY HEART TO SEE HIM DOWN IN THE FILTH WITH THE REST OF US.

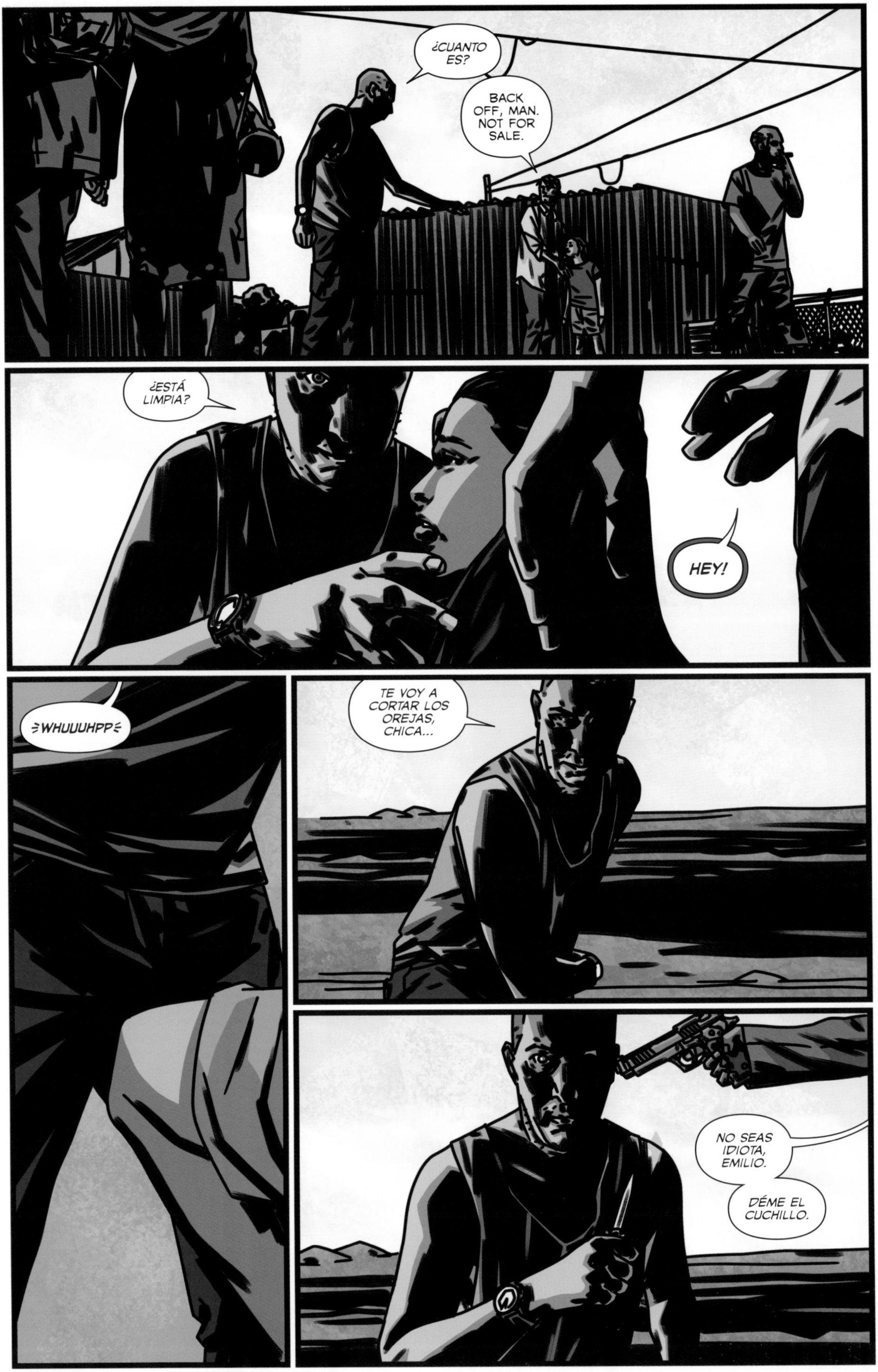
¿CUANTO ES?
BACK OFF, MAN. NOT FOR SALE.
¿ESTÁ LIMPIA?
HEY!
WHUUUHPP
TE VOY A CORTAR LOS OREJAS, CHICA...
NO SEAS IDIOTA, EMILIO.
DÉME EL CUCHILLO.

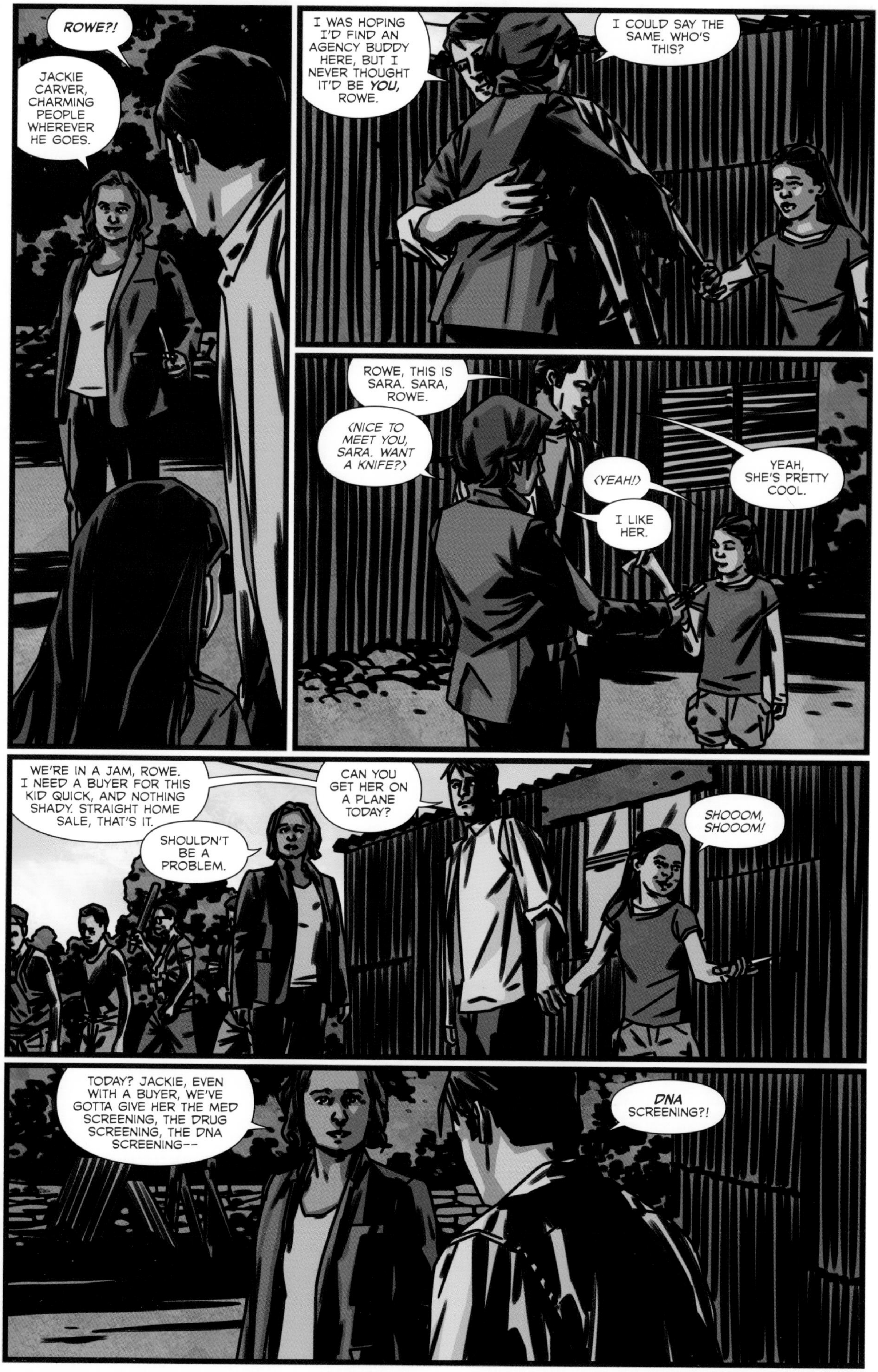

ROWE?!
JACKIE CARVER, CHARMING PEOPLE WHEREVER HE GOES.
I WAS HOPING I'D FIND AN AGENCY BUDDY HERE, BUT I NEVER THOUGHT IT'D BE YOU, ROWE.
I COULD SAY THE SAME. WHO'S THIS?
ROWE, THIS IS SARA. SARA, ROWE.
<NICE TO MEET YOU, SARA. WANT A KNIFE?>
<YEAH!>
I LIKE HER.
YEAH, SHE'S PRETTY COOL.
WE'RE IN A JAM, ROWE. I NEED A BUYER FOR THIS KID QUICK, AND NOTHING SHADY. STRAIGHT HOME SALE, THAT'S IT.
SHOULDN'T BE A PROBLEM.
CAN YOU GET HER ON A PLANE TODAY?
SHOOOM, SHOOOM!
TODAY? JACKIE, EVEN WITH A BUYER, WE'VE GOTTA GIVE HER THE MED SCREENING, THE DRUG SCREENING, THE DNA SCREENING--
DNA SCREENING?!

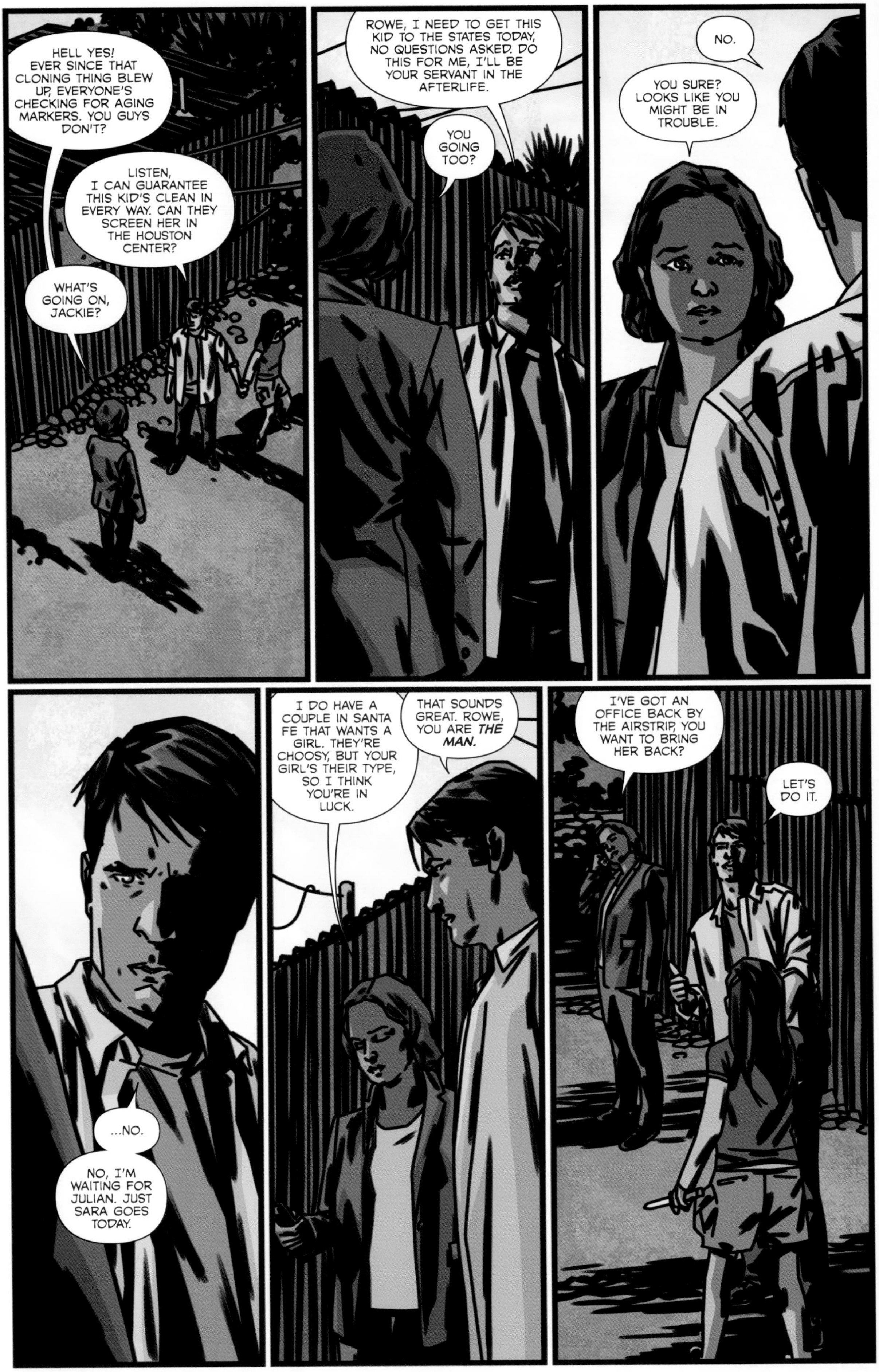
HELL YES! EVER SINCE THAT CLONING THING BLEW UP, EVERYONE'S CHECKING FOR AGING MARKERS. YOU GUYS DON'T?
LISTEN, I CAN GUARANTEE THIS KID'S CLEAN IN EVERY WAY. CAN THEY SCREEN HER IN THE HOUSTON CENTER?
WHAT'S GOING ON, JACKIE?
ROWE, I NEED TO GET THIS KID TO THE STATES TODAY, NO QUESTIONS ASKED. DO THIS FOR ME, I'LL BE YOUR SERVANT IN THE AFTERLIFE.
YOU GOING TOO?
NO.
YOU SURE? LOOKS LIKE YOU MIGHT BE IN TROUBLE.
...NO.
NO, I'M WAITING FOR JULIAN. JUST SARA GOES TODAY.
I DO HAVE A COUPLE IN SANTA FE THAT WANTS A GIRL. THEY'RE CHOOSY, BUT YOUR GIRL'S THEIR TYPE, SO I THINK YOU'RE IN LUCK.
THAT SOUNDS GREAT. ROWE, YOU ARE ***THE MAN.***
I'VE GOT AN OFFICE BACK BY THE AIRSTRIP, YOU WANT TO BRING HER BACK?
LET'S DO IT.

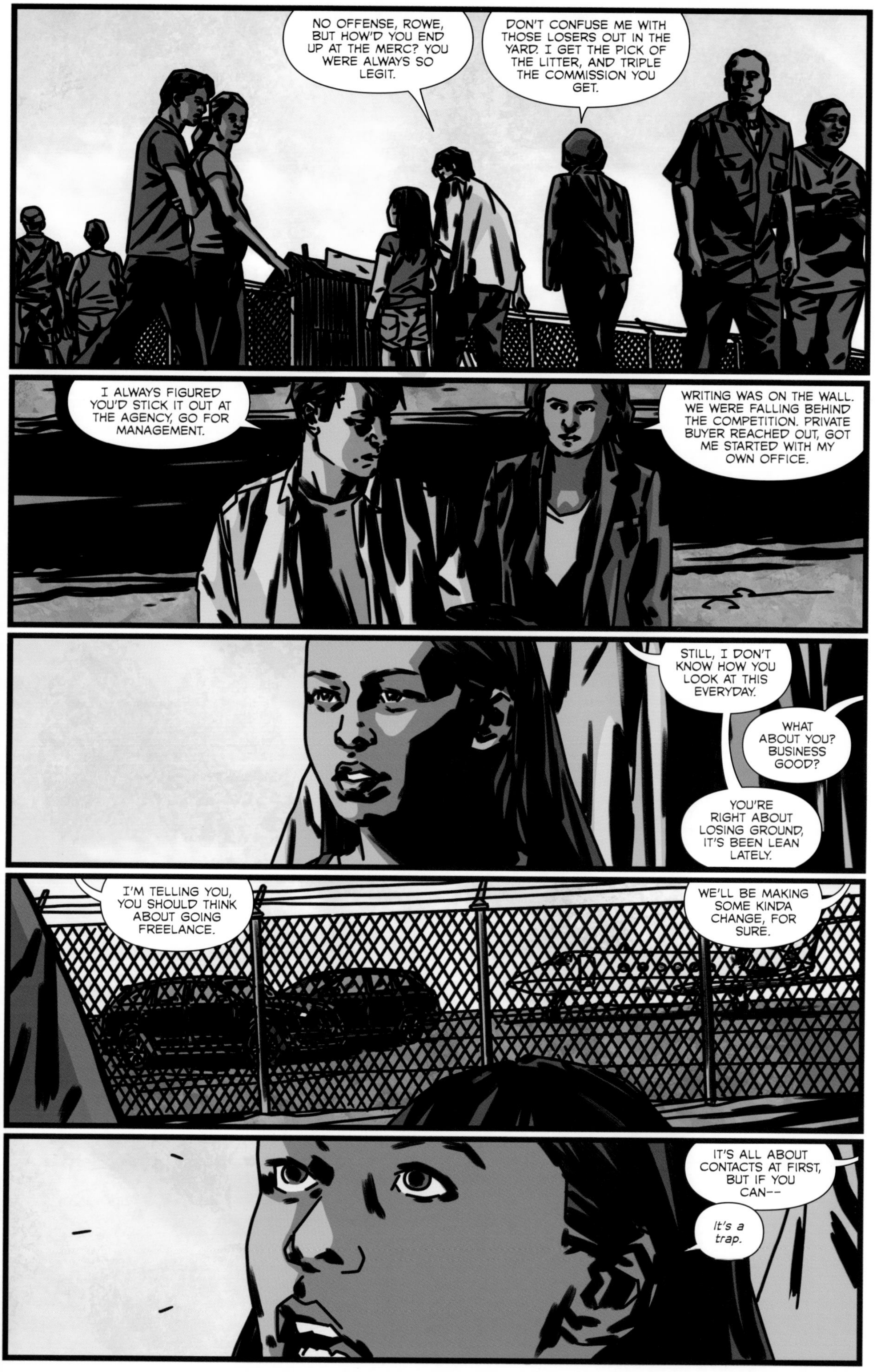
NO OFFENSE, ROWE, BUT HOW'D YOU END UP AT THE MERC? YOU WERE ALWAYS SO LEGIT.
DON'T CONFUSE ME WITH THOSE LOSERS OUT IN THE YARD. I GET THE PICK OF THE LITTER, AND TRIPLE THE COMMISSION YOU GET.
I ALWAYS FIGURED YOU'D STICK IT OUT AT THE AGENCY, GO FOR MANAGEMENT.
WRITING WAS ON THE WALL. WE WERE FALLING BEHIND THE COMPETITION. PRIVATE BUYER REACHED OUT, GOT ME STARTED WITH MY OWN OFFICE.
STILL, I DON'T KNOW HOW YOU LOOK AT THIS EVERYDAY.
WHAT ABOUT YOU? BUSINESS GOOD?
YOU'RE RIGHT ABOUT LOSING GROUND, IT'S BEEN LEAN LATELY.
I'M TELLING YOU, YOU SHOULD THINK ABOUT GOING FREELANCE.
WE'LL BE MAKING SOME KINDA CHANGE, FOR SURE.
IT'S ALL ABOUT CONTACTS AT FIRST, BUT IF YOU CAN--
It's a trap.

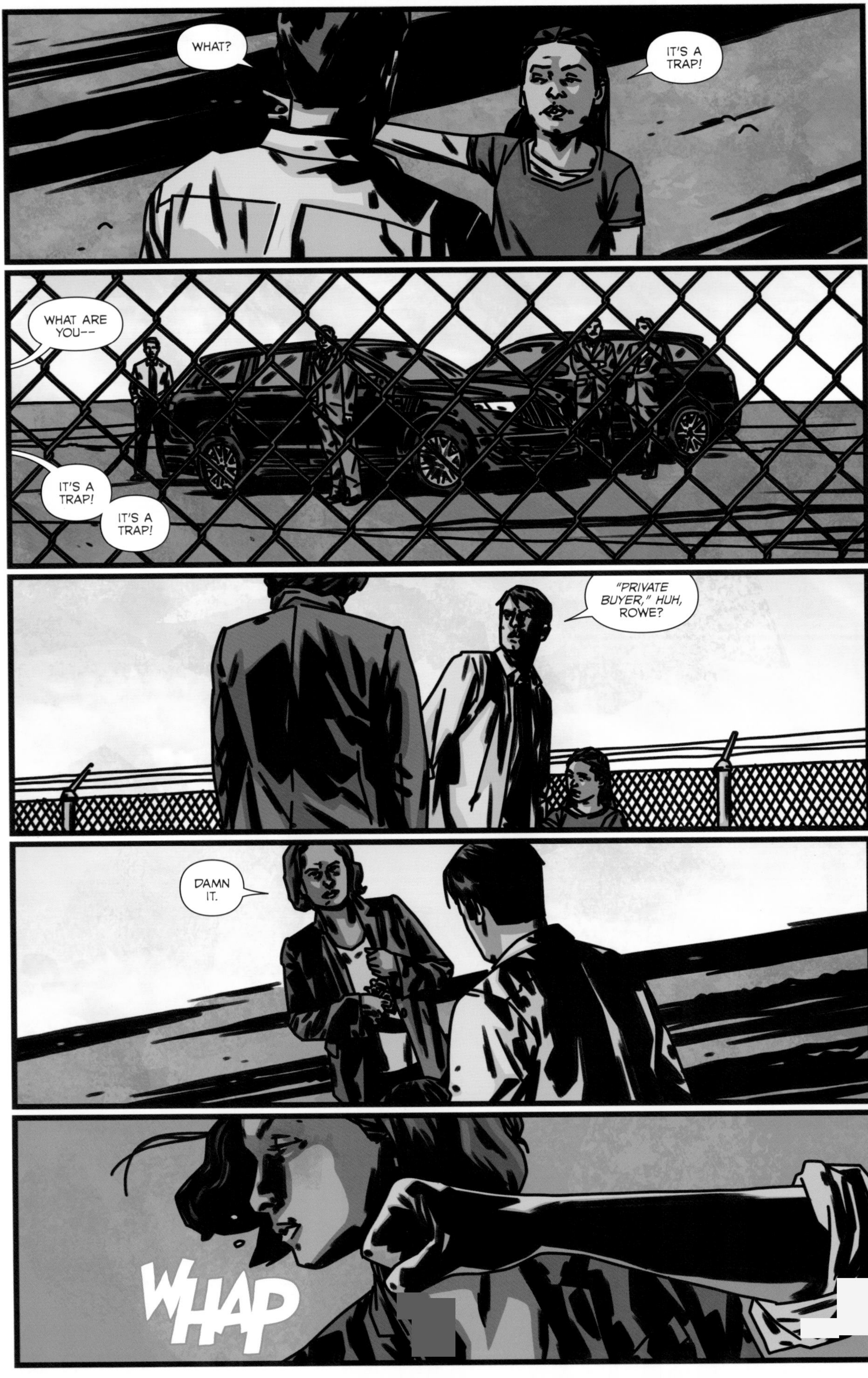
WHAT?
IT'S A TRAP!
WHAT ARE YOU--
IT'S A TRAP!
IT'S A TRAP!
"PRIVATE BUYER," HUH, ROWE?
DAMN IT.
WHAP

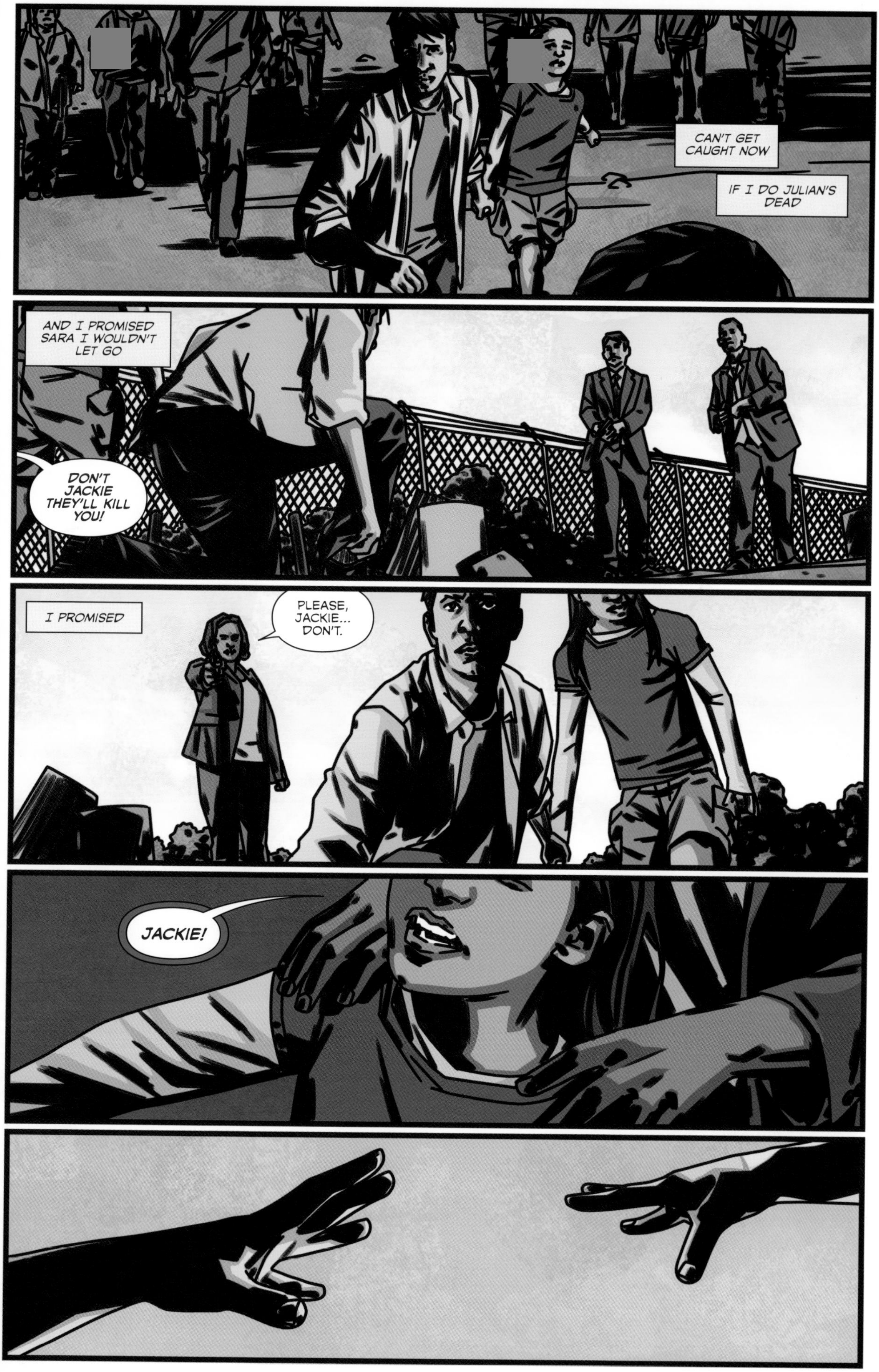
CAN'T GET CAUGHT NOW
IF I DO JULIAN'S DEAD
AND I PROMISED SARA I WOULDN'T LET GO
DON'T JACKIE THEY'LL KILL YOU!
I PROMISED
PLEASE, JACKIE... DON'T.
JACKIE!

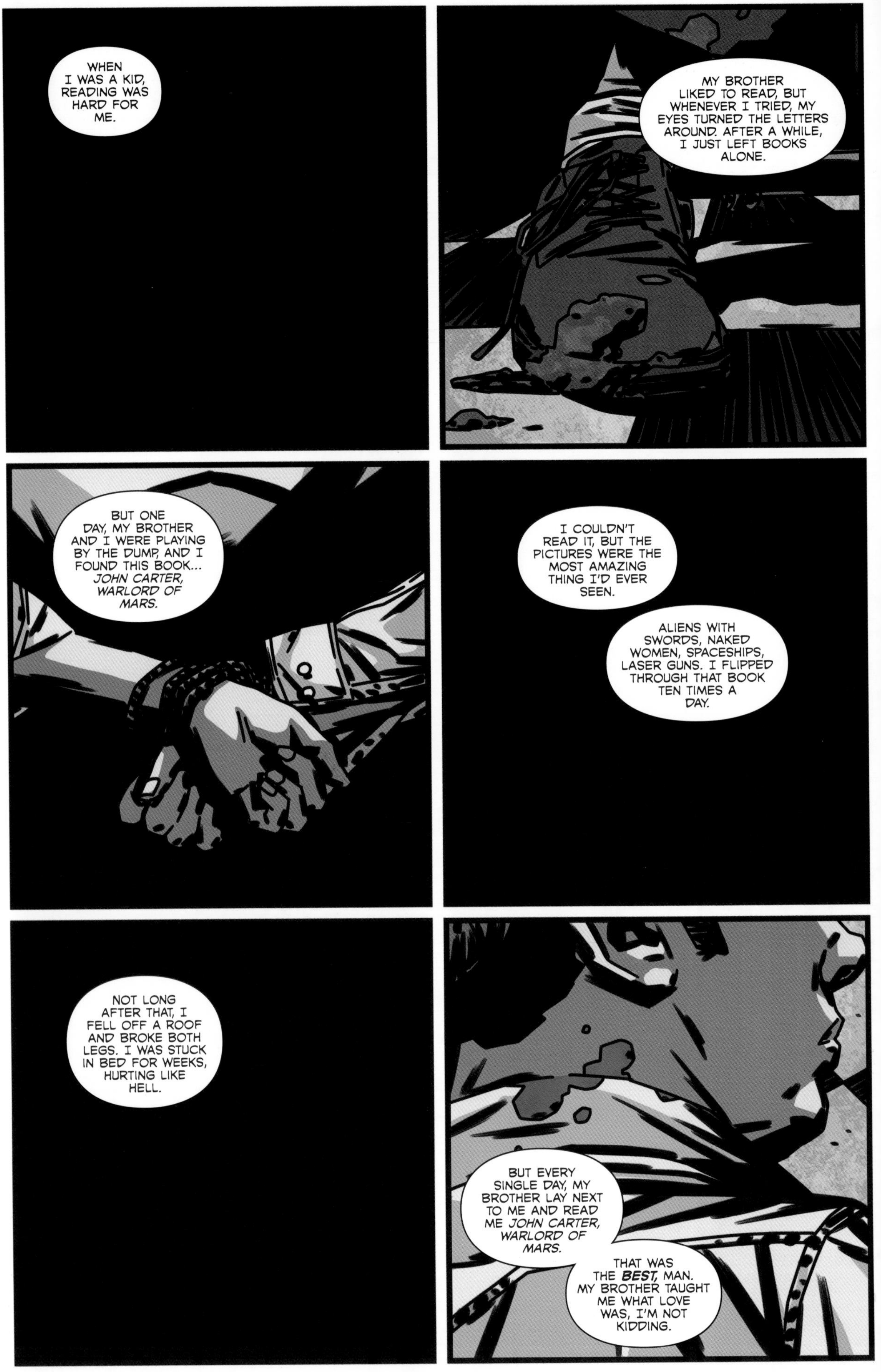
WHEN I WAS A KID, READING WAS HARD FOR ME.
MY BROTHER LIKED TO READ, BUT WHENEVER I TRIED, MY EYES TURNED THE LETTERS AROUND. AFTER A WHILE, I JUST LEFT BOOKS ALONE.
BUT ONE DAY, MY BROTHER AND I WERE PLAYING BY THE DUMP, AND I FOUND THIS BOOK... *JOHN CARTER, WARLORD OF MARS.*
I COULDN'T READ IT, BUT THE PICTURES WERE THE MOST AMAZING THING I'D EVER SEEN.
ALIENS WITH SWORDS, NAKED WOMEN, SPACESHIPS, LASER GUNS. I FLIPPED THROUGH THAT BOOK TEN TIMES A DAY.
NOT LONG AFTER THAT, I FELL OFF A ROOF AND BROKE BOTH LEGS. I WAS STUCK IN BED FOR WEEKS, HURTING LIKE HELL.
BUT EVERY SINGLE DAY, MY BROTHER LAY NEXT TO ME AND READ ME *JOHN CARTER, WARLORD OF MARS.*
THAT WAS THE ***BEST,*** MAN. MY BROTHER TAUGHT ME WHAT LOVE WAS, I'M NOT KIDDING.

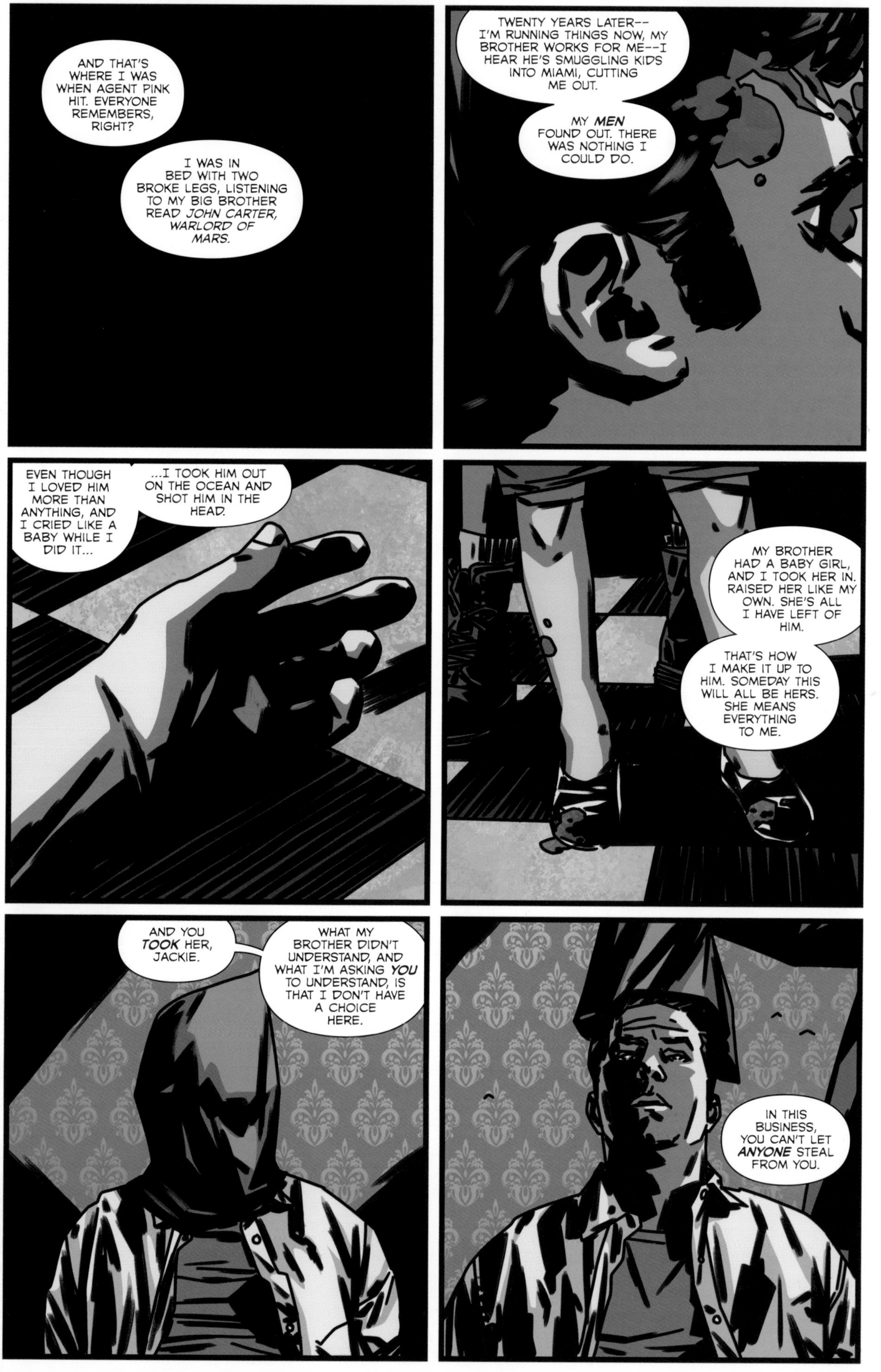
AND THAT'S WHERE I WAS WHEN AGENT PINK HIT. EVERYONE REMEMBERS, RIGHT?
I WAS IN BED WITH TWO BROKE LEGS, LISTENING TO MY BIG BROTHER READ JOHN CARTER, WARLORD OF MARS.
TWENTY YEARS LATER-- I'M RUNNING THINGS NOW, MY BROTHER WORKS FOR ME--I HEAR HE'S SMUGGLING KIDS INTO MIAMI, CUTTING ME OUT.
MY MEN FOUND OUT. THERE WAS NOTHING I COULD DO.
EVEN THOUGH I LOVED HIM MORE THAN ANYTHING, AND I CRIED LIKE A BABY WHILE I DID IT...
...I TOOK HIM OUT ON THE OCEAN AND SHOT HIM IN THE HEAD.
MY BROTHER HAD A BABY GIRL, AND I TOOK HER IN. RAISED HER LIKE MY OWN. SHE'S ALL I HAVE LEFT OF HIM.
THAT'S HOW I MAKE IT UP TO HIM. SOMEDAY THIS WILL ALL BE HERS. SHE MEANS EVERYTHING TO ME.
AND YOU TOOK HER, JACKIE.
WHAT MY BROTHER DIDN'T UNDERSTAND, AND WHAT I'M ASKING YOU TO UNDERSTAND, IS THAT I DON'T HAVE A CHOICE HERE.
IN THIS BUSINESS, YOU CAN'T LET ANYONE STEAL FROM YOU.

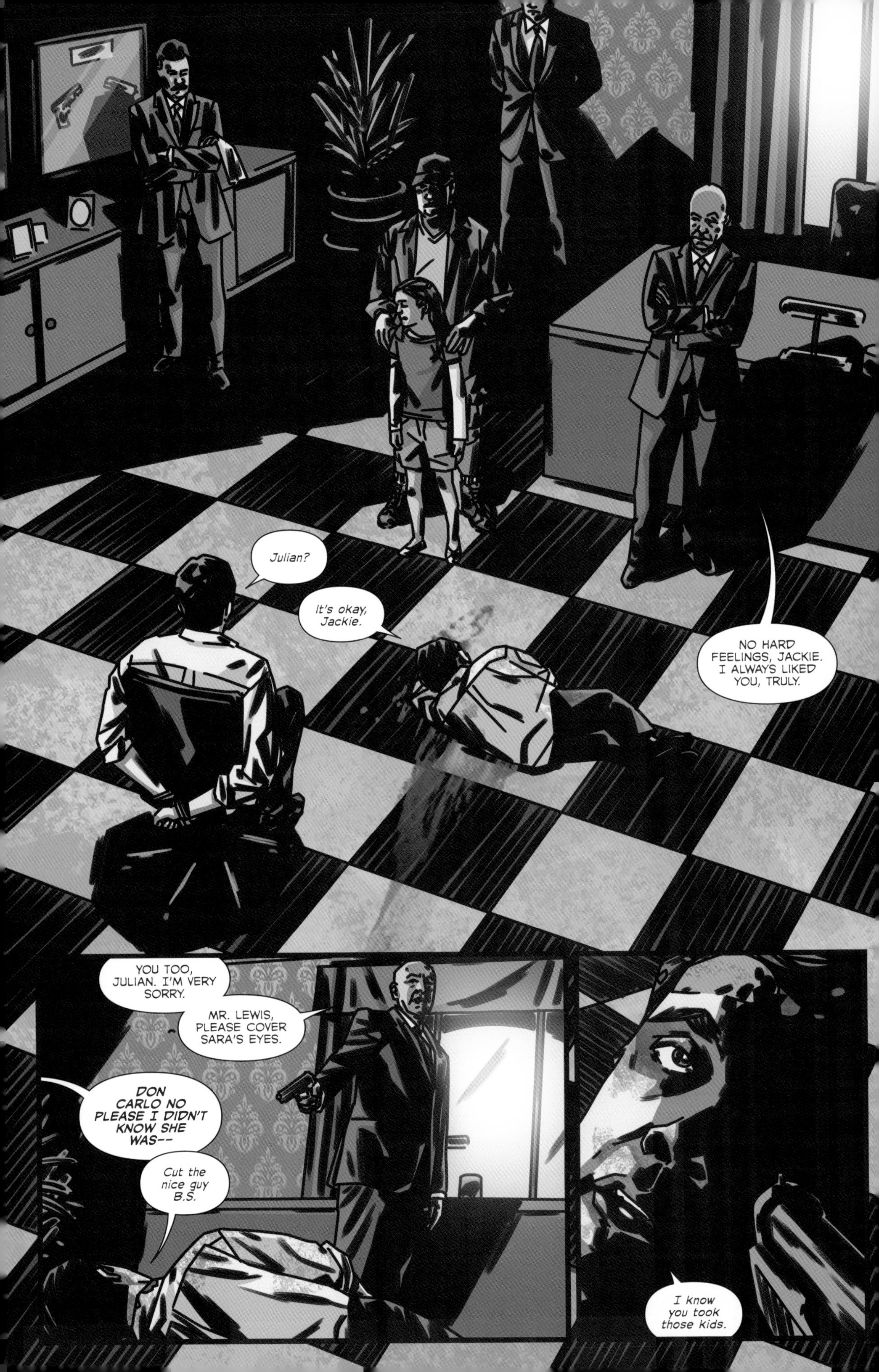
Julian?
It's okay, Jackie.
NO HARD FEELINGS, JACKIE. I ALWAYS LIKED YOU, TRULY.
YOU TOO, JULIAN. I'M VERY SORRY.
MR. LEWIS, PLEASE COVER SARA'S EYES.
DON CARLO NO PLEASE I DIDN'T KNOW SHE WAS--
Cut the nice guy B.S.
I know you took those kids.

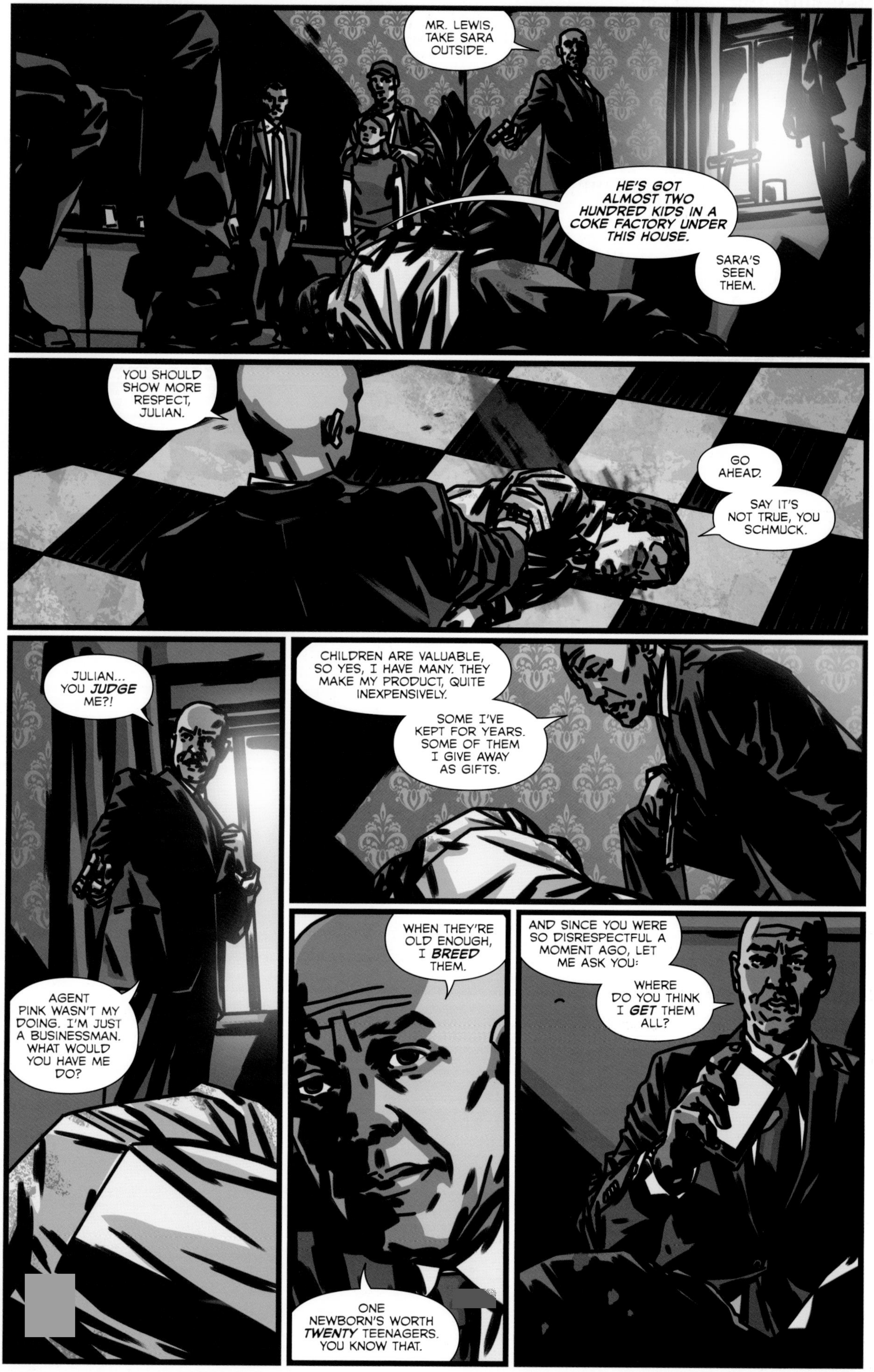

MR. LEWIS, TAKE SARA OUTSIDE.
HE'S GOT ALMOST TWO HUNDRED KIDS IN A COKE FACTORY UNDER THIS HOUSE.
SARA'S SEEN THEM.
YOU SHOULD SHOW MORE RESPECT, JULIAN.
GO AHEAD.
SAY IT'S NOT TRUE, YOU SCHMUCK.
JULIAN... YOU *JUDGE* ME?!
AGENT PINK WASN'T MY DOING. I'M JUST A BUSINESSMAN. WHAT WOULD YOU HAVE ME DO?
CHILDREN ARE VALUABLE, SO YES, I HAVE MANY. THEY MAKE MY PRODUCT, QUITE INEXPENSIVELY.
SOME I'VE KEPT FOR YEARS. SOME OF THEM I GIVE AWAY AS GIFTS.
WHEN THEY'RE OLD ENOUGH, I *BREED* THEM.
ONE NEWBORN'S WORTH *TWENTY* TEENAGERS. YOU KNOW THAT.
AND SINCE YOU WERE SO DISRESPECTFUL A MOMENT AGO, LET ME ASK YOU:
WHERE DO YOU THINK I *GET* THEM ALL?

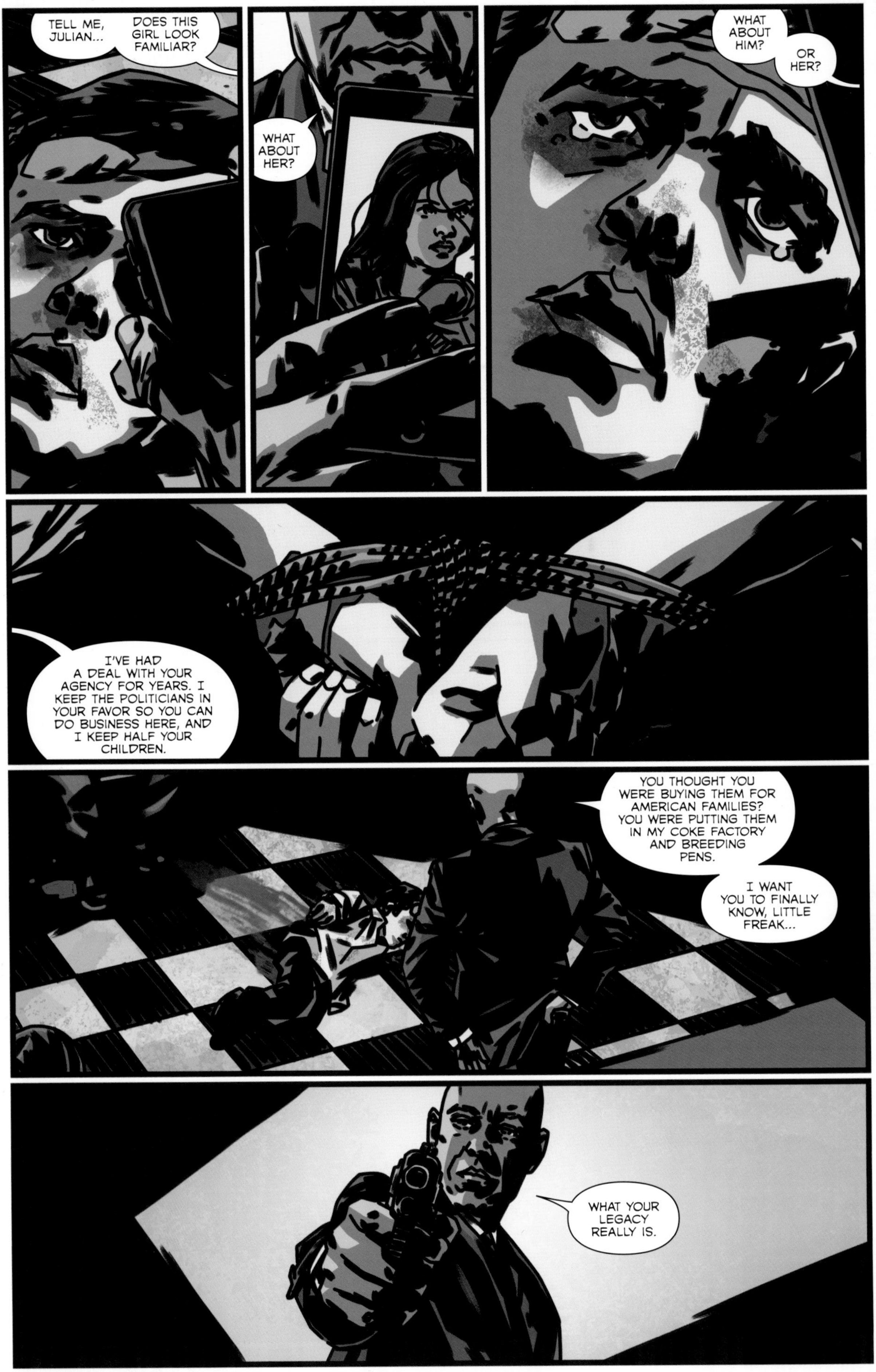
TELL ME, JULIAN...
DOES THIS GIRL LOOK FAMILIAR?
WHAT ABOUT HER?
WHAT ABOUT HIM?
OR HER?
I'VE HAD A DEAL WITH YOUR AGENCY FOR YEARS. I KEEP THE POLITICIANS IN YOUR FAVOR SO YOU CAN DO BUSINESS HERE, AND I KEEP HALF YOUR CHILDREN.
YOU THOUGHT YOU WERE BUYING THEM FOR AMERICAN FAMILIES? YOU WERE PUTTING THEM IN MY COKE FACTORY AND BREEDING PENS.
I WANT YOU TO FINALLY KNOW, LITTLE FREAK...
WHAT YOUR LEGACY REALLY IS.

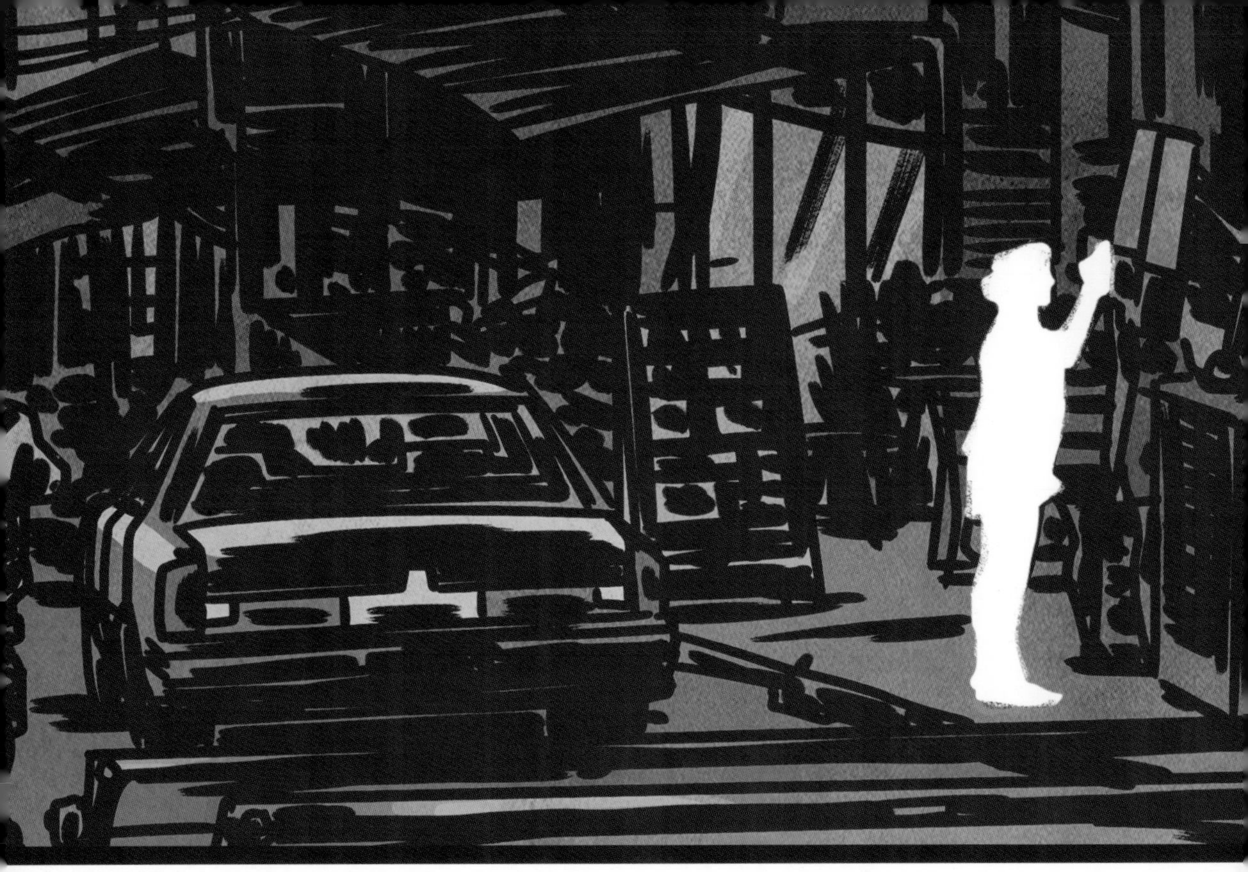

FOUR

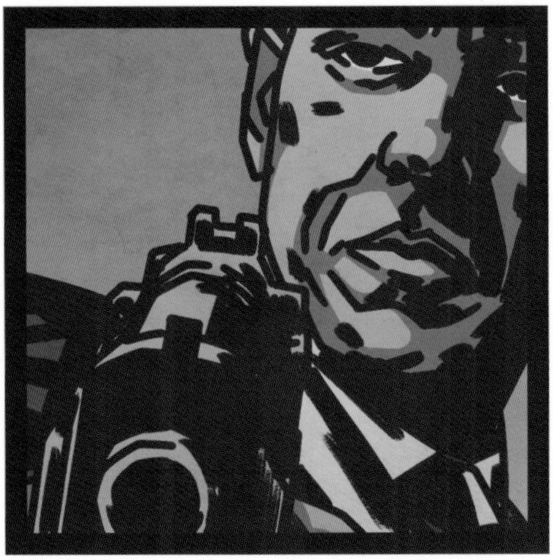

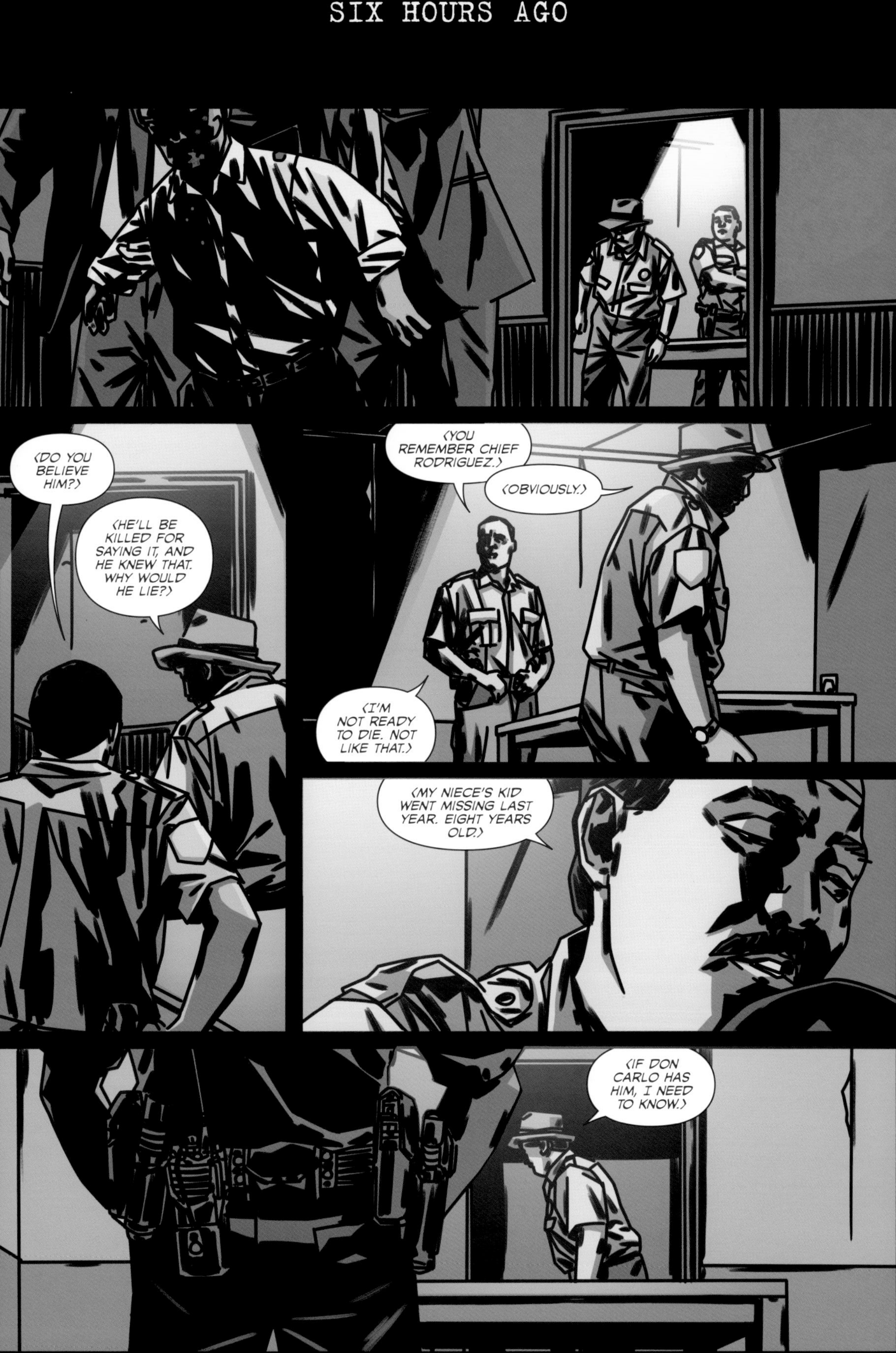
SIX HOURS AGO
‹DO YOU BELIEVE HIM?›
‹HE'LL BE KILLED FOR SAYING IT, AND HE KNEW THAT. WHY WOULD HE LIE?›
‹YOU REMEMBER CHIEF RODRIGUEZ.›
‹OBVIOUSLY.›
‹I'M NOT READY TO DIE. NOT LIKE THAT.›
‹MY NIECE'S KID WENT MISSING LAST YEAR. EIGHT YEARS OLD.›
‹IF DON CARLO HAS HIM, I NEED TO KNOW.›

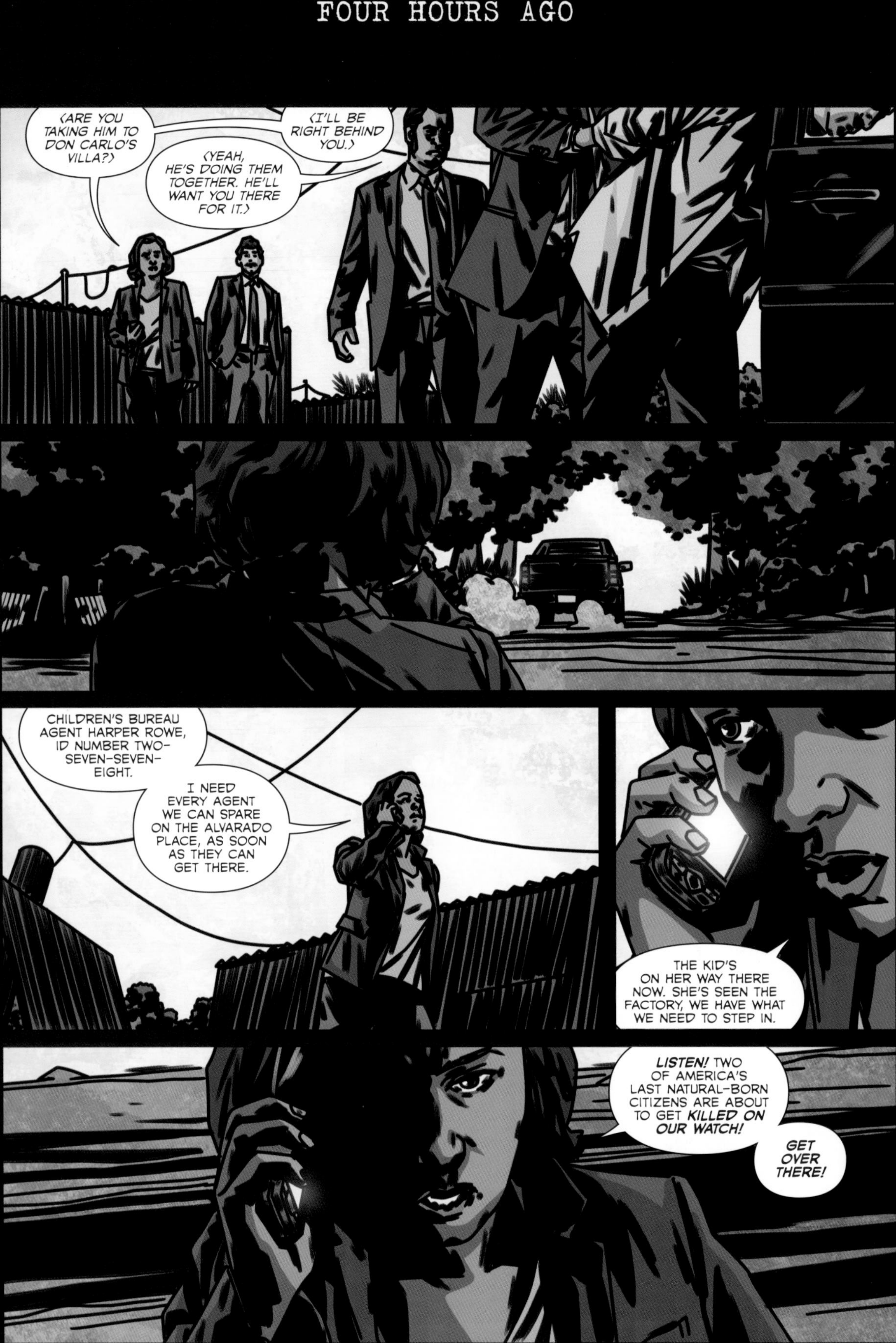
FOUR HOURS AGO
‹ARE YOU TAKING HIM TO DON CARLO'S VILLA?›
‹YEAH, HE'S DOING THEM TOGETHER. HE'LL WANT YOU THERE FOR IT.›
‹I'LL BE RIGHT BEHIND YOU.›
CHILDREN'S BUREAU AGENT HARPER ROWE, ID NUMBER TWO-SEVEN-SEVEN-EIGHT.
I NEED EVERY AGENT WE CAN SPARE ON THE ALVARADO PLACE, AS SOON AS THEY CAN GET THERE.
THE KID'S ON HER WAY THERE NOW. SHE'S SEEN THE FACTORY, WE HAVE WHAT WE NEED TO STEP IN.
LISTEN! TWO OF AMERICA'S LAST NATURAL-BORN CITIZENS ARE ABOUT TO GET KILLED ON OUR WATCH!
GET OVER THERE!

NINETY SECONDS AGO

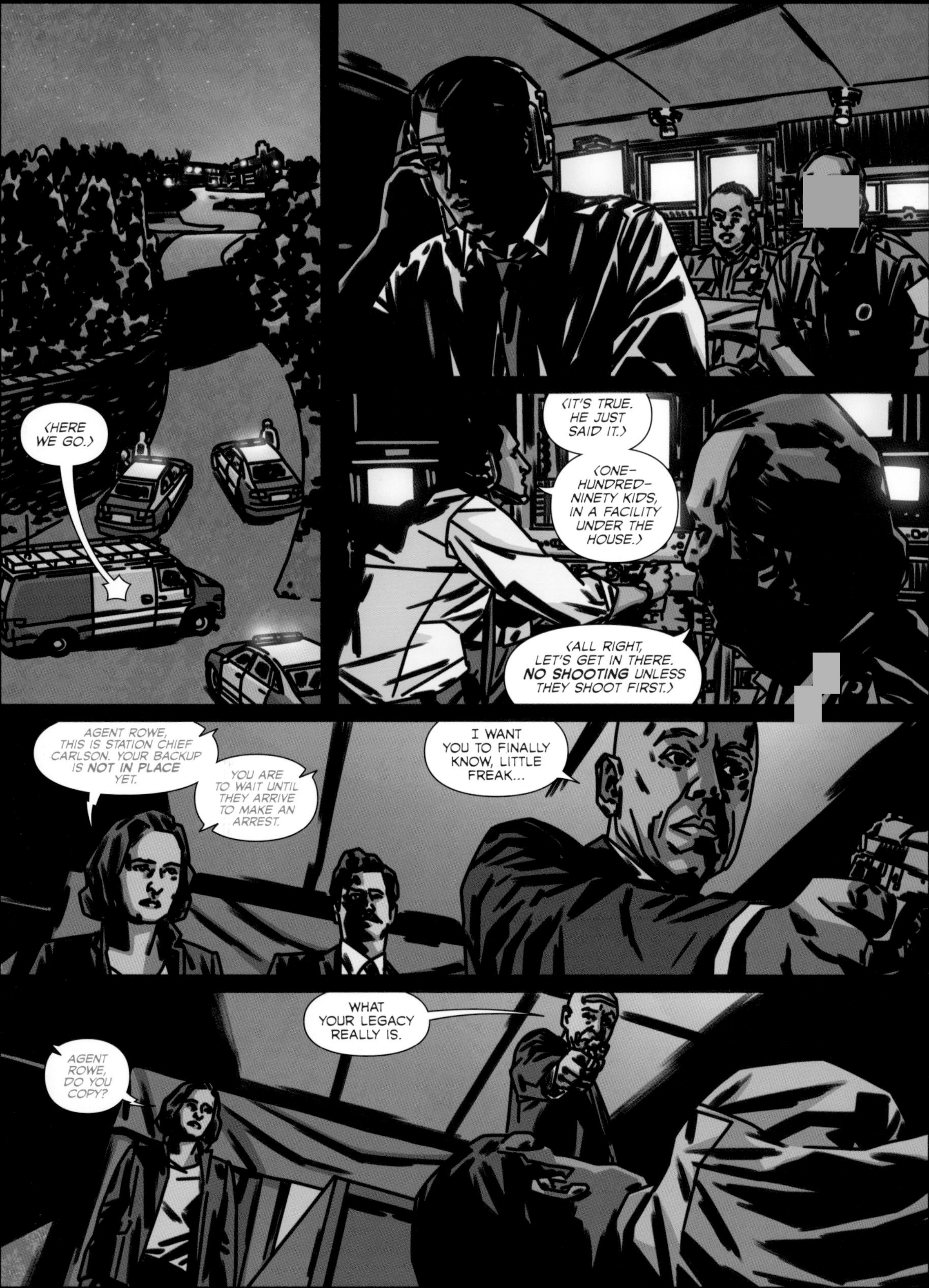
⟨HERE WE GO.⟩
⟨IT'S TRUE. HE JUST SAID IT.⟩
⟨ONE-HUNDRED-NINETY KIDS, IN A FACILITY UNDER THE HOUSE.⟩
⟨ALL RIGHT, LET'S GET IN THERE. NO SHOOTING UNLESS THEY SHOOT FIRST.⟩
AGENT ROWE, THIS IS STATION CHIEF CARLSON. YOUR BACKUP IS NOT IN PLACE YET.
YOU ARE TO WAIT UNTIL THEY ARRIVE TO MAKE AN ARREST.
I WANT YOU TO FINALLY KNOW, LITTLE FREAK...
WHAT YOUR LEGACY REALLY IS.
AGENT ROWE, DO YOU COPY?

NOW

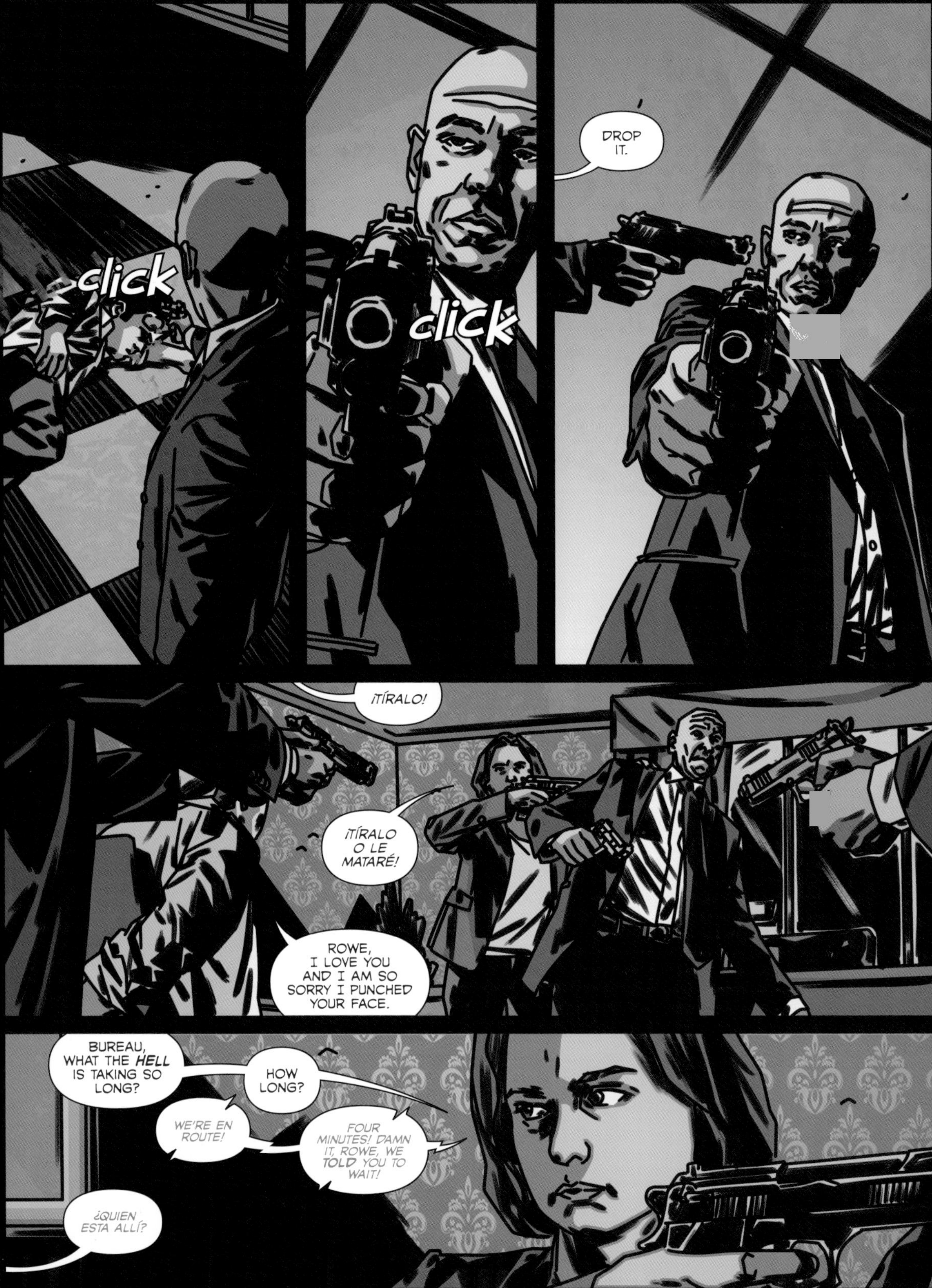
click
click
DROP IT.
¡TÍRALO!
¡TÍRALO O LE MATARÉ!
ROWE, I LOVE YOU AND I AM SO SORRY I PUNCHED YOUR FACE.
BUREAU, WHAT THE HELL IS TAKING SO LONG?
WE'RE EN ROUTE!
HOW LONG?
FOUR MINUTES! DAMN IT, ROWE, WE TOLD YOU TO WAIT!
¿QUIEN ESTA ALLÍ?

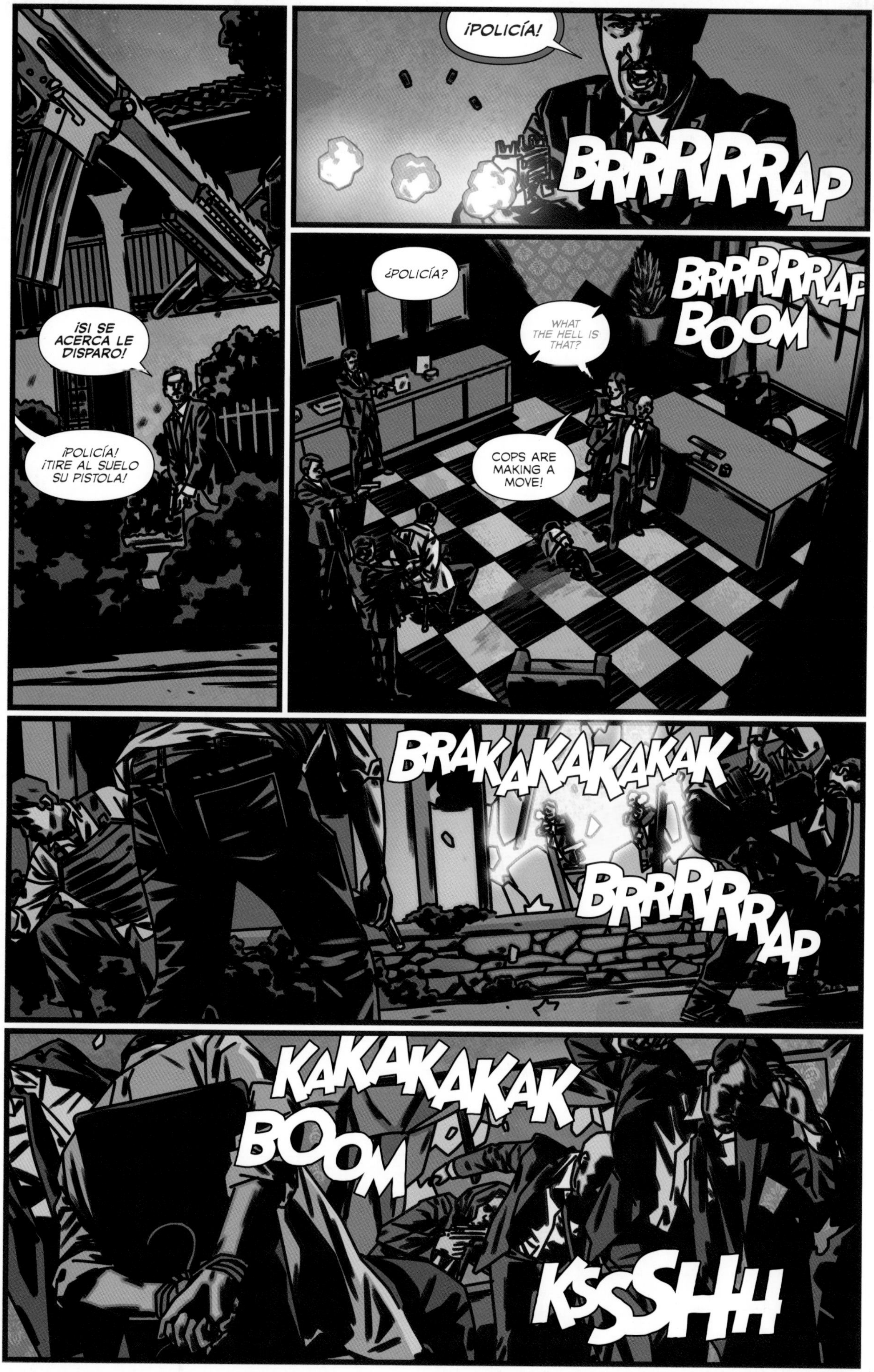
¡SI SE ACERCA LE DISPARO!
¡POLICÍA! ¡TIRE AL SUELO SU PISTOLA!
¡POLICÍA!
BRRRRRRAP
¿POLICÍA?
BRRRRRRAP
BOOM
WHAT THE HELL IS THAT?
COPS ARE MAKING A MOVE!
BRAKAKAKAKAKAK
BRRRRRRAP
KAKAKAKAKAK
BOOM
KSSSHHH

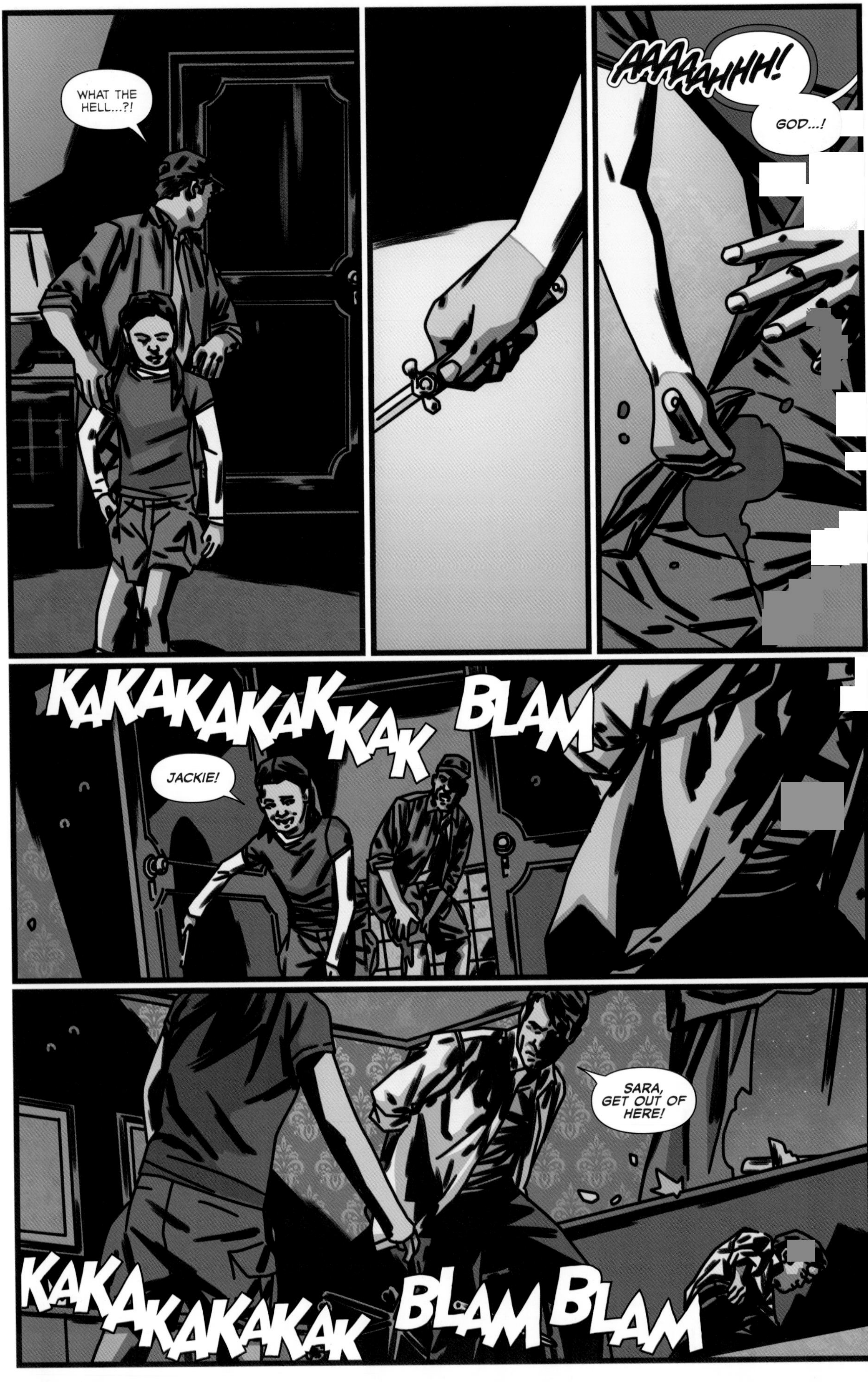
WHAT THE HELL...?!
AAAAAHHH!
GOD...!
KAKAKAKAKAKKAK
BLAM
JACKIE!
SARA, GET OUT OF HERE!
KAKAKAKAKAKAK
BLAM
BLAM

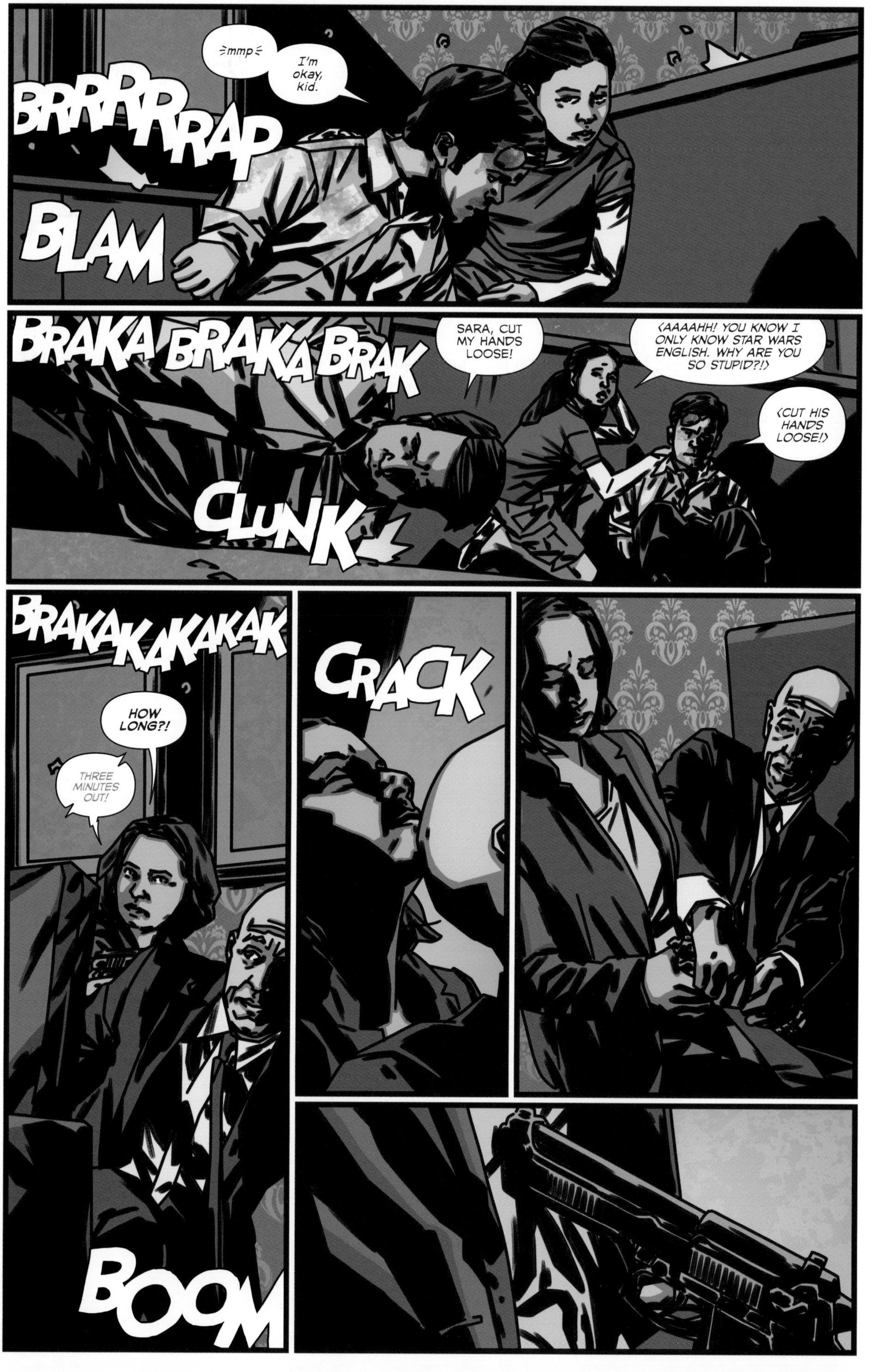

BRRRRRAP
BLAM
=mmp=
I'm okay, kid.
BRAKA BRAKA BRAK
SARA, CUT MY HANDS LOOSE!
‹AAAAHH! YOU KNOW I ONLY KNOW STAR WARS ENGLISH. WHY ARE YOU SO STUPID?!›
‹CUT HIS HANDS LOOSE!›
CLUNK
BRAKAKAKAKAKAK
HOW LONG?!
THREE MINUTES OUT!
CRACK
BOOM

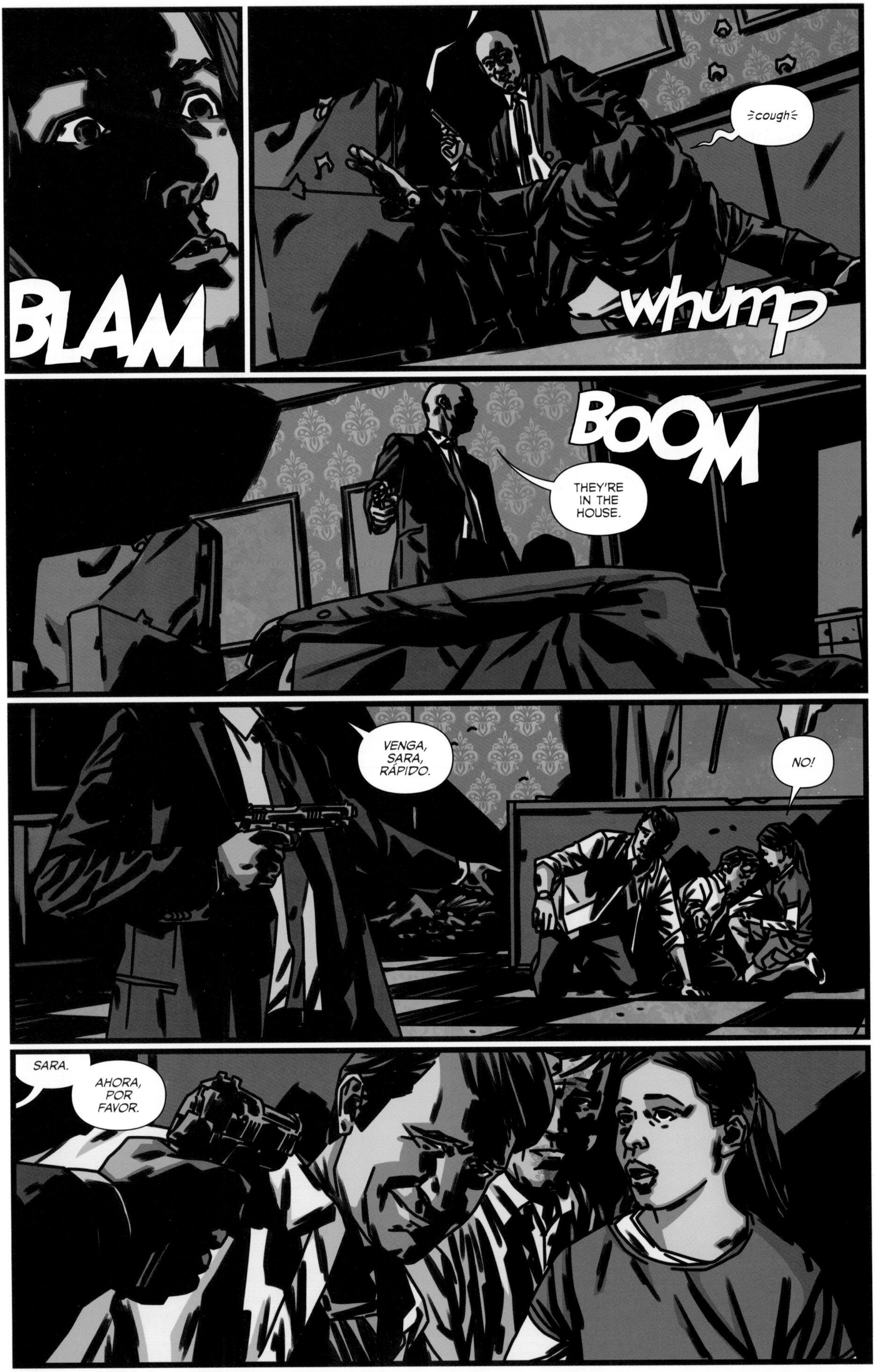
BLAM
cough
whump
BOOM
THEY'RE IN THE HOUSE.
VENGA, SARA, RÁPIDO.
NO!
SARA.
AHORA, POR FAVOR.

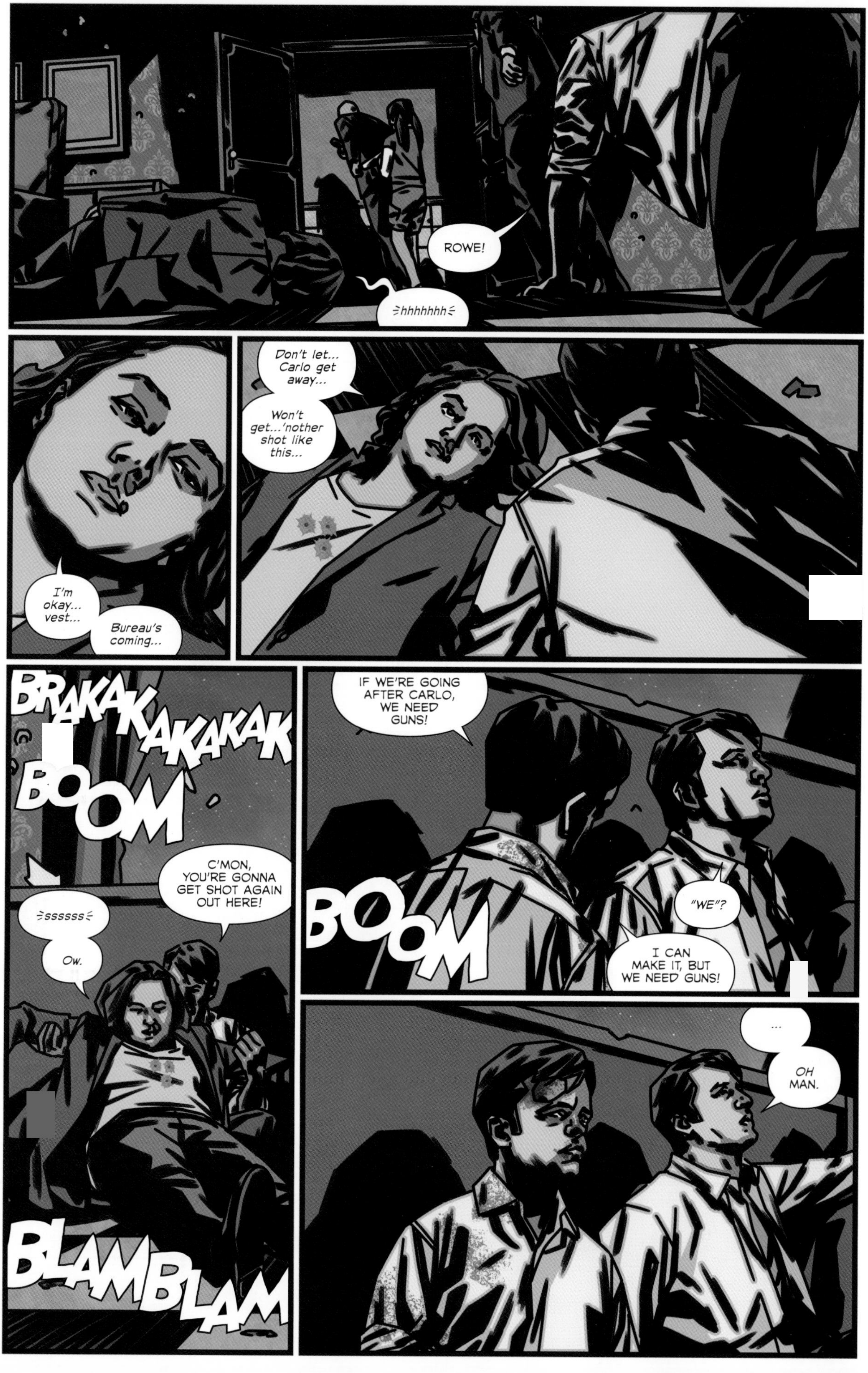
ROWE!
hhhhhhh
I'm okay... vest...
Bureau's coming...
Don't let... Carlo get away...
Won't get...'nother shot like this...
BRAKAKAKAKAK
BOOM
C'MON, YOU'RE GONNA GET SHOT AGAIN OUT HERE!
ssssss
Ow.
BLAMBLAM
IF WE'RE GOING AFTER CARLO, WE NEED GUNS!
BOOM
"WE"?
I CAN MAKE IT, BUT WE NEED GUNS!
...
OH MAN.

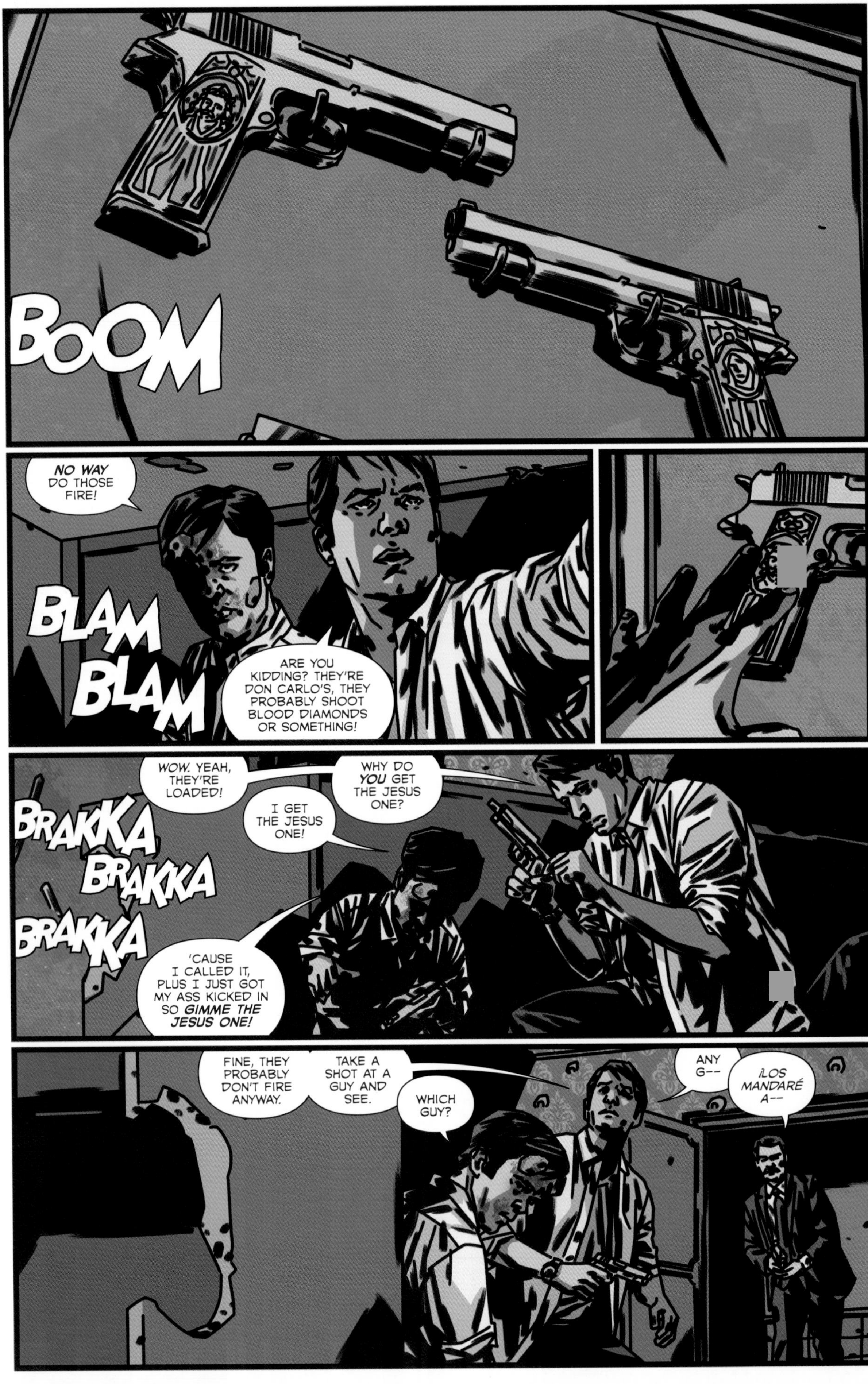
BOOM
NO WAY DO THOSE FIRE!
BLAM BLAM
ARE YOU KIDDING? THEY'RE DON CARLO'S, THEY PROBABLY SHOOT BLOOD DIAMONDS OR SOMETHING!
BRAKKA BRAKKA BRAKKA
WOW. YEAH, THEY'RE LOADED!
I GET THE JESUS ONE!
WHY DO YOU GET THE JESUS ONE?
'CAUSE I CALLED IT, PLUS I JUST GOT MY ASS KICKED IN SO GIMME THE JESUS ONE!
FINE, THEY PROBABLY DON'T FIRE ANYWAY.
TAKE A SHOT AT A GUY AND SEE.
WHICH GUY?
ANY G--
¡LOS MANDARÉ A--

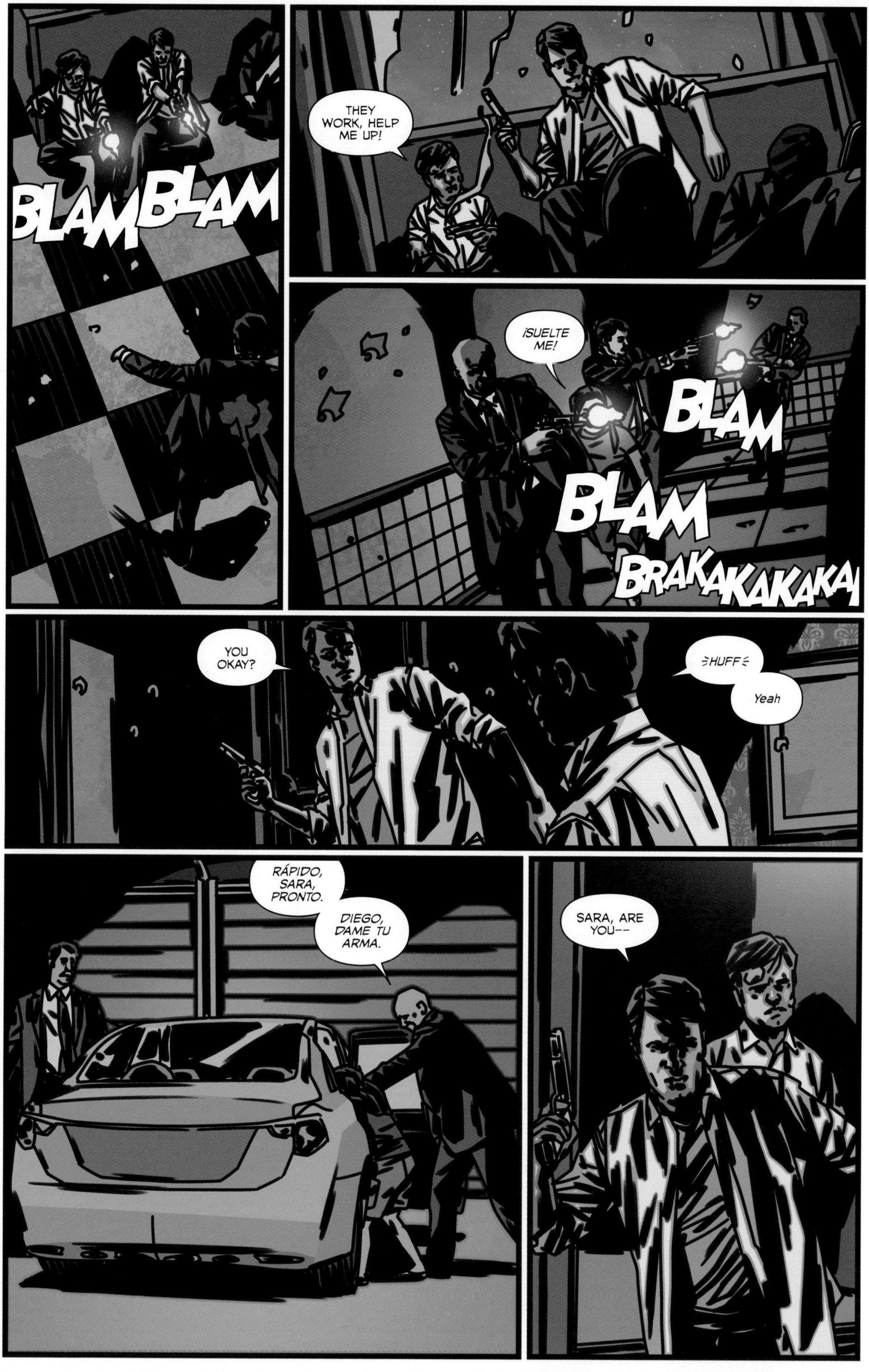
BLAM BLAM
THEY WORK, HELP ME UP!
¡SUELTE ME!
BLAM
BLAM
BRAKAKAKAKAKA
YOU OKAY?
HUFF
Yeah
RÁPIDO, SARA, PRONTO.
DIEGO, DAME TU ARMA.
SARA, ARE YOU--

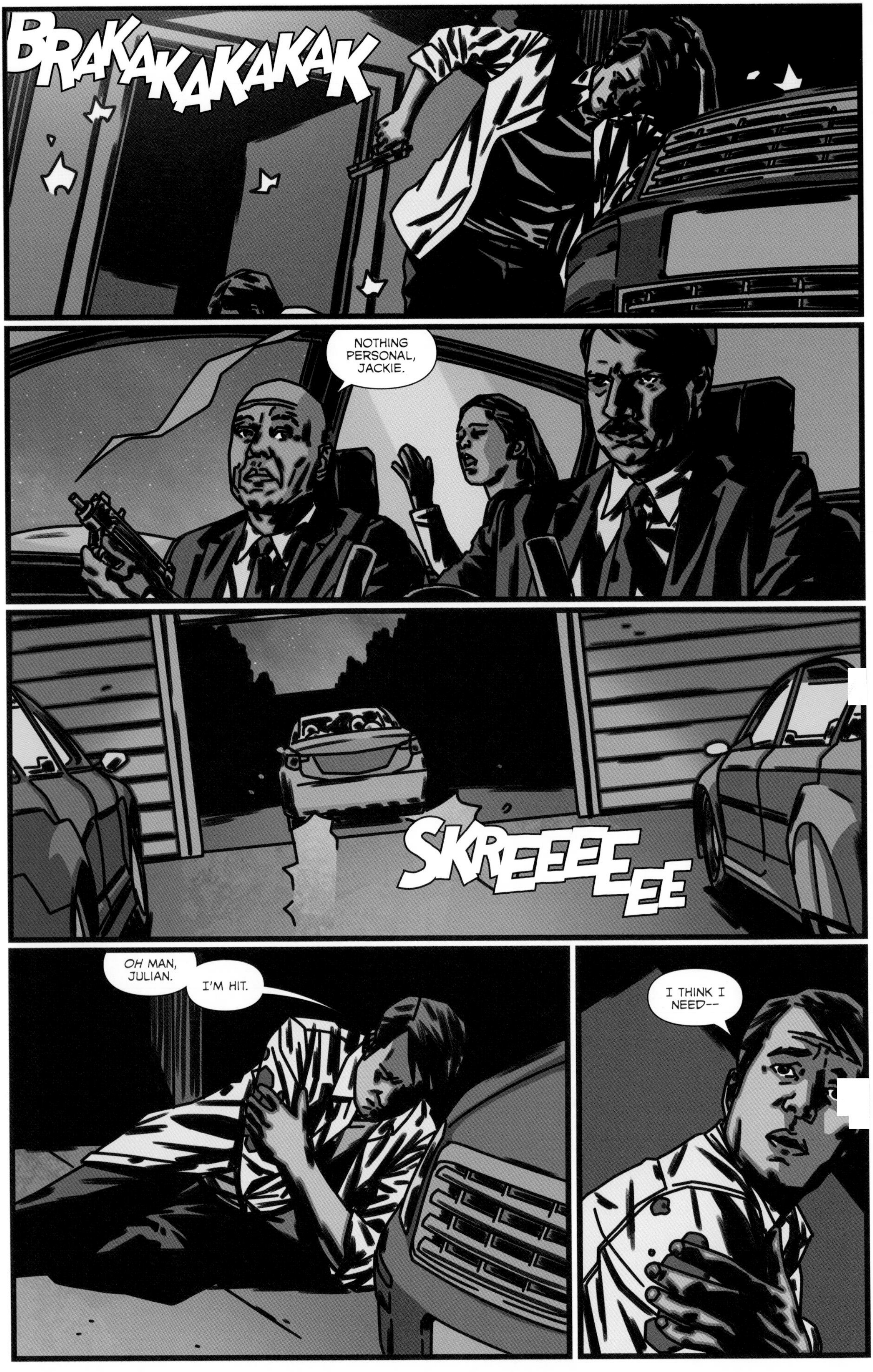
BRAKAKAKAKAKAK
NOTHING PERSONAL, JACKIE.
SKREEEEEEE
OH MAN, JULIAN.
I'M HIT.
I THINK I NEED--

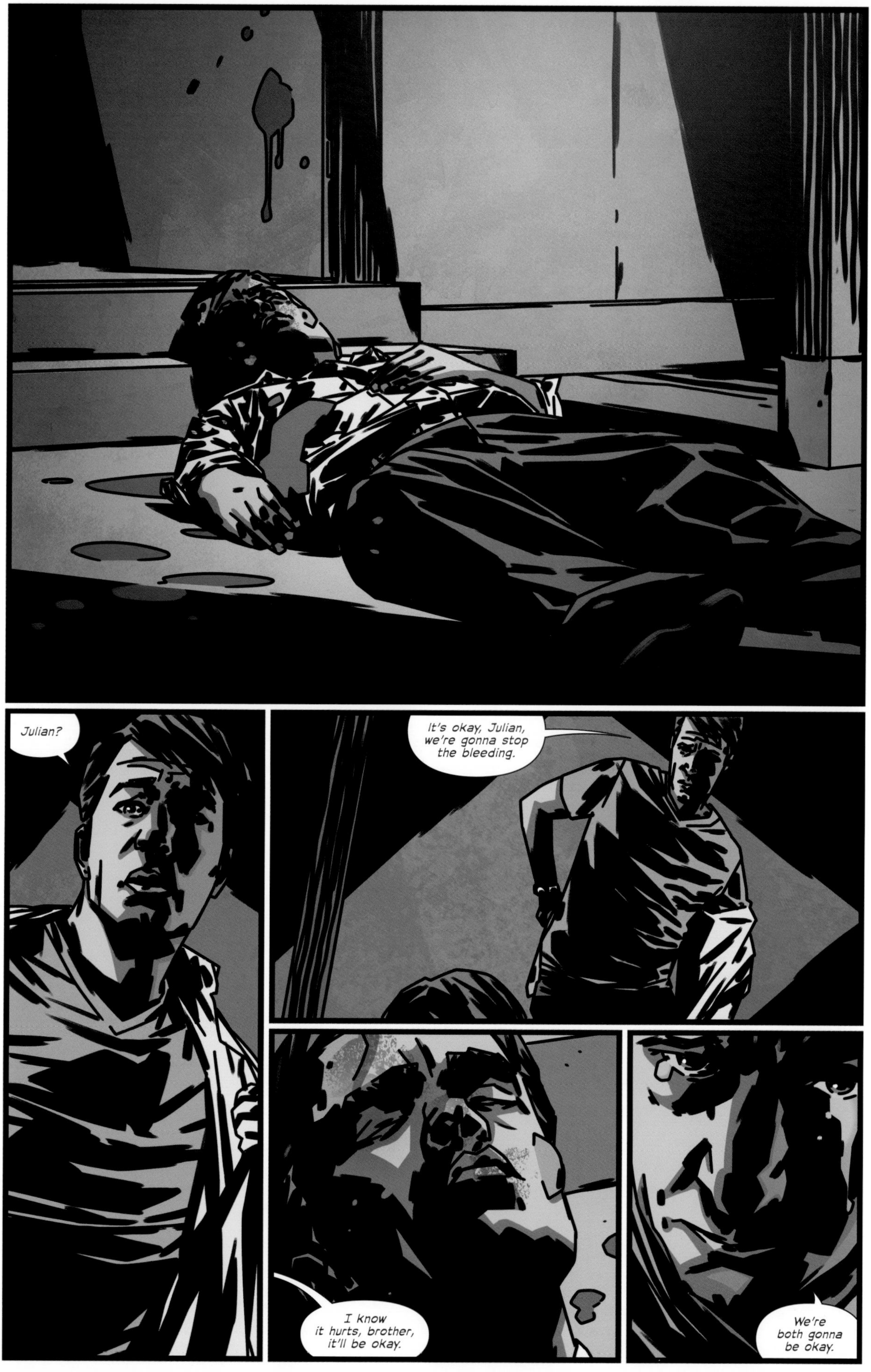
Julian?
It's okay, Julian, we're gonna stop the bleeding.
I know it hurts, brother, it'll be okay.
We're both gonna be okay.

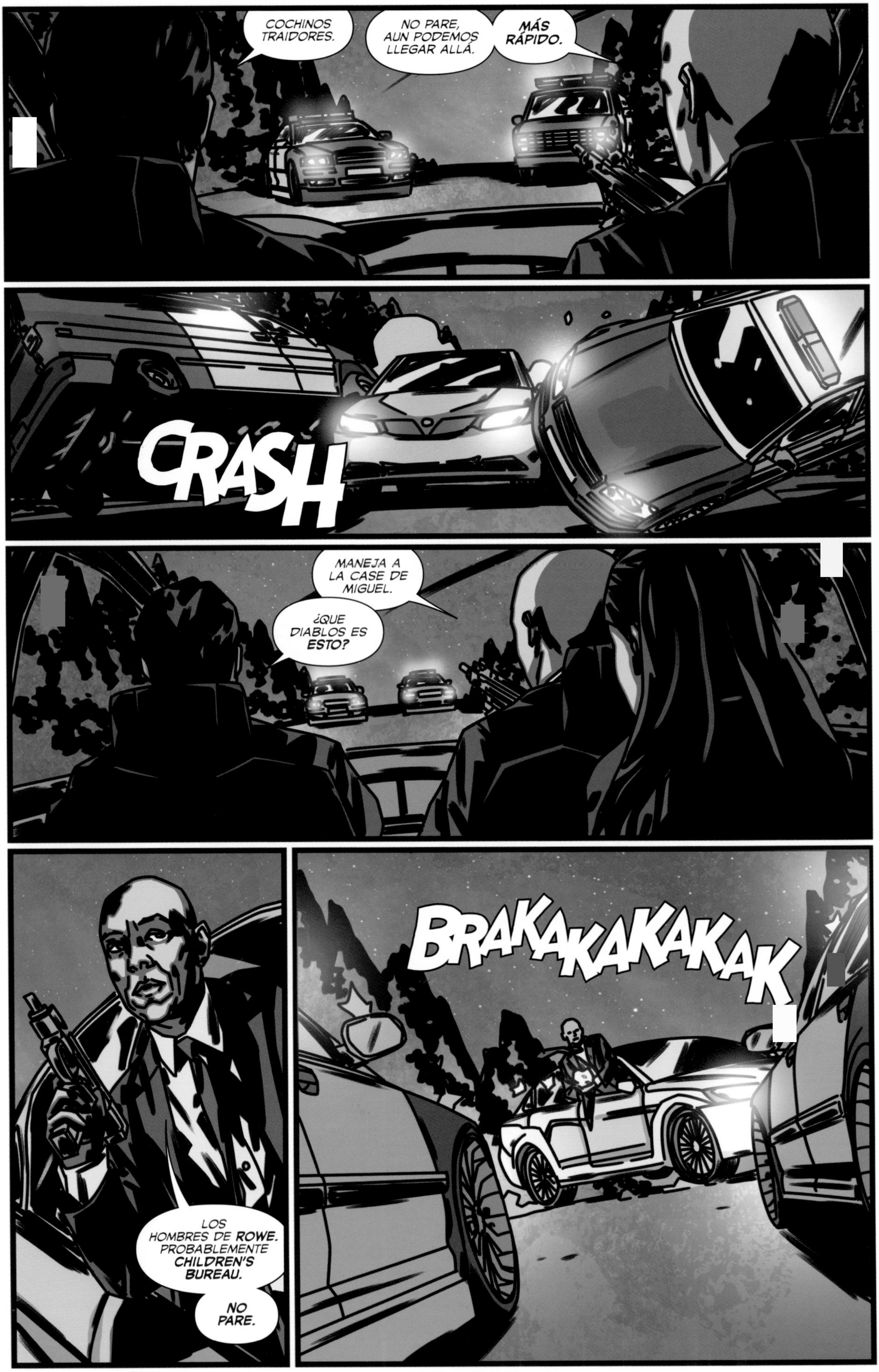
COCHINOS TRAIDORES.
NO PARE, AUN PODEMOS LLEGAR ALLÁ.
MÁS RÁPIDO.
CRASH
MANEJA A LA CASE DE MIGUEL.
¿QUE DIABLOS ES ESTO?
LOS HOMBRES DE ROWE. PROBABLEMENTE CHILDREN'S BUREAU.
NO PARE.
BRAKAKAKAKAKAK

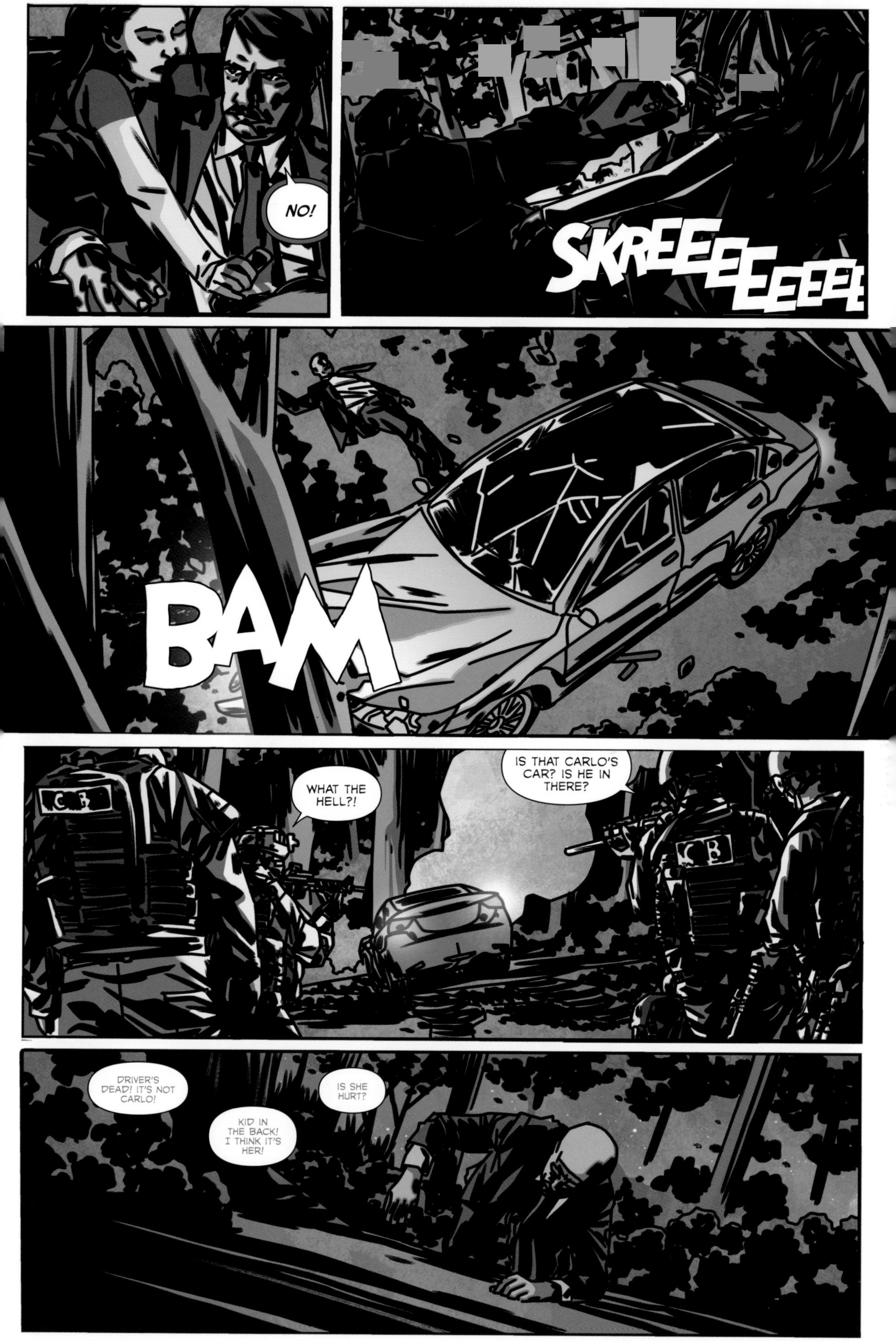
NO!
SKREEEEEEEEEE
BAM
WHAT THE HELL?!
IS THAT CARLO'S CAR? IS HE IN THERE?
DRIVER'S DEAD! IT'S NOT CARLO!
KID IN THE BACK! I THINK IT'S HER!
IS SHE HURT?

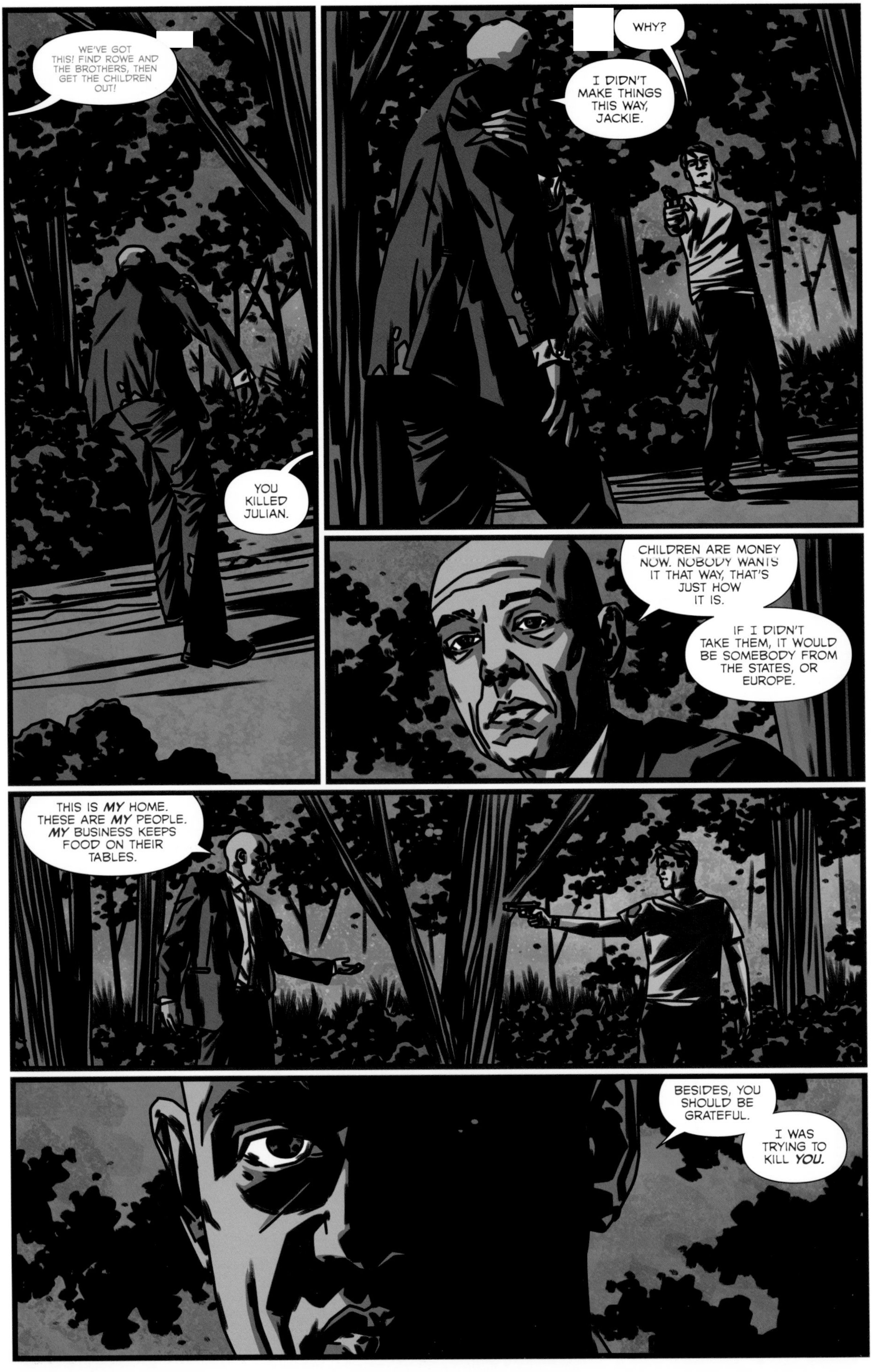
WE'VE GOT THIS! FIND ROWE AND THE BROTHERS, THEN GET THE CHILDREN OUT!
YOU KILLED JULIAN.
WHY?
I DIDN'T MAKE THINGS THIS WAY, JACKIE.
CHILDREN ARE MONEY NOW. NOBODY WANTS IT THAT WAY, THAT'S JUST HOW IT IS.
IF I DIDN'T TAKE THEM, IT WOULD BE SOMEBODY FROM THE STATES, OR EUROPE.
THIS IS *MY* HOME. THESE ARE *MY* PEOPLE. *MY* BUSINESS KEEPS FOOD ON THEIR TABLES.
BESIDES, YOU SHOULD BE GRATEFUL.
I WAS TRYING TO KILL *YOU.*

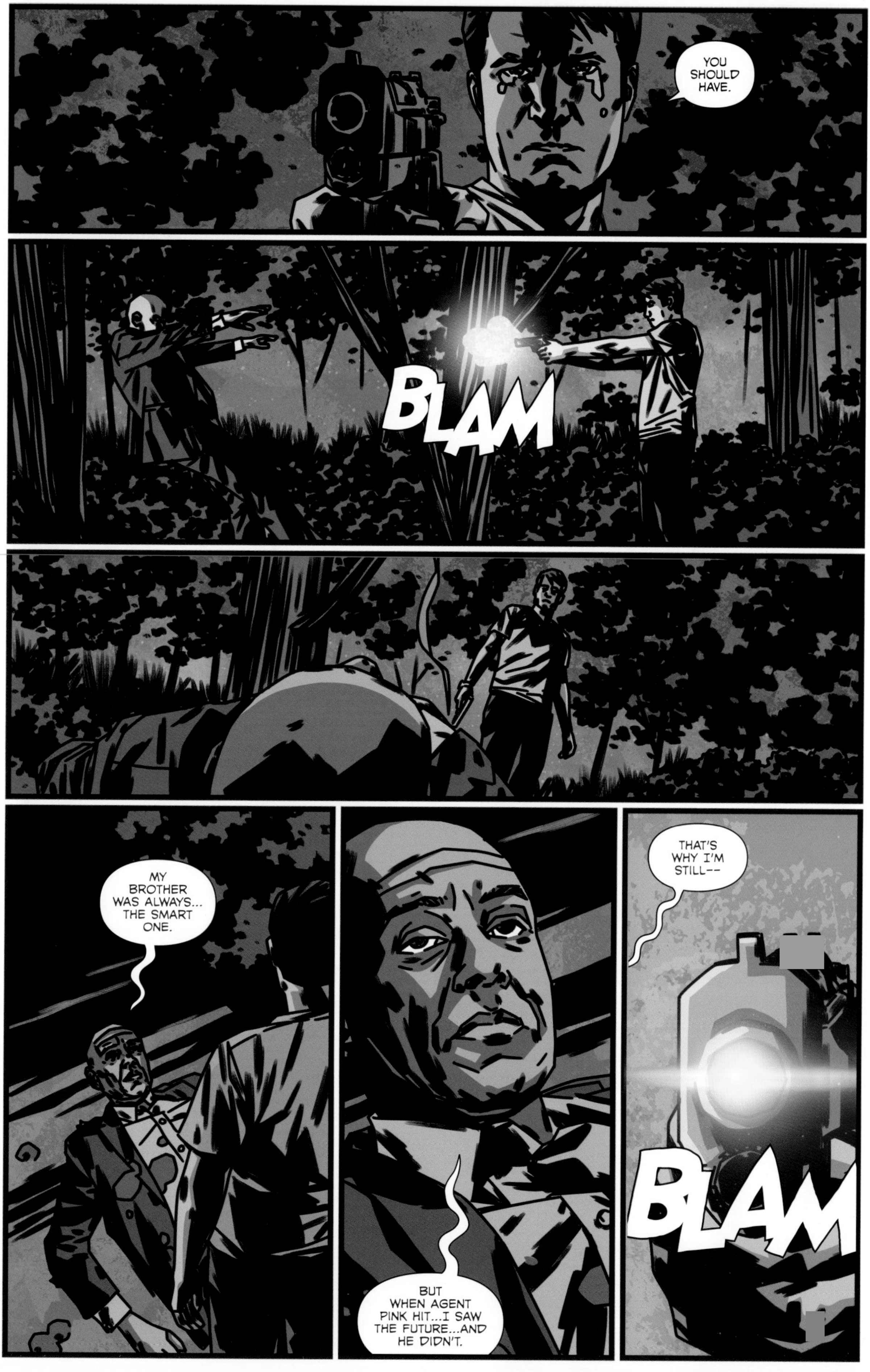
YOU SHOULD HAVE.
BLAM
MY BROTHER WAS ALWAYS... THE SMART ONE.
BUT WHEN AGENT PINK HIT...I SAW THE FUTURE...AND HE DIDN'T.
THAT'S WHY I'M STILL--
BLAM

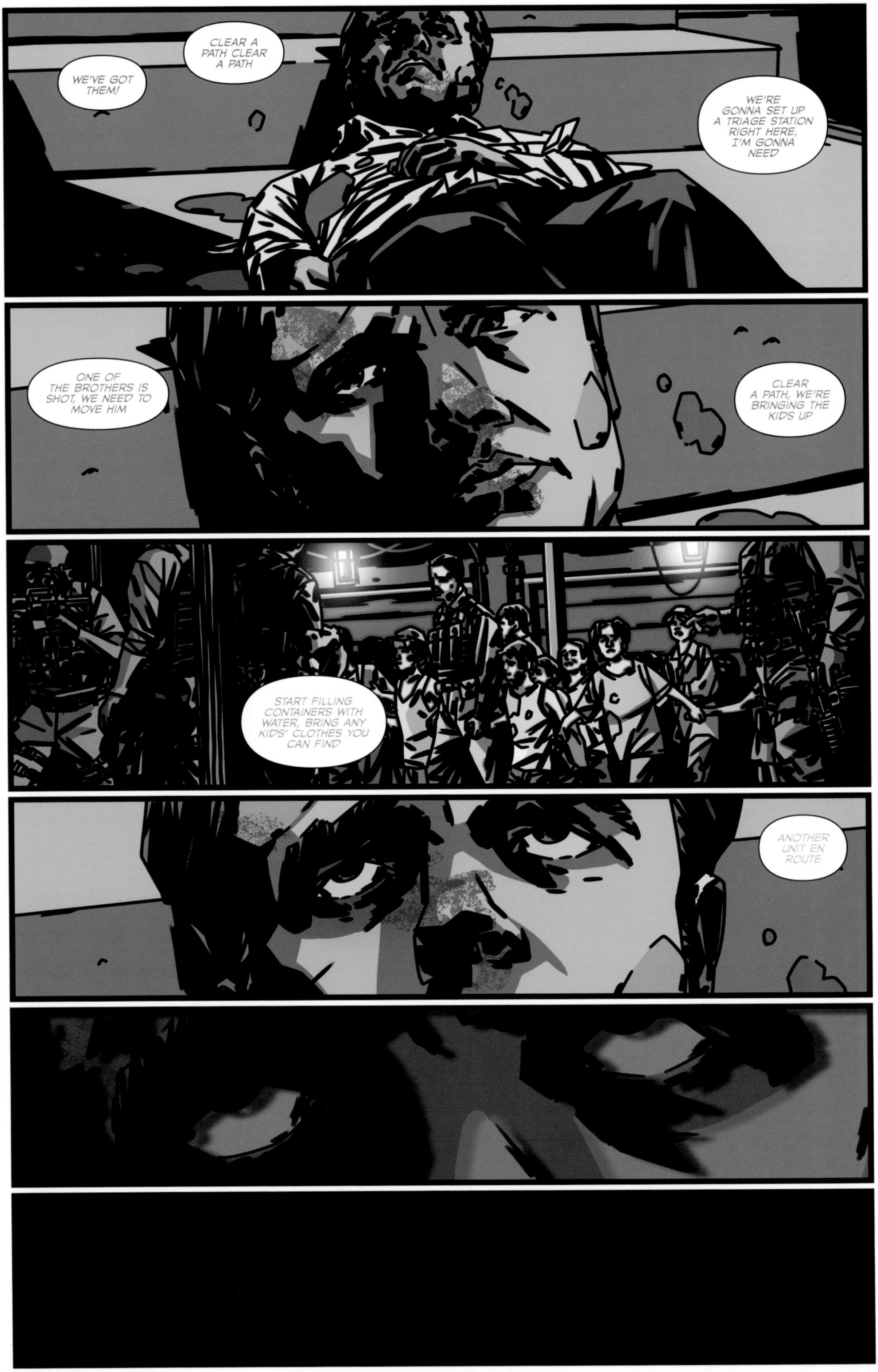

WE'VE GOT THEM!
CLEAR A PATH CLEAR A PATH
WE'RE GONNA SET UP A TRIAGE STATION RIGHT HERE, I'M GONNA NEED
ONE OF THE BROTHERS IS SHOT, WE NEED TO MOVE HIM
CLEAR A PATH, WE'RE BRINGING THE KIDS UP
START FILLING CONTAINERS WITH WATER, BRING ANY KIDS' CLOTHES YOU CAN FIND
ANOTHER UNIT EN ROUTE

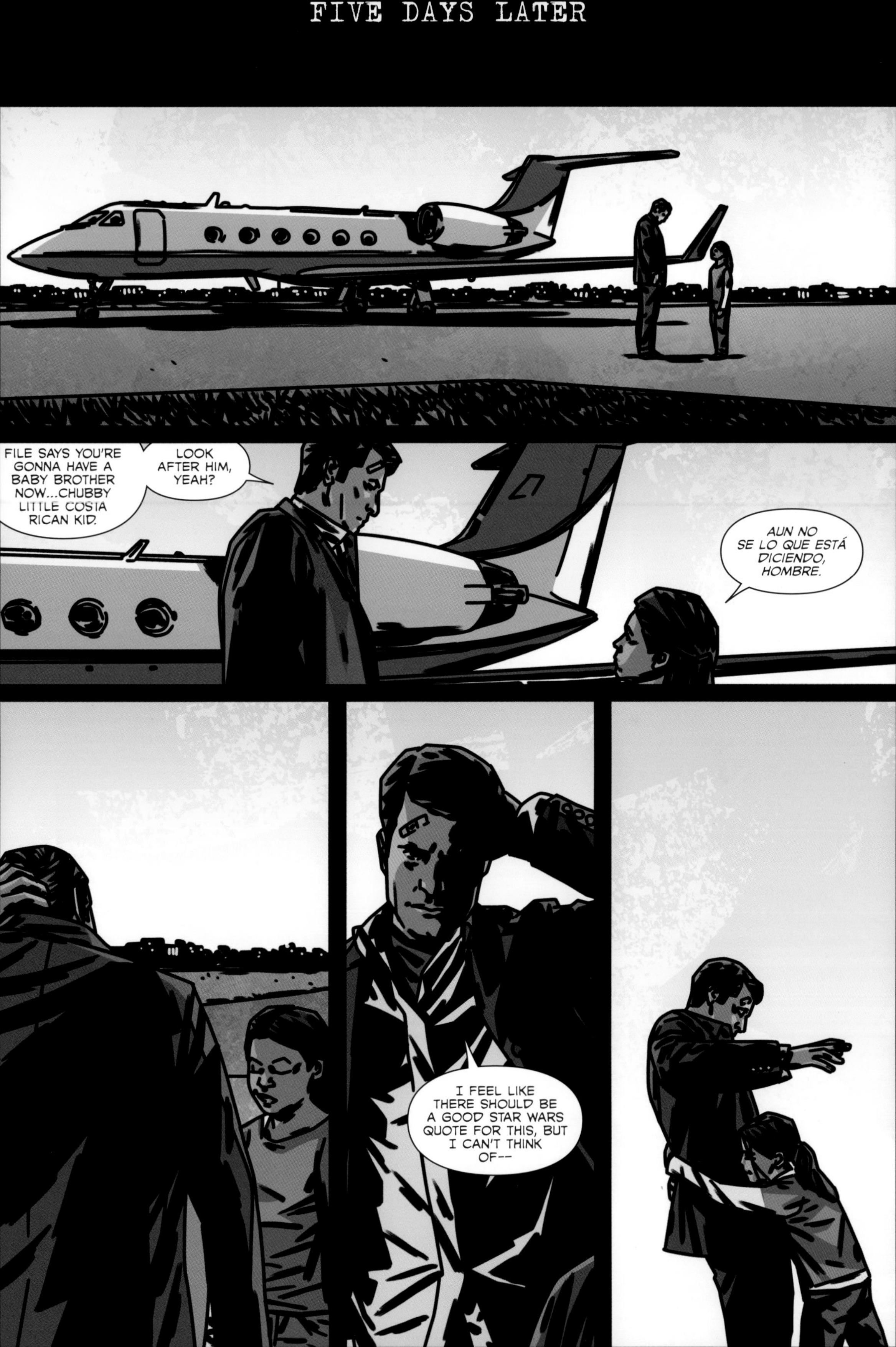
FIVE DAYS LATER
FILE SAYS YOU'RE GONNA HAVE A BABY BROTHER NOW...CHUBBY LITTLE COSTA RICAN KID.
LOOK AFTER HIM, YEAH?
AUN NO SE LO QUE ESTÁ DICIENDO, HOMBRE.
I FEEL LIKE THERE SHOULD BE A GOOD STAR WARS QUOTE FOR THIS, BUT I CAN'T THINK OF--

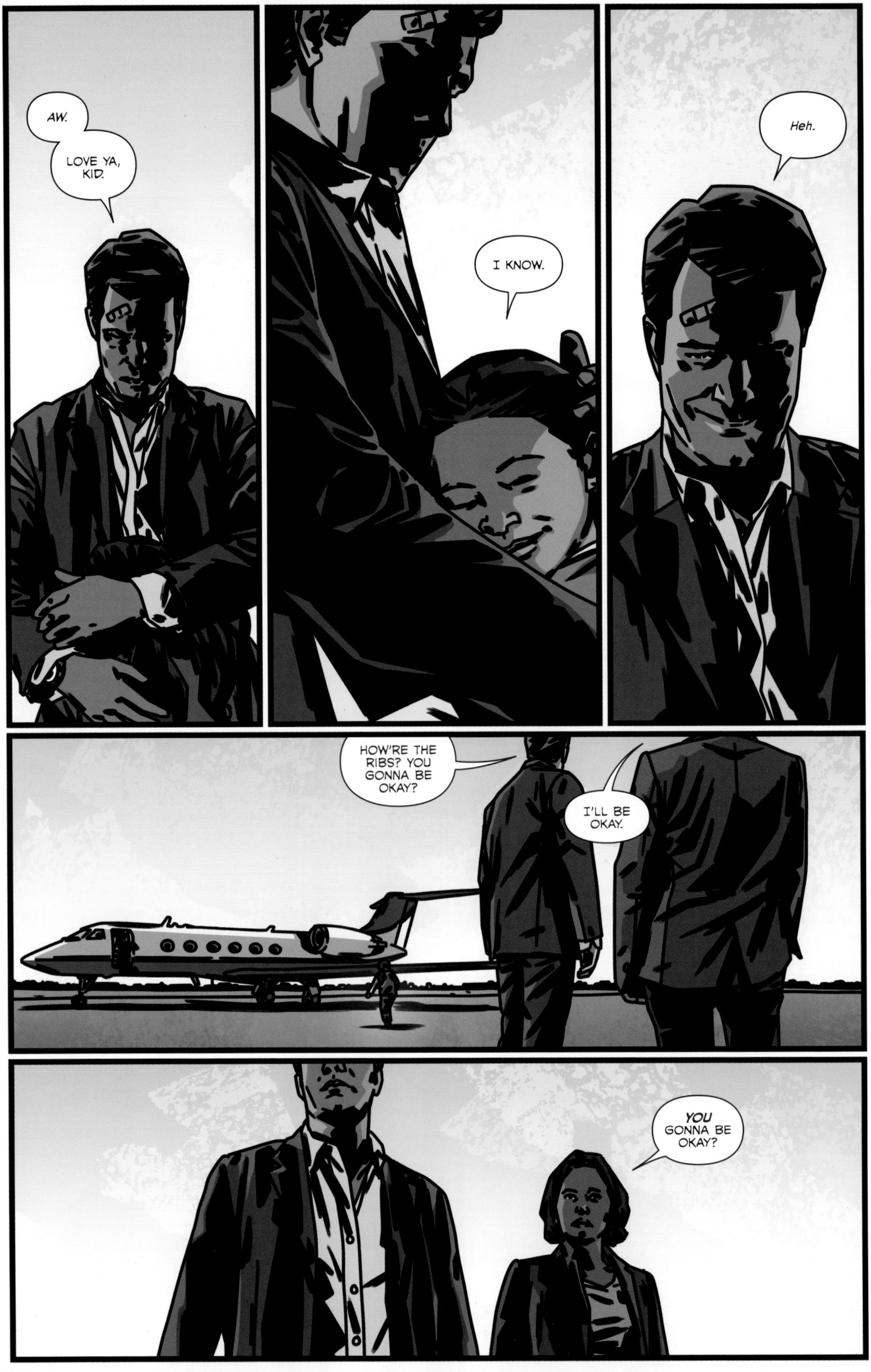
AW.
LOVE YA, KID.
I KNOW.
Heh.
HOW'RE THE RIBS? YOU GONNA BE OKAY?
I'LL BE OKAY.
YOU GONNA BE OKAY?

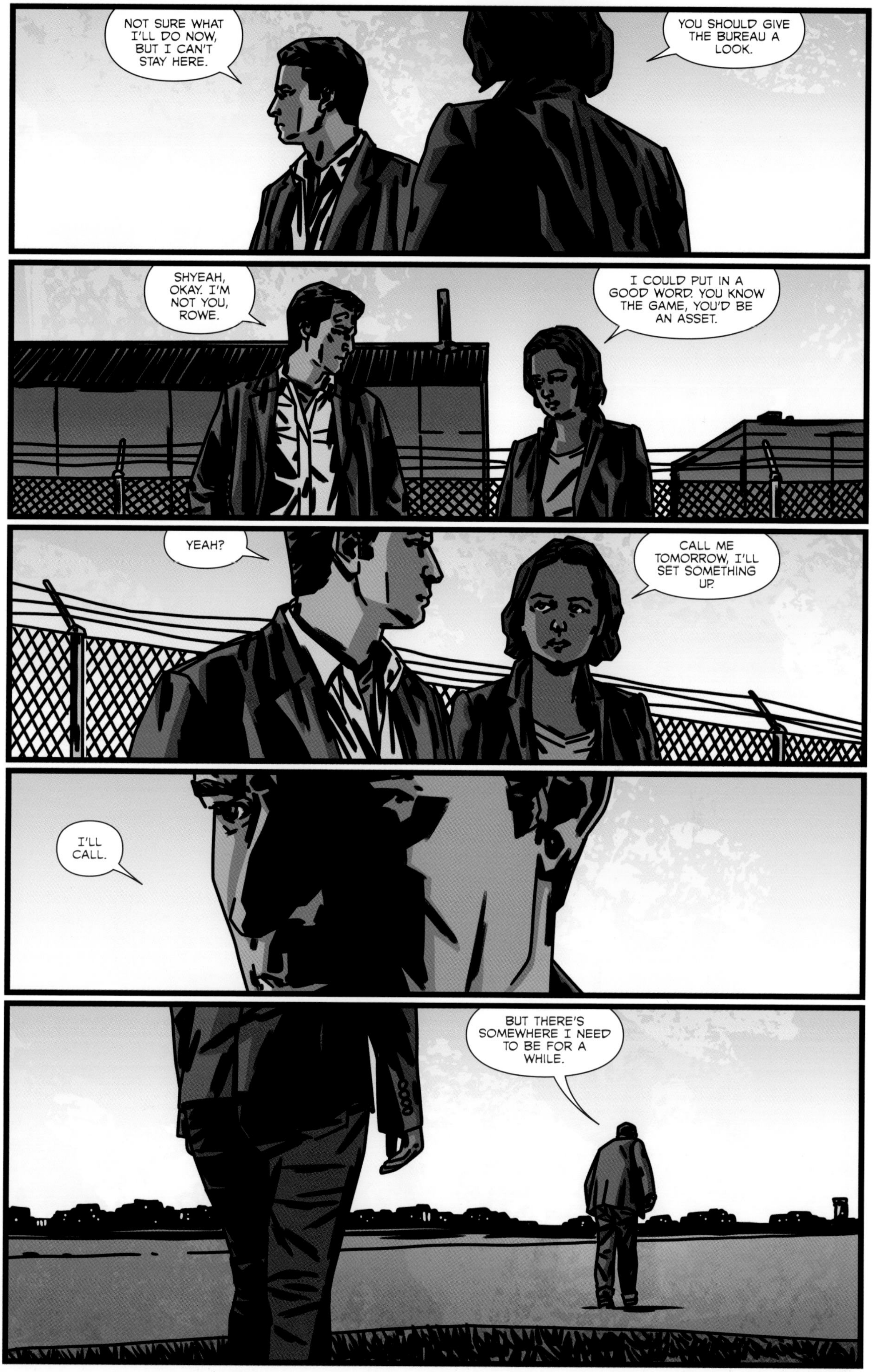
NOT SURE WHAT I'LL DO NOW, BUT I CAN'T STAY HERE.
YOU SHOULD GIVE THE BUREAU A LOOK.
SHYEAH, OKAY. I'M NOT YOU, ROWE.
I COULD PUT IN A GOOD WORD. YOU KNOW THE GAME, YOU'D BE AN ASSET.
YEAH?
CALL ME TOMORROW, I'LL SET SOMETHING UP.
I'LL CALL.
BUT THERE'S SOMEWHERE I NEED TO BE FOR A WHILE.

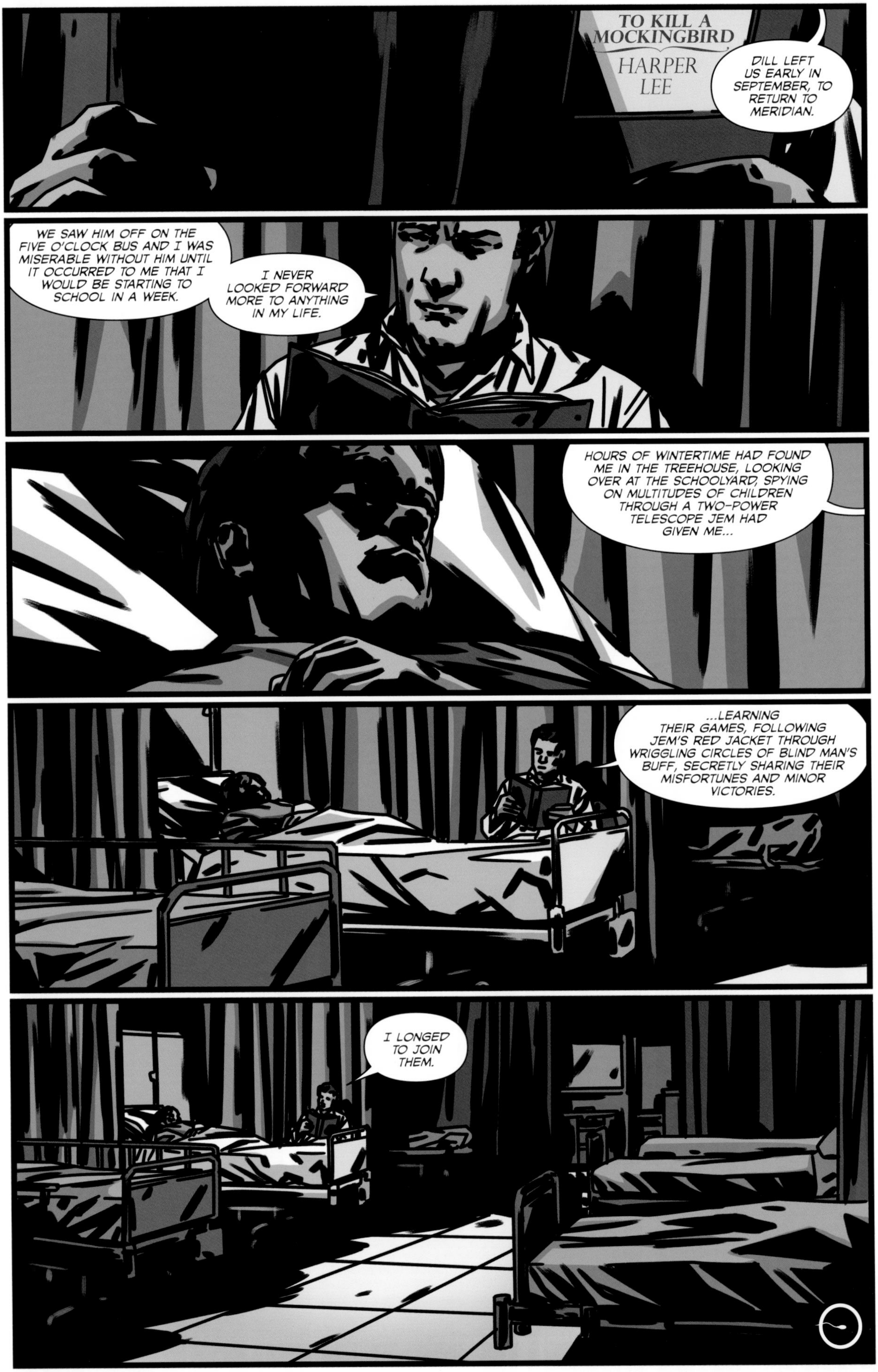
TO KILL A MOCKINGBIRD
HARPER LEE
DILL LEFT US EARLY IN SEPTEMBER, TO RETURN TO MERIDIAN.
WE SAW HIM OFF ON THE FIVE O'CLOCK BUS AND I WAS MISERABLE WITHOUT HIM UNTIL IT OCCURRED TO ME THAT I WOULD BE STARTING TO SCHOOL IN A WEEK.
I NEVER LOOKED FORWARD MORE TO ANYTHING IN MY LIFE.
HOURS OF WINTERTIME HAD FOUND ME IN THE TREEHOUSE, LOOKING OVER AT THE SCHOOLYARD, SPYING ON MULTITUDES OF CHILDREN THROUGH A TWO-POWER TELESCOPE JEM HAD GIVEN ME...
...LEARNING THEIR GAMES, FOLLOWING JEM'S RED JACKET THROUGH WRIGGLING CIRCLES OF BLIND MAN'S BUFF, SECRETLY SHARING THEIR MISFORTUNES AND MINOR VICTORIES.
I LONGED TO JOIN THEM.

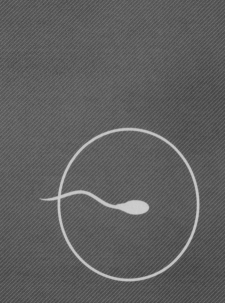

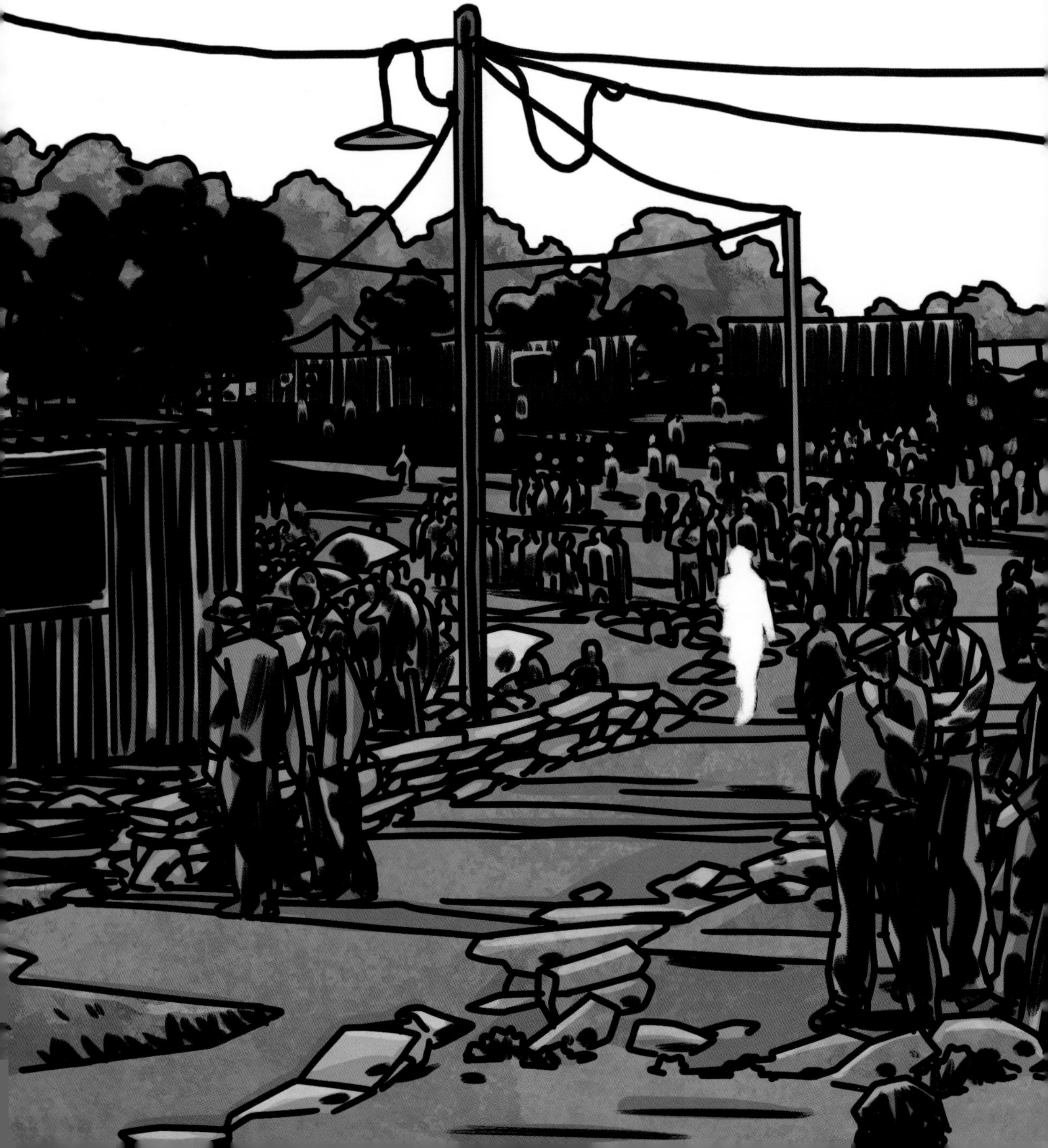

COVER GALLERY

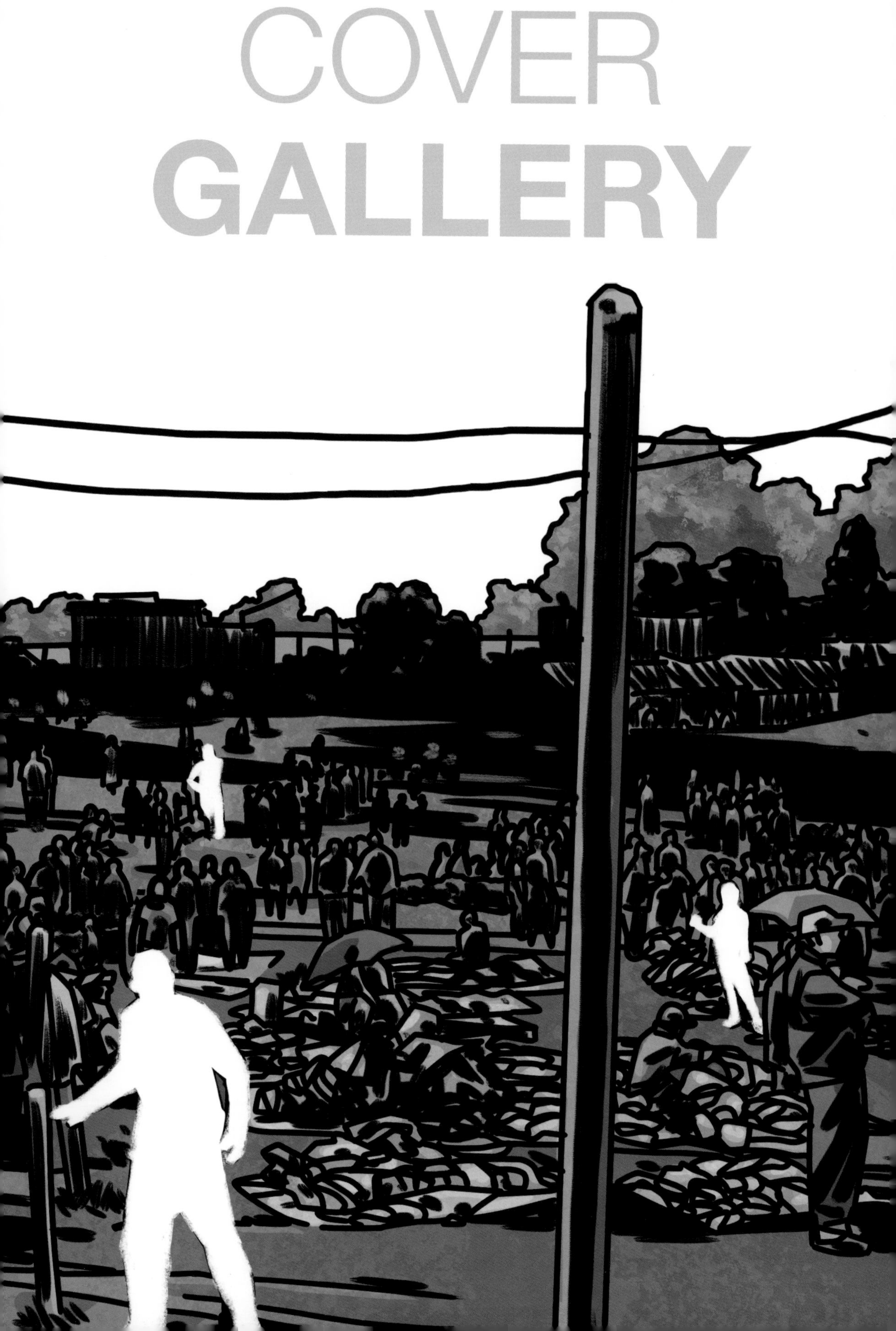

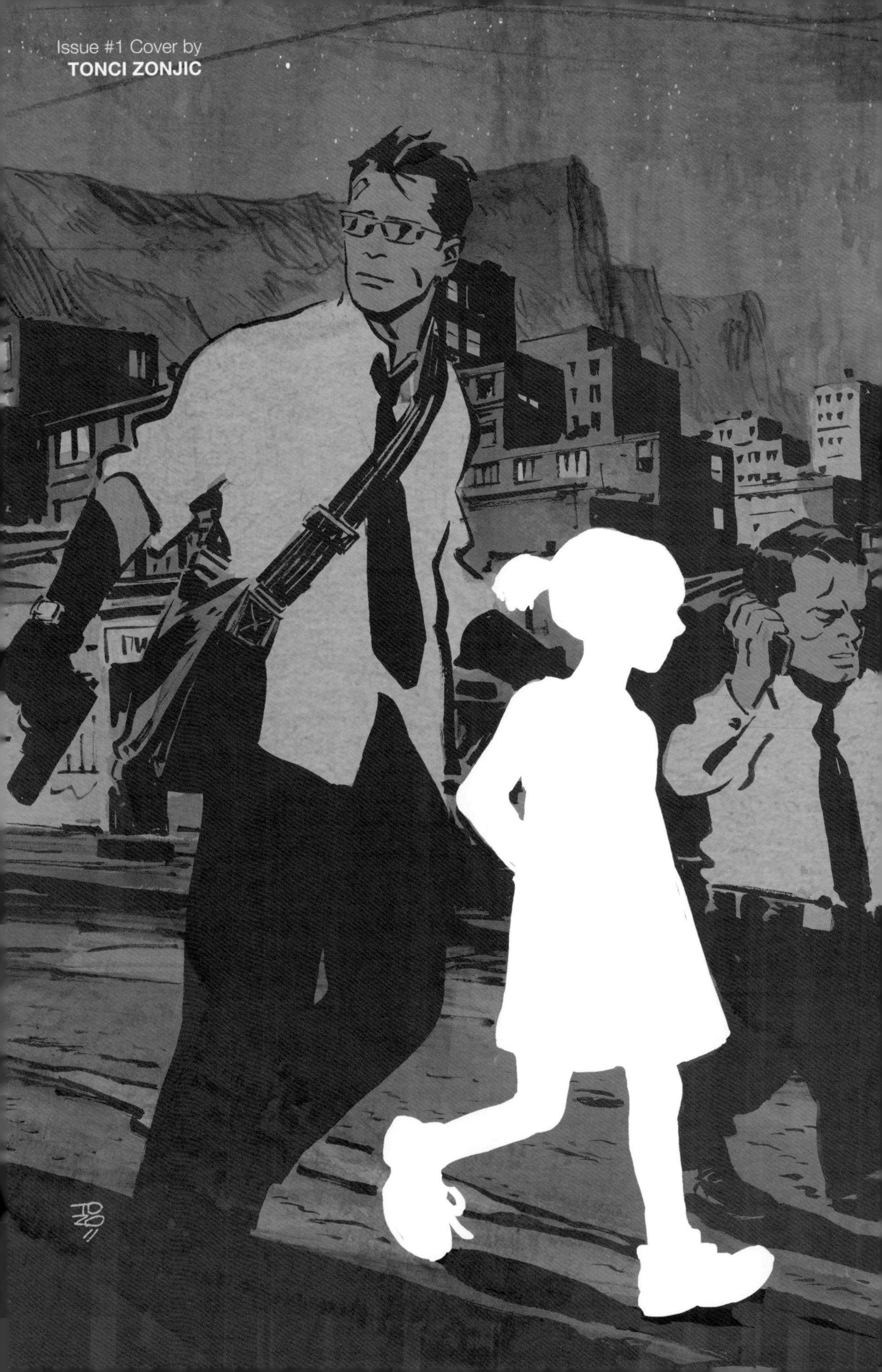

Issue #1 Cover by
TONCI ZONJIC

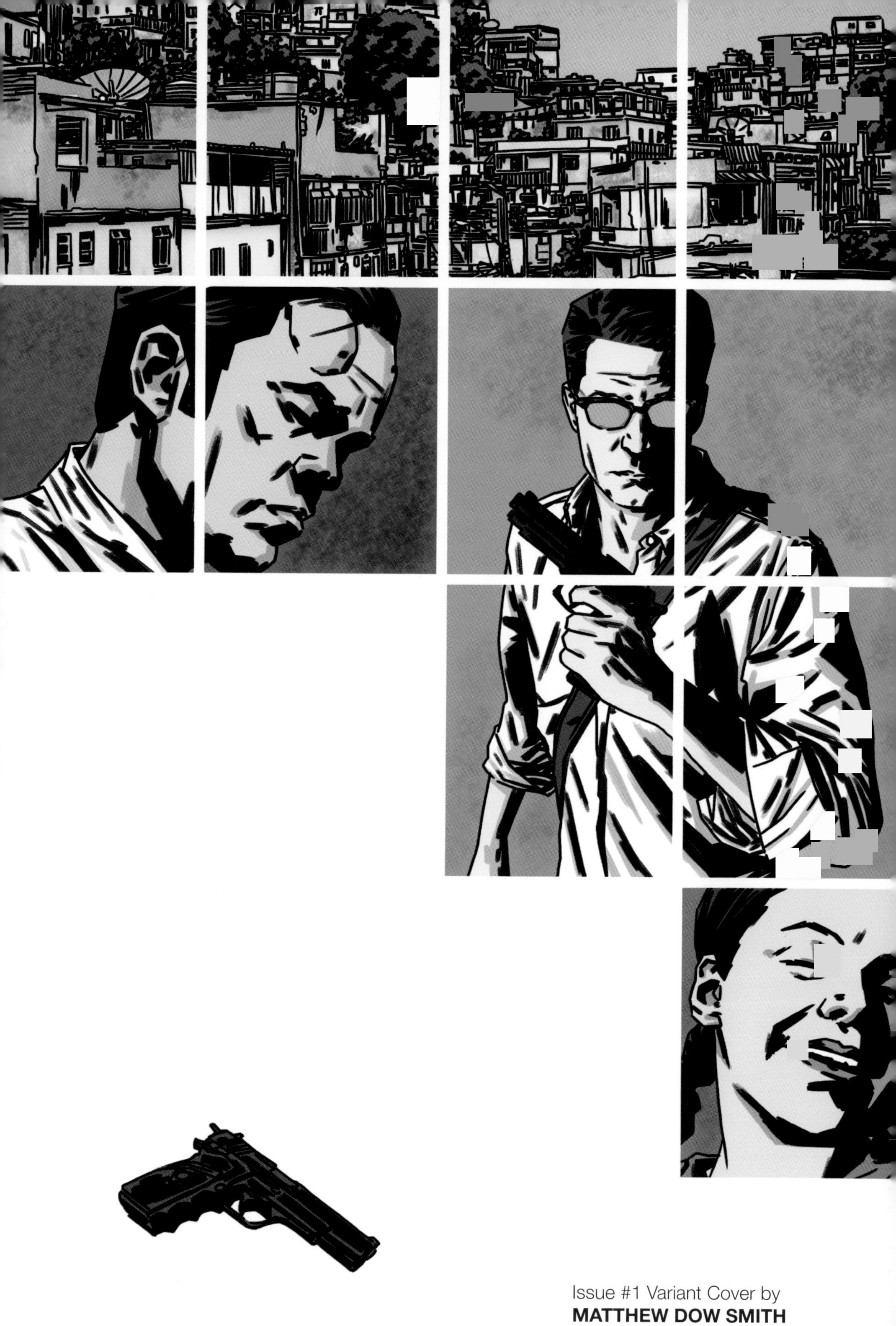

Issue #1 Variant Cover by
MATTHEW DOW SMITH

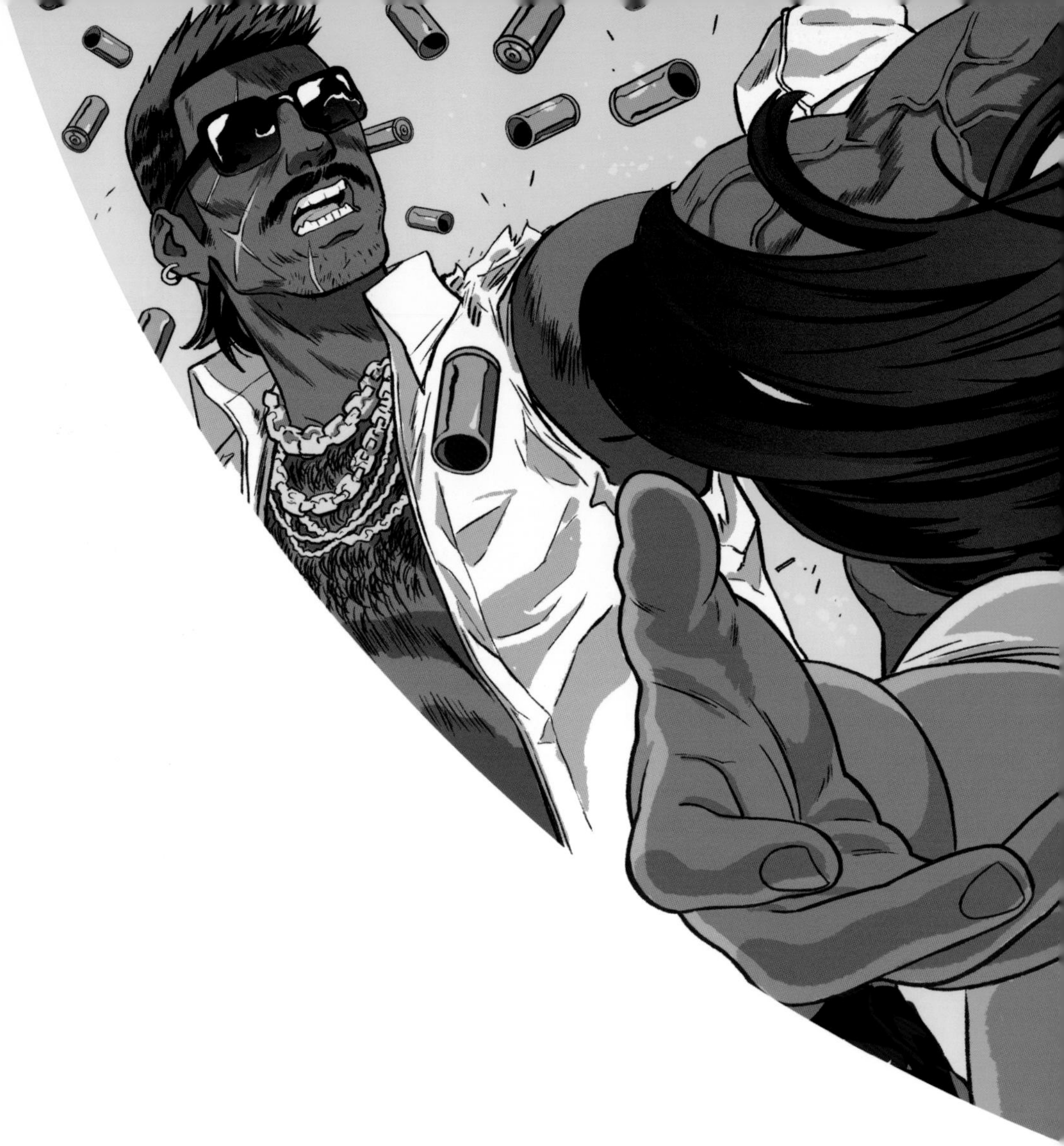

Issue #1 BOOM! Ten Years Variant Cover by
FELIPE SMITH

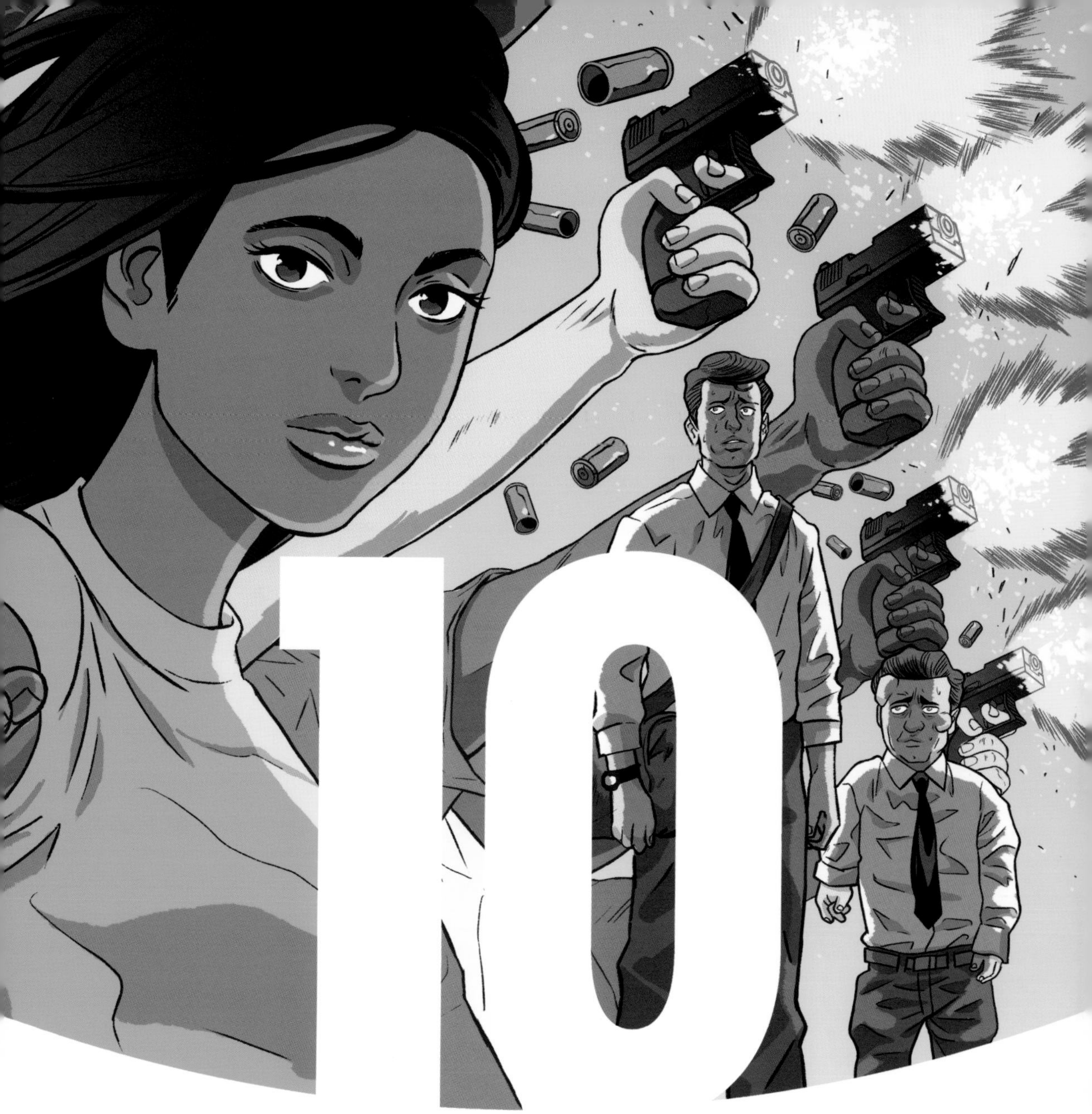

10

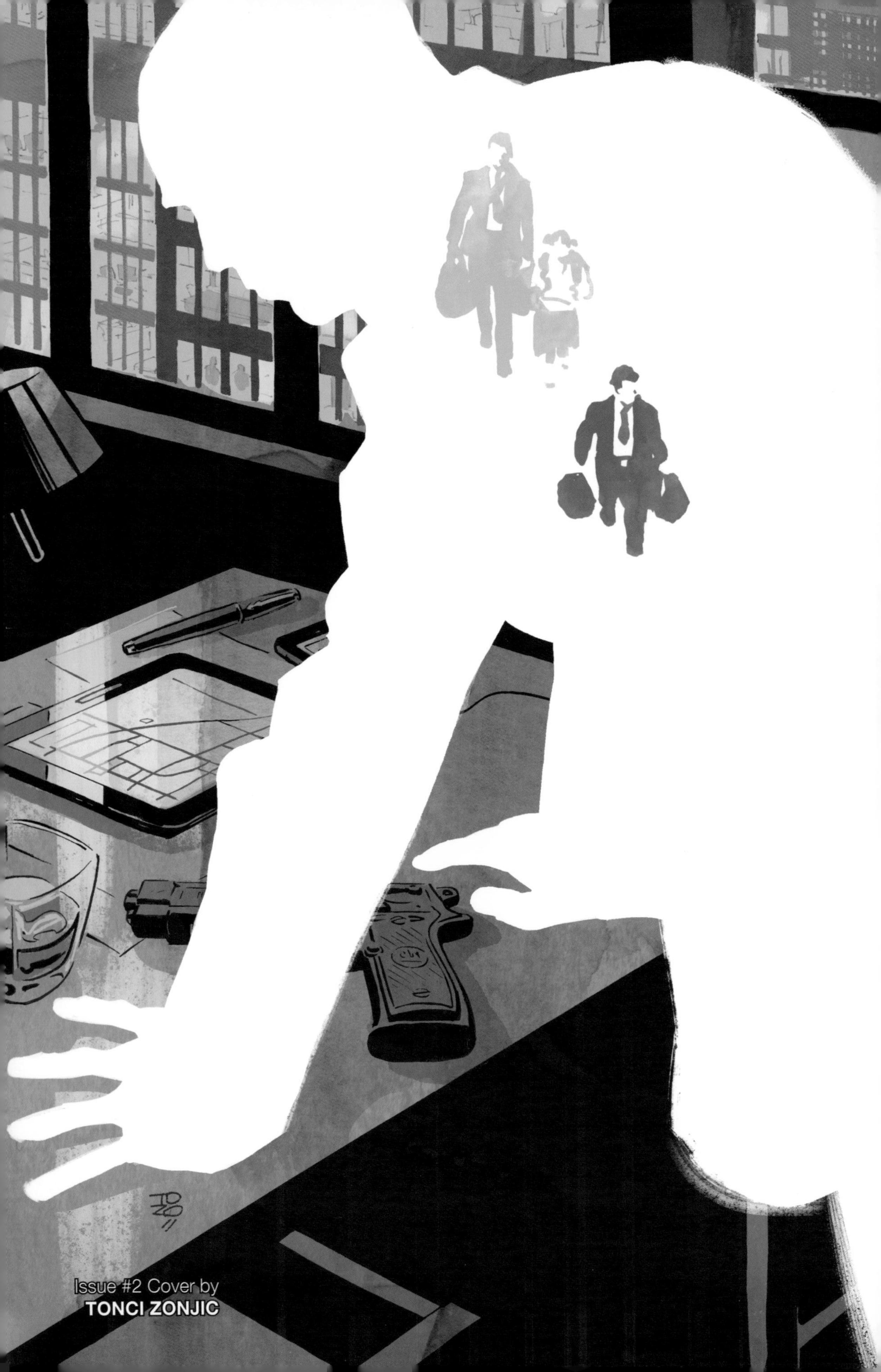

Issue #2 Cover by
TONCI ZONJIC

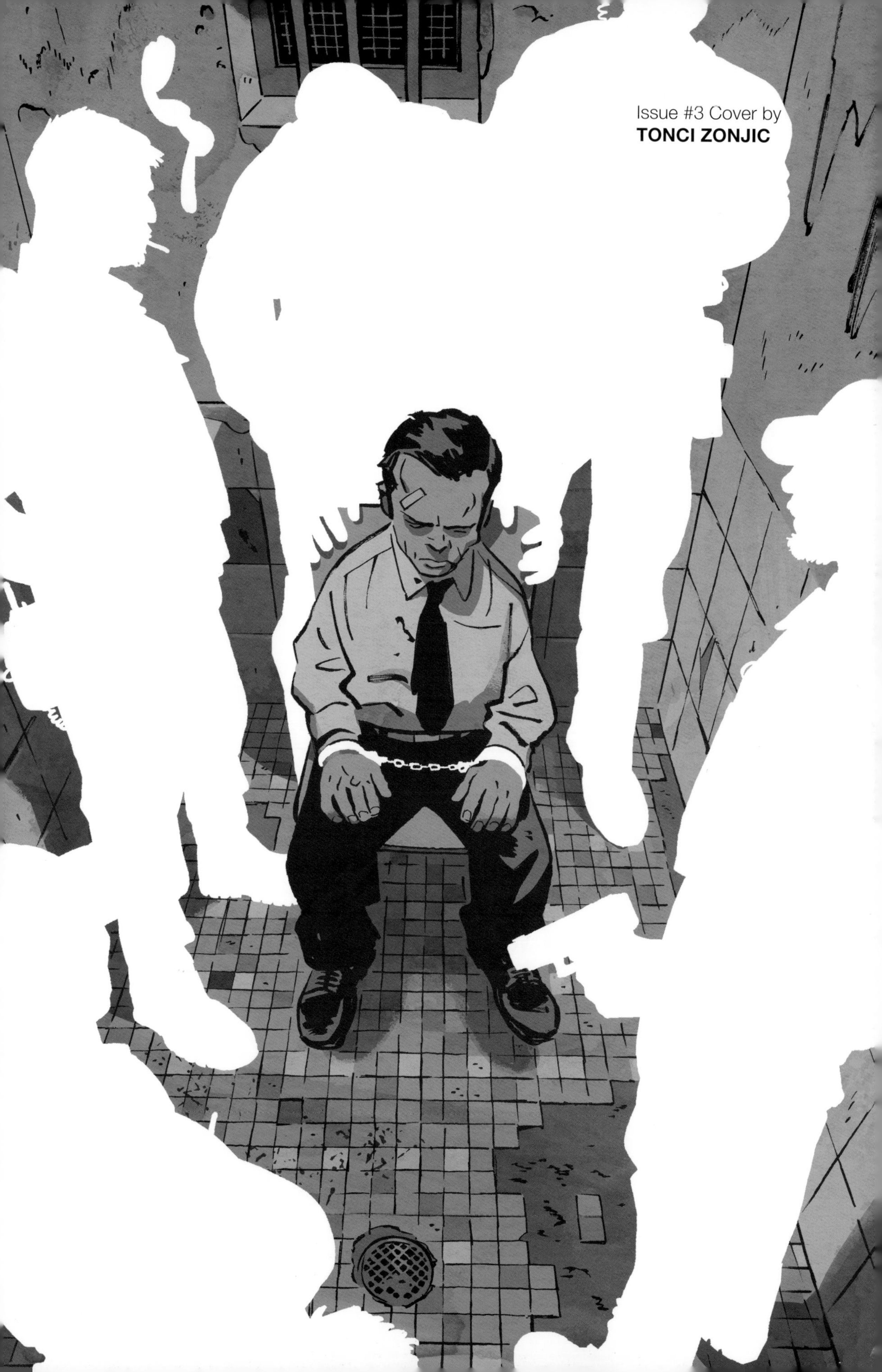
Issue #3 Cover by
TONCI ZONJIC

Issue #4 Cover by
TONCI ZONJIC

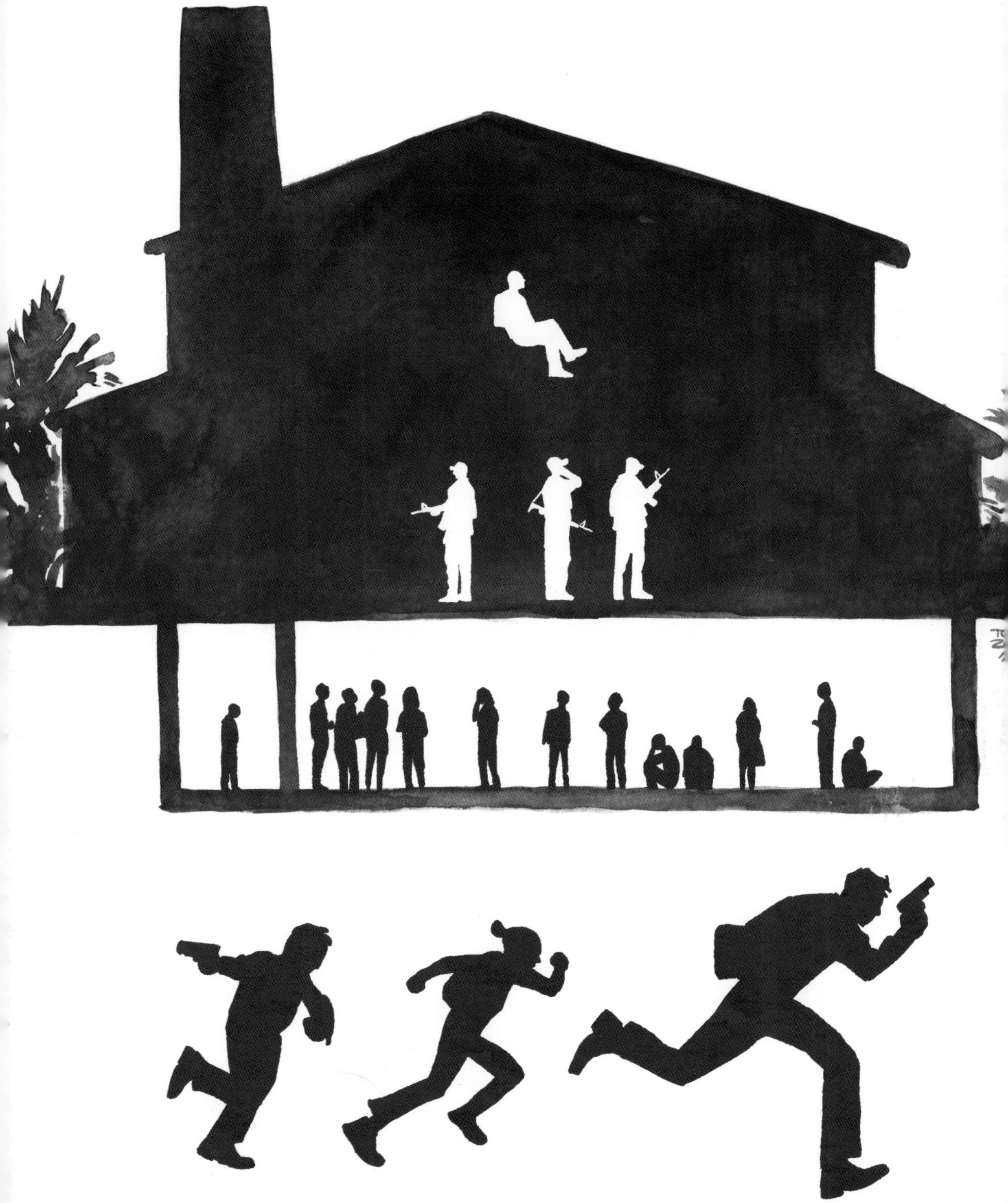

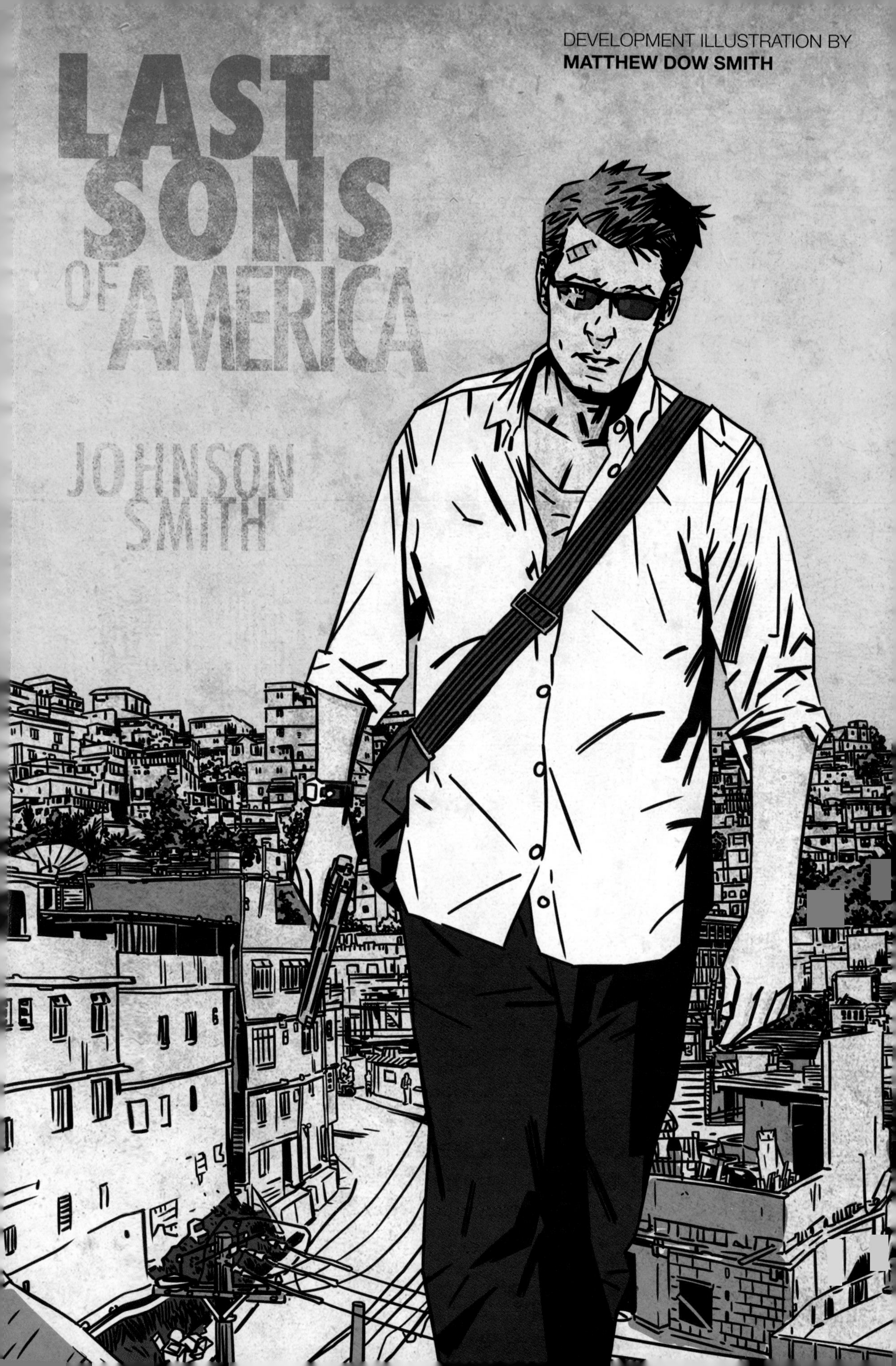
DEVELOPMENT ILLUSTRATION BY
MATTHEW DOW SMITH
LAST
SONS
OF AMERICA
JOHNSON
SMITH

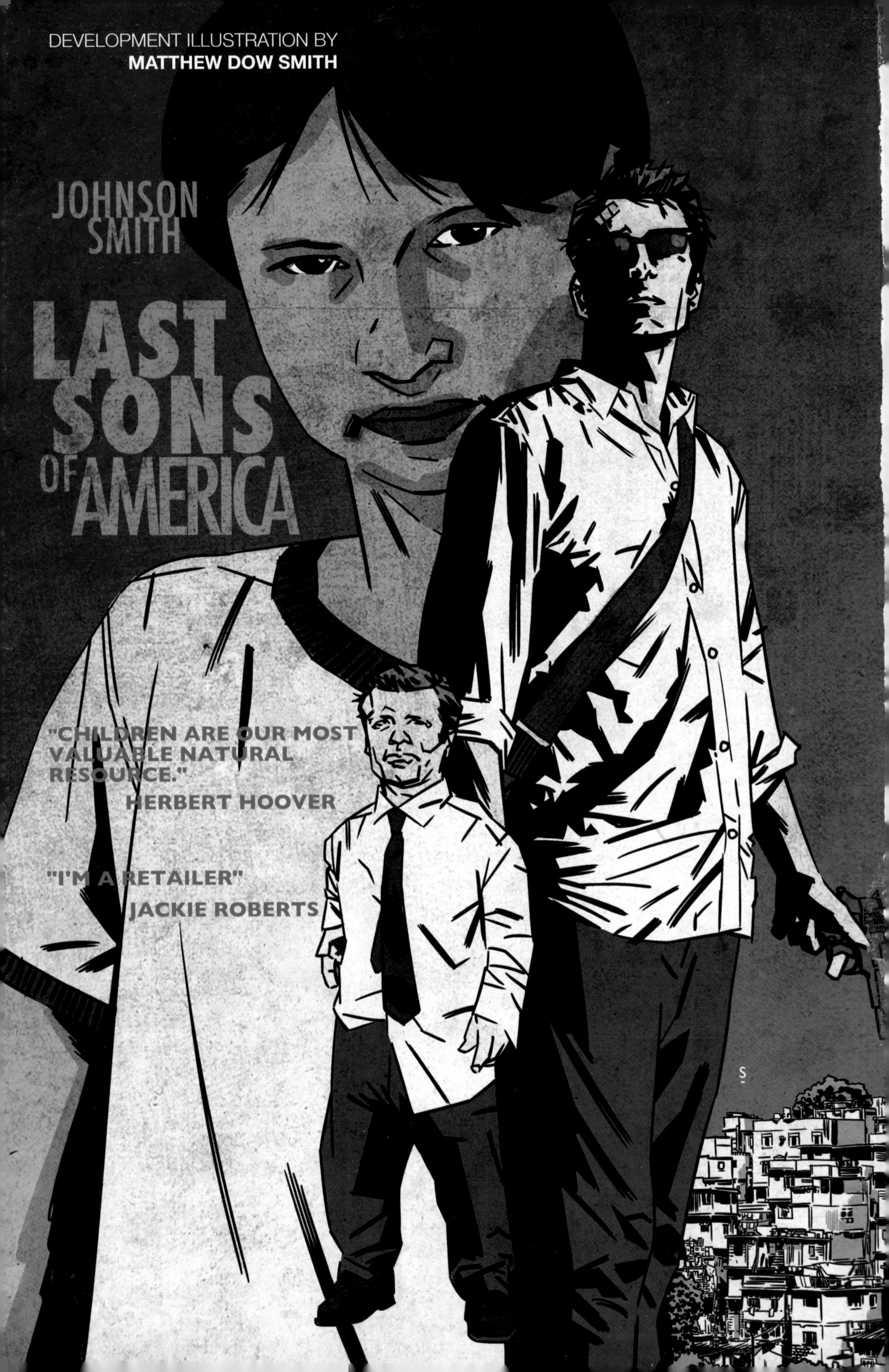
DEVELOPMENT ILLUSTRATION BY
MATTHEW DOW SMITH
JOHNSON
SMITH
LAST
SONS
OF AMERICA
"CHILDREN ARE OUR MOST VALUABLE NATURAL RESOURCE."
HERBERT HOOVER
"I'M A RETAILER"
JACKIE ROBERTS